THE NEW SMALL

THE NEW
small

How a New Breed of Small Businesses Is
Harnessing the Power of Emerging Technologies

PHIL SIMON

Motion
New Jersey

Production Director:
Kristen Eckstein
Imagine! Studios, LLC
http://www.artsimagine.com

Cover Designer:
Luke Fletcher
http://www.fletcherdesigns.com

Editor:
Kathleen Atkins
http://www.kathleenatkins.net

Proofreaders:
John Pierce
http://www.flyingspress.com

Karen Gill

Book Website Developer:
Shiri Amram
http://www.shiridesignstudio.com

Published by Motion Publishing, LLC
Caldwell, New Jersey

ISBN-13:
978-0-9829302-3-6

Library of Congress Control Number:
2010918004

To my favorite tweeps: Julie Hunt Consulting (@juliebhunt)
and Robert Lavigne, PMP (@RLavigne42)

TABLE OF CONTENTS

In a world where I feel so small I can't stop thinking big.

Neil Peart, Rush, "Caravan"

FOREWORD: THE NOT-SO REVOLUTION

This book is about me. Let me explain.

Phil wrote it for lots of people who are dealing with small business issues, and I am one of them. He just didn't realize that he wrote it for people like me, but he did. You see, I hang with the authors who have written
books that touch on some of the same subjects covered in *The New Small*.
Of course, Phil knows this. He spends time with them, too.

Phil and I are part of a new movement that's afoot. I dare not say *revolution* (the dreaded "R" word), because it's smaller than that. But many of us
have left the cubicle farm, opting to start our own shops. We are starting
and growing our own small businesses, propelled by a different management ethos and empowered by the exciting technologies discussed in this
book.

I am writing this while sitting in our office in Portland, ME, with my
right-hand man, Rob. We run a distributed company, just like Fuentek, the
subject of Chapter 13. We're helping people find new business by building virtuous cycles, a topic covered in Chapter 15. These are just a few of
the subjects I believe in deeply. And there are many more covered in this
important book.

See? Phil wrote this book for me. He just didn't know it at the time.

So, you now know what this book is generally about. But who reads
Forewords, anyway? Three groups of people:

- Obsessives. (I get it.)

- People who want the bigger story.

- People who are evaluating whether to buy this book.

Maybe you are sick of working in a faceless office. Perhaps you own a
small business because you wanted to validate your soul and your heart.

You might want to understand—and then use—the technologies that everyone seems to be raving about. Or you could be an entrepreneur with a nifty idea. If you meet any of the above criteria, this is the book for you.

If you're part of the second group, the bigger story is that you're not alone and that we're here for you. Some people cringe when they hear the word *technology*. You might be worried that *The New Small* will read a bit like a book written for the online generation. Yes and no. Much of what the folks living in front of screens are discovering will really help small businesses of many flavors. In other words, this is *not* a book that only techies will understand. On the contrary, Phil profiles many "bricks and real world" businesses, including a law firm, a dental office, and a restaurant. These are twentieth-century businesses doing twenty-first-century things. If they can, you can.

In Phil's book, you'll find a blizzard of valuable tips, lessons, and observations, backed by some incredible stories. You'll get a sense that some of the content is perfect for you, and some of it just might not apply to your business. Of course, this is true with all books of this type. But don't worry. You'll know which is which in no time. And don't be surprised if an "Aha!" moment comes from an unexpected source.

The New Small is kind of a big deal. You'll want to get out a pen because you are going to be marking it up quite a bit. And when you come to the conclusion that it's the book for you, buy a few copies and give them to the people in the groups mentioned above. We might as well keep the revolution going, right?

Check that. Let's not use the "R" word.

Chris Brogan
CEO of Human Business Works
http://www.humanbusinessworks.com
November 2010

PREFACE

A pessimist sees the difficulty in every opportunity; an optimist sees the opportunity in every difficulty.

—Winston Churchill

A Little Yarn about Tim

Back in November of 2009, I was riding a spin bike at my gym in West Caldwell, NJ. A guy next to me was reading a book, and the two of us soon started talking. It turns out that, like me, the man was a long-time technology professional. Not surprisingly, we clicked instantly and began an interesting conversation, fueled at least in my case by endorphins. Twenty years my senior, the guy (Tim) had been around the block a few more times than I had—although he had a young spirit. Tim and I were surprised to find out that I used to work for his then-employer (call it "Company X"), a massive consulting firm with tens of thousands of employees in hundreds of offices all over the globe. Tim asked what I was doing now, and I told him that, in addition to consulting, I also write and speak about technology-related topics. The conversation quickly turned to "emerging technologies," the theme of my then-unreleased second book—*The Next Wave of Technologies*. At that point, Tim's demeanor suddenly changed.

"Man, I wish that Company X did more with clouds and SaaS,"[1] Tim lamented. "I mean, we host webinars and hold meetings, but we don't really

---

[1] Software as a service (SaaS) is a way of effectively deploying software by the transaction or license; it requires only a web browser and no traditional installations and upgrades. If you're still not clear about it here, don't worry. We'll cover it in more detail later in the book.

do anything truly innovative for our clients. Our business is still primarily about putting butts in seats. I just don't see that changing anytime soon."

"It's not like we use these new technologies anyway," Tim continued, a bit wistfully. "We sure don't practice what we preach. I'd love to help our clients embrace the future—and work for a company that did the same."

Tim wasn't exaggerating; I had worked for Company X for a few years before I went out on my own. I knew all too well that its management tended to suffer from a myopic focus on quarterly earnings, a bureaucratic culture, and a general aversion to change. Despite having a wide variety of tools that ostensibly encourage workplace flexibility and collaboration, it relied on outdated methods such as massive voice mail and e-mail blasts. Consultants rued long and tedious conference calls after a long day at a client site.

At a high level, Tim and I were talking about *The Innovator's Dilemma*, Clayton M. Christensen's classic business text about the difficulties that companies face as they mature: the very products, services, and conditions that have enabled businesses to achieve some level of success now inhibit their future success. The dilemma represents a fundamental challenge for all businesses. Success is fleeting, and change is permanent. At some point, most organizations—particularly large ones—struggle with having to stick to their knitting while concurrently cannibalizing their business models. It's not an easy task, and the business landscape is littered with organizations too slow to adapt to forthcoming change. Tim's company was stuck squarely in the middle of this quandary.

I thought a great deal about that conversation after I returned home and in the following days. Tim was hardly the first consultant in history to feel burned out. People who work at large consulting outfits face challenges unlike people with so-called normal jobs, whatever those are. Consultants are not paid to go to the same office every day. We are expected to be road warriors, available at our clients' beck and call. Tim faced additional stress because he was a partner with profit and loss (P&L) responsibilities.

As I reflected, I realized that the source of Tim's frustration was not simply his employer or the travel required. Although Company X faced its own internal obstacles (as do many large organizations), there was something else going on.

Consider Company X's typical clients. Only a certain type of organization can afford to use a large consulting firm in the first place. It's doubtful that even very large small businesses (an interesting oxymoron) with $2M in annual revenue would consider using Company X. And the feeling is probably mutual. In all likelihood, Company X would never even bid on a $20,000 piece of business from what they would consider to be a mom-and-pop store. In other words, consultancies and clients tend to stick to their own kind. Rare is the large company that hires a boutique consulting firm.[2] Rarer still is the small business that brings in a Big Four management consulting firm.

Tim's frustration also stemmed from the nature of Company X's clients. At least for the next few years, in his current role, it was extremely unlikely that Tim would work with the kinds of companies deploying the emerging technologies that we were discussing, at least in any meaningful way. The companies implementing the kinds of technologies that Tim wanted to deploy weren't usually multinational corporations. They were small businesses.[3]

So, let's summarize what we know about Tim:

- He works for a big consulting firm.
- He wants to help his clients deploy new technologies.
- He wants to increase his level of engagement with his clients. In other words, he wants to help them more.

At the same time, though:

- Both with its clients and internally, Company X is struggling with emerging technologies and has been unable to change its business model.
- Company X tends to attract big clients, as do most large consulting outfits.
- Big clients are averse to change and tend to have myriad internal issues preventing meaningful change from happening.
- Even big clients that wanted to deploy an emerging technology had major restrictions. Because of the Great Recession, 2009 information technology (IT) budgets were anything but robust.[i]

So, is it any surprise that Tim wasn't happy? Is the cure to his malaise really all that difficult to discern? Something had to give, and in early 2010, it finally did.

Tim didn't get a raise or a new boss. He didn't cut back his hours. Nor did he get a bigger office, a new title, or more direct reports. None of that would have mattered to him. Tim started a new job. He's still the same smart, affable guy. But there's something different about him. He's happier, and for one reason: he's no longer swimming against the stream he's in. He's able to accomplish more in his new role. He helps his clients successfully

---

[2] This brings to mind the old adage at big companies: "No one ever got fired for hiring IBM."

[3] While definitions of the term vary, businesses with 100 or fewer employees are generally considered small. Those with 100 to 999 employees are considered to be medium-sized.

use new technologies and grow their businesses. He's not obsessed with finding billable work for his team. The roadblocks no longer frustrate him because they're not there—at least not nearly to the same degree.

Did Tim join another large consulting firm? No, he's working at a small company in New Jersey that sells SaaS-based applications to smaller clients. His new employer has a fraction of the employees and resources of his previous one. Tim's doing more with less. He's able to provide real solutions to his clients for three reasons:

- His employer has *fewer* resources.
- He encounters fewer internal obstacles at work, allowing him to help his clients effect more meaningful change.
- He's working with small clients.

No longer does he focus on maximizing his team's billable hours, submitting reports to different levels of management, proving that he's toeing the company line, or worrying about maintaining his clients' excessively complex systems and architectures.

He's able to think about—and do—what's in his company's and his clients' best short- and long-term interests. Freed from the bureaucracy of his previous environment, Tim couldn't be happier. And he's not alone.

Tim now works for—and just as important for someone in his shoes, *with*—a new breed of companies. Collectively, I call this group of fascinating small businesses *the New Small*. This book is about these companies, what they're doing, how they're doing it, and why so many highly skilled people want to work for them.

Phil Simon
Caldwell, NJ, USA
November 2010

Endnotes

i   http://www.zdnet.com/blog/btl/gartners-worst-case-for-2009-it-budgets-isnt-so-bad/10403

ACKNOWLEDGMENTS

This book could not have come together so quickly without the help of Team Simon, including my production head, Kristen Eckstein of Imagine! Studios, my rocking cover designer Luke Fletcher, my diligent proofreaders John Pierce and Karen Gill, and my awesome editor Kathleen Atkins. It was an incredible thrill to work with such talented folks.

Special thanks also go to each of the small business owners, founders, and employees who so generously let me into their lives and their businesses. This book is first and foremost a collection of their stories. Although I can do research as well as the next person, books stuffed with dry statistics on technology adoption have never interested me, even if I'm the one doing the writing. Strike that: *especially* if I'm doing the writing. This book simply wouldn't have been possible without so much cooperation, collaboration, and input from people already very busy running their businesses. Again, thank you.

Next up are the usual suspects—my longtime Carnegie Mellon friends Scott Berkun, David Sandberg, Michael Viola, Joe Mirza, and Chris McGee. A tip of the hat to Jill Dyché, Tony Fisher, Craig Heyrman, Thor Sandell, Brian and Heather Morgan, Rosalinda Cifuentes, Karen Gill, MJ Stabinski-Heckman, Pamela Redmond Satran, John Spatola, Joanne Lam, Ellen French, Marc Paolella, Angela Kubisky, web developer extraordinaire Shiri Amram, Sue Collier, Matt Carlson, and Bruce Webster.

My heroes from Rush (Geddy, Alex, and Neil), Dream Theater (Jordan, John, John, and James), and Porcupine Tree (Steven, Colin, Gavin, John, and Richard) have given me many years of creative inspiration through their music. Keep on keepin' on.

Next up: my parents, Linda and Sandy Simon. I'm not here without you.

The Kickstarter Crowd

Special thanks to the people who preordered and backed the book on Kickstarter.[1] I really appreciate the faith that you showed in the project and me. These stellar folks include:

The good folks at WhatARacquet and DataFlux, Timeview, Romaxy, J. Allard, Crysta Anderson, Mark Rowatt Anderson, Rose Aulik, Josh Austin, Rob Bell, Alan Berkson, Scott Berkun, Shahrooz Bhopti, Andrew Botwin, Paul Boudreau, Patrick Buckley, Tom Carchrae, Dalton Cervo, Robert Charette, Si Chen, Niraj Chhabra, Sue Collier, Jason Collins, Jennifer Cullari, The DeAngelo Family, Michelle Deibel, Leo Dinicola, Tamara Dull, Scott Erichsen, Jaime Fitzgerald, DJ Fusion/FuseBox Radio, Louis Galipeau, Jose Gonzalez, Andrew Gossen, Pat Gray, Mike Guiry, Gordon Hamilton, Todd Hamilton, Jim Harris, Kevin Haughwout, Mark Hayes, Doug Hensch, Liz Hersey, Colin Hickey, Robert Hillard, Julie Hunt, Naynish Jhaveri, Lonnie Johnson, Dylan Jones, Dan Keldsen, Fernando Labrada, Robert Lavigne, Jerry Levine, Lachlan Macpherson, Chef Tony Marciante, Barbara Haiss Martin, Erika McAnn, Tom McClintock, Wayne McDermott, William McKnight, Deanna McNeil, Rob Metting, Jimmy Mikusi, Vinnie Mirchandani, Patrick Mooney, Joe Mulligan, Rich Murnane, John Nicholls, Ken O'Connor, Thomas Oldervoll, Matt O'Malley, Joseph O'Toole, Rob Paller, Mike Petrucci, Charles Proctor, Erik X. Raj, Jacqueline Roberts, Cian Robinson, John Roccesano, Brian Rosenberg, Jeremy Rothschild, Terri Rylander, Roger Salazar, Damien Santer, Steve Sarsfield, Jack Sauer, Frank Scavo, Laura Schoppe, Eric Schreier, Dayce Schrieber, Julian Schwarzenbach, Susan Scrupski, Moneet Singh, Marisa Smith, Brenda Somich, Jack Spain, James Standen, Doug Steinschneider, Donna Strano, Daniel Teachey, Megan Torrance, Martin Traub-Werner, Nick Turner, Mikhail Ushanov, Brian Van Horne, Kathryn Velvel, Paul Vento, Margaret L. Wade, Ray Wang, Jill Wanless, Mike West, Dawn Westerberg, Jake Wyant, and Jon P. Yarger.

[1] See http://www.kickstarter.com/projects/705402671/the-new-small-my-third-book. It was quite inspirational to see so many people back the book when it was just a draft.

INTRODUCTION

Knowledge of what is possible is the beginning of happiness.

—George Santayana

Three main questions underlie this book:

- Which emerging technologies does the New Small use?
- How does the New Small select and deploy these technologies?
- How and where can we find meaningful work?

Which Emerging Technologies Does the New Small Use?

An astonishing variety of websites, applications, tools, and platforms is available to every type and size of business these days.[1] Many of these are relatively unknown and underutilized. Tens of millions of people work in small businesses and simply don't have the time to get their arms around the dizzying array of options today for everything from e-mail to productivity suites. As a result, too many small businesses make do with old standbys when superior and less expensive alternatives often exist.

How Does the New Small Select and Deploy These Technologies?

Although I certainly hope that you learn a great deal about emerging technologies from this book, I have two ulterior motives in writing it. On one level, I want to communicate the ethos of the New Small. Irrespective

---

[1] I learned a tremendous amount talking to the owners of these fascinating companies.

of location, industry, and company size, this is a pragmatic and innovative group of companies. The technologies are not as important as the problems and challenges that these businesses face.

Contrast this with large corporations. Although it's hardly true across the board, I have seen big companies buy expensive applications because a VP or an executive thinks they should. They then struggle to figure out what to do with their expensive new tools.

Remember that this book is about *small* businesses that lack the margin of error that many corporations take for granted. To this end, I have detailed many internal decision-making processes of the New Small. What did these companies do when a particular technology or system could no longer meet their needs? You don't just read about the specific tools that a company uses. Rather, you'll discover:

- Why they were chosen
- How people use them
- How they've evolved
- What was learned in making the jump

New Small founders are hardly infallible; they make mistakes—as we will see. This book isn't a sales brochure for the latest and greatest toys.

How and Where Can We Find Meaningful Work?

Finally, a significant part of this book focuses on how we work—and only indirectly on technology. It's about how we choose to spend our professional lives and what we do to put food on our tables. I want you to be inspired reading this book, just as I was writing it. To me at least, this is an uplifting text—one that I hope will motivate people pondering whether to start a small business. As you will soon see, this doesn't have to be just a dream.

Put simply, the New Small understands one critical thing: *Work doesn't have to suck.* You will read about people who actually enjoy their jobs—many of whom *love* going to work each day. Quite a few New Small founders come from big, political corporate environments and would never return; they have seen the light. At the other end of the spectrum are the founders of DODOcase and Voices.com, serial entrepreneurs who never had any interest in climbing the corporate ladder. Whatever their backgrounds, they share one fundamental belief: Work can actually be fulfilling. It need not be reduced to salary, ego, title, who has the corner office, or organizational politics. Rather, it can—*and should*—involve:

- Knowing the names of your colleagues—even if you've never met them in person

- Taking care of your customers
- Making a true difference at work
- Working smarter, not harder
- Constantly learning on the job
- Solving different problems
- Becoming indispensable
- Gaining valuable skills and learning new tools
- Not knowing what to expect each day
- Being treated with respect—and doing the same to others
- Feeling free to disagree with your boss
- Being a part of something great

Now, I've seen plenty of recruiting pitches in my day. Many executives in large companies claim that the preceding conditions prevail in their organizations. But when you talk to their employees and customers, you usually hear a very different story. By virtue of their size, politics, cultures, and the like, old-guard organizations are almost always unable to create and maintain exciting and fulfilling environments for their employees.[2] Try as they might, their own size—and all that comes with it—prohibits them from doing many of the things they may honestly want to do.

Most big companies could not be more different from the companies you're about to discover. In the following pages, you're going to meet the New Small. Although none of them is perfect, each tries and largely succeeds in creating meaningful jobs for their employees. And their clubhouse isn't closed. In fact, the doors are wide open. People are starting successful small businesses and SOHOs (small offices/home offices) every day. And guess what? You can too.

Who Should Read This Book?

Many small businesses are struggling to get their arms around emerging technologies. Keeping up to speed isn't terribly easy to do today. There's just too much going on. To that end, I specifically wrote this book *not* as a technology consultant for other techies. By design, the book's voice is that of a small business owner (yours truly) addressing other small business owners who are curious about what they can do to increase revenue, reduce costs, and attract and retain highly desirable employees.

---

[2] Again, not everyone *wants* to work in such an environment. Some people just want to collect a paycheck, and there's absolutely nothing wrong with that.

This book is about what the New Small is doing on a number of levels—and why this makes them special. It also demystifies each of the Five Enablers for those who stand to benefit from using them—even though they may be technologically challenged. Of course, to understand the ins and outs of cloud computing or social networks, one should buy a book about each—and there are many. This is a book for those who wonder if there are better ways to use technology. It addresses questions such as these:

- Do I have to be some type of expert to improve my company's use of technology? Answer: No.

- Can my business use powerful technologies at a fraction of the cost of its current ones? Answer: Probably.

- If I start my own business, do I need to spend most of my seed money on expensive technologies? Answer: Probably not.

- Is it "all or nothing" with emerging technologies? Answer: Hardly. There are degrees and levels of adoption.

By the end of this book, you will see that, despite the wide variety of small businesses covered in this book, there's really only one fundamental thing unique about the New Small: The owners and employees of these companies were simply willing to embrace a different way of doing things. They didn't rely upon what they learned while working in large companies or upon conventional wisdom. These people aren't inherently smarter, nor are they more tech-savvy.

What's more, membership in the group is *not* limited to a specific industry or a type of company. You are welcome to join the New Small as well. This book shows you how to join the club—and transform your small business in the process. The only requirement is an open mind.

Beyond current small business owners, this is a book for those who are thinking about joining the ranks of the entrepreneurs. That's not to say that this book will walk you through all of the legal, financial, and administrative hurdles required to open your own shop, much less successfully cultivate a client base. It won't. You have to read a different book for that. Nor will it provide a checklist for how to enable your applications in the cloud or create a mobile application. But if you're thinking about starting a small business and are curious about how similar companies are taking advantage of emerging technologies, you're reading the right book.

Finally, employees of big companies will benefit from this book. As you'll soon discover, many larger organizations have quite a bit to learn from their smaller counterparts. This is particularly true today, especially with respect to deploying technology and managing people. While it's hardly simple for big companies to turn on a dime, it behooves them to know what progressive smaller outfits are doing—and how they are doing it.

Methodology: Selecting the New Small

With so many small businesses doing so many interesting things with emerging technologies, you might wonder how I chose the companies profiled in this book. Admittedly, this was more art than science. There's just no way that I could measure or capture statistics to identify the most innovative or progressive companies.

I started out by posting my intentions to interview small business owners on my own website, different LinkedIn groups, social networking sites, and Help A Reporter Out.[3] The response was pretty overwhelming; I quickly had more replies than I could realistically manage. There was just no way that I could profile every company, and to be truthful, some small businesses were using emerging technologies much more extensively—and with better results—than others.

Remember that many small businesses are privately held, and as such, keep their cards pretty close to their vests. I certainly didn't need to see companies' profit and loss statements (P&Ls) or balance sheets, but I did hope that people would be honest about the states of their companies. I didn't want to quote anonymous sources. Nor did I want to use pseudonyms, as I had in my first book. Some prospective interviewees had fascinating stories to tell, but for a variety of reasons, could not divulge details such as the number of full-time employees. One health care organization in particular had a great story to tell. I spoke with its CEO and asked point-blank, "How many full-time employees work there?" He gave a verbose answer to the question. Reading between the lines, I could tell that the company relied pretty extensively on contractors and outsourced help—not that there's anything wrong with that.[4] I assumed that it employed fewer than five full-time individuals. After a brief discussion, the CEO decided not to divulge the precise number; he feared that disclosure would hurt his company's brand and reputation with its clients. Onward I marched.

I also wanted New Small founders to talk freely about any mistakes they made while adopting new technologies. Let me be clear: my intent in this book is not to accentuate the negative. Still, most organizations of any size don't successfully deploy new technologies in a linear fashion; there are errors in judgment and execution that, with hindsight, seem obvious later. I explained to each potential contributor that I was writing a book as a small business owner for other small business owners. Neglecting lessons learned ran the risk of turning this book into a glorified marketing brochure for all things technology. I wasn't willing to do that.

---

3   Help A Reporter Out (http://www.helpareporter.net) is a site that allows reporters, authors, writers, and researchers to find people willing to talk about different issues. I have been on the "interviewee" side of the virtual table more than once.

4   One of *Seinfeld's* best lines.

Last, I didn't want to repeatedly profile the same type of company. Without question, as a writer, I am heavily influenced by Malcolm Gladwell's books. Like many others, I really enjoy the way that he ties together ostensibly disparate people and trends in books like *Blink*, *Outliers*, and *The Tipping Point*. He finds the common ground in apparently unrelated areas. I have endeavored to do the same. In fact, I did this in my first book, *Why New Systems Fail*. But *The New Small* is a very different book for several reasons.

First, I can actually use real company and individual names. I didn't have to get creative with pseudonyms because New Small founders, owners, and employees were justifiably proud of what they had done. They *wanted* to talk to me and share their wisdom and experiences so others could benefit. Second and more important, the lessons that the New Small teaches us in the following pages are much more normative than negative. The companies profiled show us what most small businesses—and large organizations, for that matter—ought to be doing right now.[5] As a result, I enjoyed the writing process immensely.

On a more general level, I was fortunate enough to receive many responses to my queries, many of which came from software, consulting, and other high-tech companies. Most of these companies were taking advantage of emerging technologies. Not only was I able to avoid profiling the same type of company again and again, I could pay attention to the challenges that small businesses faced in a range of industries.

So although this book is by no means a definitive guide on deploying any one type of technology or application (much less every one), I have tried to include as many different types of small businesses and industries as possible—while keeping the book at a reasonable length. Those expecting to find a comprehensive list of technologies required for *every* industry will ultimately be disappointed. It's not a directory or reference manual. This is a book of stories: it's about people and small businesses.

Two Disclaimers: Big Isn't Necessarily Bad

I certainly don't want readers to misinterpret the central message of *The New Small*. By virtue of its title, the book focuses on companies of a particular size. I often contrast New Small companies to larger and often more bureaucratic organizations that, by comparison, typically have more—and more severe—problems. In no way do I mean to imply that all big companies are inherently bad places to work. They are not all run by greedy or aloof senior management, nor do they employ only incompetent people. I certainly don't believe that all small businesses are progressive, idyllic, and inherently good. Nor do I think that big companies are evil, bureaucratic,

---

[5] *Why New Systems Fail* provides many case studies, but, with one exception, they are examples of what *not* to do.

soulless, and technologically backward. Put it this way: this book is pro-small, not anti-big.

Also, from a technology standpoint, I am certainly not implying that large companies never embrace anything new. Indeed, stories abound about how the biggest of organizations are embracing the technologies discussed in this book. For example, consider Delta Air Lines, a company that is neither new nor small. Founded in the 1920s, today it has more than 81,000 employees and $28B US in sales.[i] On August 12 of 2010, *The Associated Press* reported that Delta is now allowing passengers to book tickets via Facebook, rather than through its website. Delta has "launched a new 'Ticket Window' on Facebook that will allow passengers to book directly on the social media site. It's the first time an airline has allowed customers to reserve flights on Facebook, although nearly all major U.S. airlines use Facebook and Twitter to promote sales."[ii]

Although interesting, you won't find many stories like this one in this book.[6] Big companies such as Delta, General Electric, and BMW are certainly doing worthy things on the technology front. However, this book is about small businesses harnessing the power of emerging technologies.

Book Layout

This book is broken into four sections.

Part I: Trends and the Five Enablers

The current technology revolution is fundamentally not about whether companies run their own servers, data centers, and software. Nor is it about who has the best applications. Rather, the revolution is about a new mindset, a new relationship between technology and work. It's about how New Small companies are using emerging technologies to focus their attention on what they do best. It's about everyone pitching in on a project. It's about the death of "that's not my job" and territorial pissing contests endemic to so many large organizations.

This part covers the major trends that are collectively driving small businesses to embrace emerging technologies. Among the trends are:

- Flexibility and agility
- Collaboration
- The explosion of content and choice
- Experimentation and acceptable risk

---

[6] For those of you interested in that type of book, check out my friend Vinnie Mirchandani's recently released book, *The New Polymath*.

- The social customer
- The war for talent

The focus then shifts to the technologies currently at the center of a revolution of sorts. They let the New Small do things simply unfathomable 10 years ago. Small businesses are competing with larger organizations right here, right now. No longer are they caught between doing without important technologies on one hand and long, expensive, and typically disappointing IT projects on the other.

Chapter 2 introduces the Five Enablers: the five specific technologies allowing the New Small to do simply amazing things. These technologies are:

- Cloud computing
- SaaS
- Free and open source software (FOSS)
- Mobility
- Social networks

We will see how the New Small is taking advantage of the Five Enablers to a much greater extent than large companies.

Part II: The New Small

Part II is the heart of the book. It details 11 small companies that are using emerging technologies in innovative ways—the New Small. They are doing more with less, striking a balance between flexibility and structure. This section does much more than list the technologies used by each company. You will learn how these companies experimented, sometimes taking two steps back in order to take a giant step forward. Amidst the successes and failures, each company continued learning and charting its own paths. Today, being small can be a tremendous asset. The little guy is doing it faster and with greater success.

Part III: Becoming One of the New Small

New Small companies adopt emerging technologies with higher success rates compared to larger organizations. However, these are *relative* terms. I've seen firsthand how small businesses struggle to implement new technologies. A point from before bears repeating: all else equal, it's easier for the New Small to deploy and use emerging technologies. *But easier doesn't mean easy.*

This part of the book examines many of the lessons learned from the companies profiled in Part II, with an eye on enabling future technology changes. You see how the smartest small businesses don't immediately and unilaterally embrace every technology that comes along. When they do, they enter into new relationships with employees, consultants, and vendors. As with any new business endeavor, there are perils all around. I cover how to avoid—or at least minimize—them.

New Small companies carefully select the technologies that make the most sense. In the process, they balance immediate short-term needs with long-term prospects for growth. However, it's just plain foolish to ignore the costs, risks, disadvantages, and limitations of the Five Enablers. These are covered as well.

Part IV: Thinking Ahead

The book will conclude with a summary chapter and a look toward the future.

So, fasten your seatbelts. We're about to embark on a journey to understand some amazing companies, some very exciting technologies, a different management ethos, and a more progressive—and I'd argue better—definition of work.

Let's start.

Endnotes

i   http://www.hoovers.com/company/Delta_Air_Lines_Inc/rfccxi-1.html
ii   http://www.msnbc.msn.com/id/38676513/ns/travel-travel_tips

Part I

TRENDS AND THE FIVE ENABLERS

Part I of this book covers the reasons that the New Small is adopting emerging technologies *en masse*. It then provides a chapter on the specific emerging technologies allowing these companies to do so much. These are the Five Enablers, and they are:

- Cloud computing
- Software as a service (SaaS)
- Free and open source software (FOSS)
- Mobility
- Social technologies

Part I lays the foundation for the rest of the book. It describes the changes taking place in the workforce as well as the technologies giving the New Small a leg up.

Chapters

1 Technology and How We Work
2 Major Trends Driving the New Small
3 The Five Enablers
4 The Continuing Search for Meaning at Work

Chapter **1**

TECHNOLOGY AND HOW WE WORK

We are all growing volcanoes approaching the hour of their eruption.

—Friedrich Nietzsche

I started working with workplace technologies way back in the mid-1990s. Over the course of my career, I have spent more than my fair share of time in front of a computer. I have used a panoply of different tools, graphical user interfaces (GUIs),[1] programming languages, operating systems, databases, system architectures, systems, productivity applications, and reporting tools. Although no one has seen and worked on everything, I have come just about as close as anyone I know. After 10 years in the corporate world, let's just say that I know my way around a computer.

I look at technology today and am simply amazed. It's so different on so many levels compared to 15 years ago. I'm old enough to remember a time *before* e-mail, Internet browsers, and Microsoft Office.[2] Back then, just about all companies used applications and systems that are very different from what they use today.

In my days as a technology consultant, I have worked with many different types of companies. I've advised single-person home-based businesses

---

[1] Including the now antiquated green screens.

[2] I absolutely despised early versions of WordPerfect, the antithesis of "what you see is what you get" or WYSIWYG. Imagine today printing out a document and having no idea about how it would be formatted.

and 50,000 employee multinational corporations—and just about all types in between. I can also lay claim to working with companies in many different industries: health care, nonprofit, telecommunications, hi-tech, public sector retail, manufacturing, and professional services. It's fair to say that all organizations use technology, with some doing so much better than others.

The Consultant's Perspective

Technology consultants are for the most part change agents. For a variety of reasons, we are contracted to help organizations move from one platform, system, or application to another. Consider a typical project for someone like me. A company purchases a new technology, and absent the requisite internal expertise, brings in consultants to make it work. Of course, we consultants can do only so much. We're not miracle workers, despite what salespeople might have said before contracts were signed—and despite what clients themselves wanted to hear. On particularly contentious or difficult projects, such as most of the ones detailed in *Why New Systems Fail*, consultants tend to shoulder most of the blame.

In my career, I've seen people make some horrendous decisions deploying new technologies. As a conscientious consultant, I attempted to steer them away from decisions ultimately not in their organization's best interests—or theirs, for that matter. Sometimes I've been successful; sometimes I've just irritated them and have had to admit defeat. This has happened to me with companies of all sizes: small, medium, and large.

Truth be told, however, I'm much more of a small business type of guy. I simply prefer working in smaller environments, where people generally rely less upon strict policies and procedures and more on plain old common sense.[3] Finding a solution to a problem tends to be more important than interminably debating the pros and cons of each alternative in endless meetings, childish bickering, internal politics, and extensive CYA.[4]

---

[3]   Again, this is a general rule. There are plenty of pragmatic folks at enormous organizations and probably just as many irrational folks at mom-and-pop stores.

[4]   Consultant-speak for "cover your ass."

Traditional Impediments to Small Business Technology Adoption

As a general rule, technology at many small businesses has historically lagged technology at larger companies for six main reasons.[5] They include these:

- Resource availability
- Perceived need
- Priorities
- Bad decisions
- IT project failure stories and statistics
- Finding the right scale

Let's explore them.

Resource Availability

Many small businesses have lacked the financial and human resources of their larger brethren. Historically, they often could not afford best-of-breed systems and technologies.

Perceived Need

Many small businesses have made do with paper files, spreadsheets, and other technological Band-Aids. Historically and at a core level, many have not recognized that they needed proper systems or applications. Although it's hard to argue that the local food store needs the same powerful and expensive inventory management systems as Walmart and Amazon, both kinds of organizations need to electronically track inventory. The only difference is scale.

Priorities

Even many small businesses that recognize the need for proper systems and applications have never deployed proper systems. At these companies, information technology (IT) folks have been primarily concerned with "keeping the lights on." The focus here has been on the usual suspects: securing the company's IT assets, maintaining networks, fighting fires, creating user and e-mail accounts, and handling hardware issues.

---

[5] Of course, there are plenty of exceptions to this rule. Some of my smaller clients have implemented amazing and simple technologies. At the same time, many larger companies have suffered from too much technology: an eye chart of overlapping legacy systems that generally got in the way of each other.

In other words, the people responsible for deploying technology have been far too busy to upgrade their company's technology. Despite recognizing the need for better technology, more compelling business priorities have forced these companies to get by with a pastiche of paper files, spreadsheets, and other "low-tech" solutions.

Bad Decisions

Many organizations originally made bad technology-related decisions that they ultimately intended to address. Unfortunately, for whatever reason, many of these mistakes have never been corrected. Even the best of intentions get derailed. Applied within the context of this book, years ago many small businesses outgrew their original, limited applications and technologies. They have not had the time, money, or desire to upgrade them.

IT Project Failure Stories and Statistics

Horror stories from other organizations have often deterred many small businesses from making the jump into new technology. To be sure, large system implementations fail more frequently and spectacularly than relatively small IT projects. However, the latter often miss their mark.

Finding the Right Scale

Many traditional client-server applications were geared toward businesses of a certain size. A small company in the midst of decent growth would typically pause to consider before buying and implementing an enterprise-wide system. Consider the following conundrum:

- Growth in the number of employees, transactions, or physical locations would make a starter system obsolete. If growth continues, in a few years, the company would have to revisit the process of choosing a new system.

- If growth abates, the company would have purchased too much technology. It would be stuck indefinitely with excessive IT support and maintenance costs, inhibiting future growth and potentially threatening the success of the company.

The scale issue often deterred many small companies from making much-needed investments in technology.

The Paradox of Dramatically Increased Choice

As has been discussed, the last five years has produced a massive technological explosion. Make no mistake: this has been an explosion of both breadth *and* depth. New technologies have emerged, as has the number of existing options *within* existing technologies. (This is true even against a backdrop of an enormous amount of simultaneous merger and acquisition activity in the software world.) As a result, today many companies are simply unsure about what to do. Although increased choice with regard to technology is hardly a bad thing, many small business owners are inundated with options, unsure about "the best" solution for their companies. Call this paralysis by analysis.

For example, consider the number of different products offered by one very large technology company. Google has done many amazing things on many different levels.[6] In recent years, it has moved far beyond merely providing the world's most popular search engine. Consider what some of the company's applications can do for its business customers:

- Allow for customized e-mail domains (Gmail for Business).

- Share and manage online schedules (Google Calendar).

- Create team websites as easily as drafting documents (Google Sites).

- Collaborate in real time on documents, presentations, and spreadsheets (Google Apps and Google Docs). Indeed, over 30 million people use these tools.[i]

- Analyze traffic data for websites (Google Analytics).[7]

And Google isn't alone. Other companies such as OpenOffice[ii] and Zoho[iii] (discussed later in this book) offer similar arrays of related, integrated, and easily deployable services aimed at small businesses, although larger organizations can use them as well.

This is not to say that software vendors have long neglected the small business market. Nothing could be further from the truth. Indeed, companies such as Sage Software[iv] have long sold applications geared toward the small business. At the risk of excessively generalizing, however, today's small business applications are far superior to their antecedents on several levels:

- They offer increased integration, both out of the box and in terms of future development after the purchase.

- They are relatively easy to deploy and customize.

---

[6] Ken Auletta's excellent book *Googled* details how Larry Page and Sergey Brin rarely strayed from their overall vision in creating a revolutionary search engine.

[7] This is hardly a comprehensive list of Google's offerings. For such a list, see http://en.wikipedia.org/wiki/List_of_Google_products.

▨ Especially for SaaS solutions, there's comparatively little internal maintenance involved.

Collectively, these factors mean that small businesses can be up and running with integrated and powerful software in a much shorter period of time than in years past. By extension, small business owners and employees can focus on growing their businesses, not on IT headaches and deployment nightmares. However, before any company can reap the benefits of these technologies, it has to choose to deploy them. For many small businesses, that's no longer an easy decision. This is the paradox of increased choice.

An Era of Constant Technological Change

In the words of Mitchell Kapor, pioneer of the personal computing revolution: "Getting information off the Internet is like taking a drink from a fire hydrant." Few would dispute that we have entered an era of severe information and technology overload. Nearly every day (or every hour, if you're like me), we seem to hear about a new technology, website, gadget, or technology-inspired event that can affect our lives. In large part, today's environment stems from what many technology pundits and thought leaders have called "the consumerization of IT."[8]

Forget the ancient times of needing to read the newspaper to know what's happening. Think back to the days in which e-mail fundamentally changed the way many of us communicate. Those days now seem quaint in comparison to today's deluge of information. We instant message (IM), tweet, text, and "friend" others from our nearly ubiquitous portable devices. Some people, particularly those in Generation Y (aka *Millenials*), think nothing about divulging amazingly personal details about themselves on social networking sites such as Facebook. Five years ago, cell phones were common, although they were hardly the minicomputers they are today. Kindles, iPads, and Nooks are just a few of the devices altering the way that we consume information. Not too long ago, almost everyone used a PC equipped with Microsoft Windows and Office. Now, mobility, cloud computing, and open source software allow for things previously unfathomable. And most important, this flurry of activity isn't letting up anytime soon.

In the world of small businesses, this flood of technology has produced mixed results. Relatively few are thriving, doing more with less. Others are seeing only mild benefits. Many if not most are standing still, unable or unwilling to effect change.

---

[8] In a nutshell, most people no longer see and touch technology only at work.

This is hardly surprising. In fact, it has *always* been the case with new technologies and inventions. In this sense, the era of Web 2.0 is not unique. Other periods rife with disruptive technologies have also brought a mixed bag of results.

So what exactly has changed now? In a word, speed.

The Challenges of Staying Current

I need to keep abreast of a wide variety of dynamic topics, not only for myself but for my clients. Trying to stay current is easier said than done. If I'm on a consulting gig for as little time as a week, I routinely wonder about what I'm missing outside my client's walls. If I'm writing a piece for one of my clients on a specific topic, such as social media, I can't help but think about what's happening in other spheres. You could say such is life for the perennially curious man in the twenty-first century. Although the old adage "So many books, so little time" is still true, it could also be updated to "So many technologies, so little time."

These technologies are changing the rules by which we live and do business. They are taking people out of their comfort zones. Today, most people in organizations of all sizes need to deal with a great deal of technology-oriented change. Although I don't have a crystal ball, I just don't see this abating anytime soon.

Books such as *Distracted: The Erosion of Attention and the Coming Dark Age*[9] and *The Shallows: What the Internet Is Doing to Our Brains*[10] cover the potential long-term effects of this frenetic pace of activity. These books ask profound questions. Have we opened a new Pandora's box? Despite the benefits of our constantly connected world, do we fully understand its costs? Do we really know all of the pros and cons of these new technologies?

For most businesses, the answer to each of these questions is a resounding no. In the spring of 2010, I spoke at a few professional organizations about emerging technologies, social media, and website design. One in particular stands out. In April, I addressed a local Chamber of Commerce in Florham Park, NJ. I spoke to a group of about 40 small business owners who wanted to know more about recent developments in technology. My talk was originally scheduled for half an hour, but I knew within five minutes that I had struck a nerve with the audience. They kept peppering me with questions about blogging, cloud computing, software as a service (SaaS), and other new topics with which they were vaguely familiar. I

[9]   By Maggie Jackson and Bill McKibben.
[10] By Nicolas Carr.

suspect that, had they not had to go work, we would have chatted all day. Our conversation lasted nearly 90 minutes.

No matter where I went, I kept thinking about small businesses' struggles with—and misconceptions about—emerging technologies. For example, in June of 2010, I needed to get my tennis racquet restrung. Rather than go to a large chain store, I try to support local businesses. I frequent the aptly named WhatARacquet close to my home. After all, I'm a local business here in northern NJ as well—although a really small one. At the time, I hadn't begun writing this book.

As I paid for my restrung racquet at the counter, I started chatting with one of WhatARacquet's co-owners, a woman named Linda. She knew that I was a tech guy and asked me whether I thought she needed a proper website or could get away with just a Facebook page. Never one lacking opinions, I offered mine: why not both?[11] I explained to her the benefits of social networks and media. She was all ears.

It seems to me that many small business owners are awash in a sea of technology they aren't using. Most haven't explored mobility, cloud computing, social technologies, and so on. They aren't keeping up with many of the changes that could significantly help them on so many levels.

Reasons for Lagging

I began to wonder about why so many small business owners seem to be unaware of the profound technological changes currently taking place. Reasons include:

- Some are just overwhelmed by the rate of change.
- Some just don't care—they don't plan to change anything if they can avoid it.
- Some are probably intimidated by these new technologies.
- Some just aren't aware. Their attention is elsewhere.
- Some subscribe to the view "If it ain't broke, don't fix it."

I suppose that this would make sense if these emerging technologies offered only marginal improvements to John Q. Business Owner. But that's just not the case. These days, many small companies ignore technologies that, at a minimum, can help them *significantly*:

- Grow their businesses
- Attract talented employees

---

[11] Why some companies don't have a Facebook presence is beyond me. Facebook recently achieved more than 500,000,000 registered users. Put another way: if Facebook were a country, only India and China would have more citizens.

- Improve access to key information
- Increase employee communication and collaboration
- Reduce costs of recruiting, IT, and marketing
- Compete with larger companies

Of course, exceptions abound. Some small businesses are using emerging technologies in creative and interesting ways to achieve these benefits. These are the New Small.

Kranzberg's Laws of Technology

Lest I paint a morbid picture of the state of small business technology adoption, let's review a little history. This is hardly the first time that massive technological change has affected the American workplace and the fundamental way that people actually perform their jobs.[12] Melvin Kranzberg spent decades lecturing about the history of technology. He is most famous for his six laws of technology, listed below:

- Technology is neither good nor bad; nor is it neutral.
- Invention is the mother of necessity.
- Technology comes in packages, big and small.
- Although technology might be a prime element in many public issues, nontechnical factors take precedence in technology-policy decisions.
- All history is relevant, but the history of technology is the most relevant.
- Technology is a very human activity—and so is the history of technology.[v]

Although technology constantly changes, Kranzberg's laws have had remarkable staying power.[13] Today, emerging technologies are allowing small businesses to do amazing things. From a technology perspective, they can act big and scale just as easily as larger players. No longer are powerful enterprise technologies necessarily too big or too expensive for small businesses. In many cases, smaller companies can do exactly what the big boys can do at a fraction of the cost.

---

[12] Perhaps the best account of this I've read is Dennis Baron's book, *A Better Pencil: Readers, Writers, and the Digital Revolution*. For centuries, people have questioned advances in the world of writing.

[13] I am reminded here of the signature Rush song "Tom Sawyer" with the apropos lyric "Changes aren't permanent, but change is."

From a people management perspective, new communication technology, for example, can be a godsend. Employees are able to work wherever and whenever they choose. Increased flexibility is, in fact, a major reason that many people work for smaller outfits or start their own shops. Other motivations include the ability to have a greater impact at work and the desire to be one's own boss. Although the reasons vary, we will see later on that many New Small founders had similar motivations in deciding to start their own businesses.

Companies of any size that lack a coherent technology strategy ultimately pay the price, and not just in terms of money wasted on failed IT projects. In such workplaces, many employees feel completely overwhelmed by too much technology; they are not sure about what they should be doing, much less how to do it.

Over the last two years, I have written a great deal about the different effects of these technologies, as well as related trends, events, and innovations. The vast majority of my writing, consulting, and speaking over the last two years has revolved around one central question: how can organizations make the best use of emerging technologies?

It's a big question, and its answer hinges on the following:

- The type and size of the organization
- The industry
- Profit margins and competition
- The specific technology
- Regulatory considerations
- The economy
- Business imperatives

I've come to one conclusion: *all else being equal, it's better to be small.*

That's right. For several reasons, it's no longer a liability to be the little guy. As mentioned earlier, the last five years have seen a massive explosion of available *and viable* business technologies that allow small businesses to compete. In general and compared to their larger counterparts, small companies are simply better able to adapt to changes and move in different directions as needed. This book illustrates how small businesses are now *leapfrogging* big companies, effectively deploying new technologies faster, more effectively, and at lower costs.

But it gets better. Yes, compared to big companies, many small businesses are adopting new technologies at both greater speed and lower cost. These represent two sources of a new competitive advantage for these nimble, agile companies. At the New Small, new technologies are enabling a completely different mindset and definition of work. Smaller outfits and start-ups are attracting top-flight talent because, to some extent, they allow work to be done anywhere: from home, on a beach, or in a coffee shop. This tech-friendly ethos is allowing employees to work on their own terms, addressing the work-life imbalance from which many people suffer (more on this in Chapters 2 and 4). In this vein, the New Small is using technology strategically to win the war for talent.

The Five Enablers

So, there's good news for small businesses on several fronts. Emerging technologies are allowing progressive companies to leap ahead of others still struggling to figure things out. But which technologies are making such a dramatic difference? There are five specific ones, and in this book, I collectively refer to them as *the Five Enablers*:

- Cloud computing
- Software as a service (SaaS)
- Free and open source software (FOSS)
- Mobility
- Social technologies

New Small companies effectively deploy and use the Five Enablers. As a result, they have the same—or even superior—technology compared to organizations 10 times their size, often at a fraction of the time and cost. What's more, these businesses go from technological laggards to leaders.

Traditional Aphorisms

For many years, many small businesses have followed traditional business aphorisms such as "do more with less," "focus on what you do best," and "never be satisfied." Progressive small businesses have always looked for ways to do things better, faster, and cheaper while concurrently maintaining focus. In this manner, the Five Enablers are merely means to traditional ends.

A Welcome Byproduct

The Five Enablers are doing so much more than allowing New Small companies to upgrade their technology and reduce their IT budgets: they are enabling employees at these companies to work in much more fulfilling jobs. As you see in the small companies profiled later in this book, fewer employees' jobs are rigidly defined and compartmentalized. Ask many owners of New Small companies to name their head of IT, for example, and they will probably say, "Well, we all sort of pitch in" or "It's probably Steven today."

The New Small is creating more meaningful jobs, and in the process, turning long-held management theories on their head. In some circles, they are reversing Scientific Management, the theory developed by Frederick Taylor in the late nineteenth century and largely adopted by many businesses around the globe. No longer does work need to be excessively specialized, repetitive, and mind-numbingly boring. Through the Five Enablers, the New Small is injecting a much-needed sense of excitement into many workplaces.

Why Now?

Astute readers will note that these technologies have existed in one form or another for quite some time. They may be more evolutionary than revolutionary. So, what has changed? First, as with bandwidth and storage, over the last 10 years these technologies have become significantly less expensive and even more powerful. The net result: by and large, small companies are now able to afford these exciting technologies. Second, deployment is far easier and more flexible. No longer do small businesses have to attempt to predict just how much technology they will need—and face dire consequences if they are wrong. As we see in Chapter 3, today a company of 200 employees can scale its technology in the same way that a 20,000-employee company can. Third, success begets more success, creating a type of network effect.[14] *Technologies become more popular because, reflexively, they are already popular.* For example, as more companies have adopted cloud computing, others have become emboldened to do the same. Lessons and case studies become available as different technologies and products become more mature. While the evolution of technology is by no means finished, with respect to the Five Enablers, we certainly understand a great deal more than we did five years ago.

---

[14] A network effect is "the resulting increased value of a product because more and more people use it. Telephones, fax machines, and computer operating systems are examples. A product's success is due to compatibility and conformity issues, not that the product or technology may be superior or inferior to the competition." See http://computer.yourdictionary.com/network-effect.

SUMMARY

This chapter has examined the reasons that many small businesses have historically been technological laggards—and why this is now changing. It also introduced the Five Enablers: the emerging technologies currently enabling the New Small to realize enormous benefits, savings, and efficiencies. The bottom line is that today there are major advantages to being small.

The next chapter will provide greater context about the nature of these technological changes in the workplace.

Endnotes

i   http://www.google.com/hostednews/afp/article/ALeqM5iBM55JyzGXlgtxrJ3gu9qt
    Cx30dA
ii http://www.openoffice.org
iii http://www.zoho.com
iv http://www.sagenorthamerica.com/products_services
v   http://en.wikipedia.org/wiki/Kranzberg%27s_laws_of_technology

Chapter 2

MAJOR TRENDS DRIVING THE NEW SMALL

*All truth passes through three stages. First,
it is ridiculed. Second, it is violently opposed.
Third, it is accepted as self-evident.*

—Arthur Schopenhauer

In the mid-1990s, there was no New Small. It simply could not have existed. Sure, there were progressive small businesses that embraced an ethos different from the rest, using technology in interesting ways. Often singled out as "quirky," these companies allowed employees to do fun things at work. They created cool cultures by creatively using the technologies available at the time. However, those technologies were not nearly as powerful as the Five Enablers. As discussed in the last chapter, small businesses have historically used inferior technologies relative to large organizations.

Times have certainly changed. We've entered a whole new world, and this chapter explores it. It covers the major trends and events in both technology and labor markets that have allowed the New Small to blossom. These eight specific trends are:

- The rise of the freemium model
- Improved offshore development
- Better outsourcing

- The explosion of software choice
- The rise of the social customer and social technologies
- The erosion of the employee-employer social compact
- The increased use of contractors
- The war for talent

The Rise of the Freemium Model

Perhaps nothing allows the New Small to do more with less than free and open source software (FOSS), discussed in more detail in Chapter 3. Collectively, the massive rise in popularity of the Internet and the adoption of broadband connections have allowed software companies and developers to distribute their wares at virtually no cost. Fifteen years ago, people like William Hurley (now of Chaotic Moon, profiled in Chapter 15) worked at Apple Computer. Software companies like Apple had to deliver their products via physical media—typically on compact discs (CDs). Manufacturing thousands of CDs costs a great deal of money, to say nothing about packing and shipping them. Back in the 1990s, some companies willingly accepted these expenses as costs of doing business. America Online (AOL) most readily comes to mind. As a whole, though, relatively few software vendors were keen to just give their stuff away. That has changed.

On March 23, 2006, venture capitalist Fred Wilson wrote a blog post entitled "My Favorite Business Model,"[i] in which he articulated the rationale behind freemium. Here is its premise:

> Give your service away for free, possibly ad supported but maybe not, acquire a lot of customers very efficiently through word of mouth, referral networks, organic search marketing, etc., then offer premium priced value added services or an enhanced version of your service to your customer base.

Freemium entered the business zeitgeist with the 2009 publication of Chris Anderson's bestselling book *Free: The Future of a Radical Price*. The popularity of freemium cannot be overstated. Innumerable companies have embraced this business model, including Skype, Pandora, Google, Facebook, Twitter, Box.Net, Trillian, and probably tens of thousands of others. In fact, these days, many if not most software vendors offer some type of free or trial version of their software. Microsoft allows as much with the web-based version of Office 2010. In 2009, *The New York Times* went so far as to claim that freemium had become "the most popular business model among web start-ups."[ii]

Freemium has become so pervasive that many people now take free goods and services as givens. This has huge implications for many areas of society and business, as Anderson demonstrates throughout his book. But I wonder whether the model is sustainable. At some point, businesses and individuals need to make money. What happens if nearly all of a company's customers opt for its free version, preferring not to pay for premium features? Well, in April of 2010, we found out. Popular social networking site Ning[iii] had to abandon the freemium model in favor of a more income-centric business model.[iv]

Many people (and I am no exception[v]) have openly wondered whether freemium is sustainable. Think about the following two scenarios. First, let's say that a company pays GoDaddy[vi] to provide web hosting services. It has a right to expect a certain level of system uptime and assistance in the event of a problem. These expectations are entirely rational.

Now, consider a company that pays nothing for a critical software application, opting to save a few bucks. One day, that program experiences a major problem. The following questions come to mind:

- Do the company's employees have a right to complain about the quality of that product?
- What about expecting timely support?
- Who's going to actually solve the problem?
- Will the problem be solved in a timely manner?
- What will be the costs of the downtime?
- Were there any security breaches or data corruption?

The answers to these questions are murky at best. The New Small realizes the inherent limitations of the freemium model. Being cost-conscious is one thing. Being foolish and excessively frugal is quite another.

Improved Offshore Development

In his wildly successful book *The World Is Flat*, Thomas L. Friedman discusses how the development of the Internet caused—and expedited—many American jobs to move offshore. Although this trend may have been a net negative for the U.S. economy, it has clearly benefited companies such as PeerPort (profiled in Chapter 9).[1] The company found a very effective and affordable offshore development team in Macronimous.[vii] Put simply, offshore development has allowed many small businesses to significantly reduce their costs. Although there are still significant risks in using offshore

---

[1] Remember Kranzberg's first law: Technology is neither good nor bad; nor is it neutral.

companies for software development projects, the New Small effectively manages these challenges.

Better Outsourcing

The term *outsourcing* originally found its way into mainstream business vocabulary in the 1980s. To be sure, there still are some major potential drawbacks. However, if done right, the practice can yield major advantages, particularly with regard to cost. And New Small companies understand this well. They freely embrace different types of outsourcing, including software development, accounting, and administrative functions such as payroll distribution. In the current environment, some small businesses are outsourcing not just discrete tasks, but *entire departments*, such as

- Human Resources (HR), through professional employment organizations (PEOs)
- Finance or Accounting, through services that provide part-time chief financial officers (CFOs) and comptrollers

Examples of the latter include Tatum[viii] and Consult Your CFO.[ix] These companies work with small businesses that lack the internal expertise to handle budgets, accounting, and the like—in other words, prime candidates for part-time CFOs. "As a new company matures, an outsourced CFO/Comptroller can assist the owner in many ways," says Ken Weil, founder and president of Consult Your CFO, itself a small business. "Specific activities are related to analysis, implementation, and oversight. Many companies simply cannot afford to hire a full-time CFO or Comptroller, especially early on." Companies like Weil's provide a key service to businesses that need a *part-time* but seasoned key financial executive.

Note that New Small companies typically do *not* outsource critical elements of their businesses. These *may* include customer service (to be discussed later in this chapter) as well as business strategy.

The Explosion of Software Choice

For several reasons, the last 10 years in the technology world have been fascinating. For one, there has been a great deal of merger and acquisition (M&A) activity, as large software vendors such as Oracle, SAP, IBM, and Microsoft have spent billions of dollars gobbling up companies with interesting products and niche focuses. What's more, there's been an explosion in the number and variety of software applications, tools, sites, and platforms available to businesses of all sizes (see "The Paradox of Dramatically Increased Choice" in Chapter 1). These include free, open source, and proprietary applications. Today, just about every type of technology seems to offer a dazzling array of viable options.

A small business that can't find an application or technology that meets its needs doesn't need to fret. Enormously powerful technologies allow companies to build new tools—and modify existing ones—relatively easily and inexpensively. Some of these technologies include:

- Robust content management systems (CMSs) allow easy publication of posts, videos, and podcasts. Examples include Drupal,[x] WordPress,[xi] and Joomla![xii]

- Software development kits (SDKs or devkits) allow developers to create applications for many software packages, frameworks, hardware platforms, computer systems, operating systems, or similar platforms.

- Application programming interfaces (APIs) allow developers to easily build real-time links and interfaces among different applications. In other words, it's far easier—and less expensive—for Application A to talk to Application B.[2] Here, many major software companies and tech giants such as Salesforce.com have followed the lead of relatively smaller outfits such as Twitter.[xiii]

I could go on, but suffice it to say for now that there is no shortage of choices available to small businesses. Much of the aforementioned M&A activity has only affected large software vendors and their large client bases. These products are so expensive that they're beyond the budgets of even the largest small businesses—and generally unnecessary anyway. New Small companies have found—or built—tools that work for them. More important, these companies constantly keep their eyes open for new alternatives.

The Rise of the Social Customer and Social Technologies

I know a little something about the inner workings of customer service because I wasn't always an author, speaker, and technology consultant. Let's go back in time to 1994. I had graduated from Carnegie Mellon University, and I was unsure about what I wanted to do with my life. I began working in customer service at Sony Electronics near my home in New Jersey. It was a decent job that involved a good deal of listening to upset customers. (No one calls customer service and waits on hold for 15 minutes just to

---

[2] Although this was possible 10 years ago, the closed nature of most APIs meant that such work was often time-consuming and difficult. It's considerably easier today.

praise your company and its products.) Sony wasn't foolish. The company wasn't about to put a recent college grad on the phone with irate parents complaining that their camcorder didn't work during their daughter's second birthday. No, I had to attend training with other new hires. I remember one statistic from that class as though I first heard it yesterday: according to Sony research, the average dissatisfied customer told 60 people about his/her experience, and I'm quite sure that that number is much higher today. That was more than 15 years ago, well before most people heard of the Internet.

In case you've been living in a bubble for the last decade, the Internet has destroyed or drastically changed many businesses. Photo printing, travel agents, and the music industry most readily come to mind. Along with creating new industries and forever altering others, it has caused seismic shifts in departments such as customer service. For a few years now, we have been hearing increasingly about the term *social customer relationship management*. Paul Greenberg, author of *CRM at the Speed of Light*, defines it as

> ...a philosophy and a business strategy, supported by a technology platform, business rules, workflow, processes, and social characteristics, designed to engage the customer in a collaborative conversation in order to provide mutually beneficial value in a trusted and transparent business environment. *It's the company's response to the customer's ownership of the conversation*[xiv] (emphasis added).

Many large companies have yet to embrace social CRM.[3] As Greenberg notes above, power has shifted to the customer. Paradoxically, relatively few companies understand this fundamental shift. How many provide excellent customer service? How many understand that customers can be their most zealous advocates—and biggest detractors? Not many, as I've argued before.[xv] In fact, Amazon.com is the exception that proves the rule. Large companies continue to struggle to understand truths the New Small knows very well:

- All customers are social—or easily can become social.
- Social CRM isn't really new at all; customers today simply have more tools and options to express their delight or discontent.

The New Small realizes that social CRM is not a threat; *it's an opportunity*. It represents innovative ways that companies can take care of their

---

[3] And many never understood the basics of plain old customer relationship management, but that's a separate discussion.

most important asset: their customers. Take away its customers, and any company ceases to exist. Period.

Part II covers small businesses such as Torrance Learning, RedSeven, and Chaotic Motion. These companies would never even dream of insisting that their customers call 1-800 numbers to resolve their issues. I laugh—as you probably will—at the very thought of RedSeven founder Michael Cady making his company's customers play "dial-a-rep" to find someone capable of helping them. It just doesn't make sense for his business. At the same time, though, outsourcing customer service to the right type of partner makes sense for small businesses hit by sudden, unexpected growth. DODOcase founders Patrick Buckley and Craig Dalton (discussed in Chapter 11) regret waiting so long to outsource the customer service function to 5anHour,[xvi] a company that specializes in customer service with plans that start at (you guessed it) $5 per hour.[4]

As a general rule, New Small companies appreciate three related trends to a much greater extent than large organizations do:

- The continued importance of customer service
- The rise of the social customer
- The proliferation of social technologies

Maria Ogneva knows a thing or two about these topics. She is the director of social media at Nimble,[xvii] a social media engagement company. In a blog post entitled "Why Your Company Needs to Embrace Social CRM,"[xviii] Ogneva offers the following definition of the social customer:

> The social customer expects you to listen and engage with her, not only when it coincides with an e-mail blast or new feature release, but rather when she needs you. And you better respond fast, in real time, or she will either move on to a competitor, or tell her friends about her bad experiences.

The New Small understands that impatient, angry, and web-savvy customers will act on their anger in a number of ways:

- Describe, in person, their bad experiences to anyone they encounter.
- In all but the most extreme cases, such as in dealings with energy and cable companies (de facto monopolies), use another company.
- Go social. They will use blogs, social networking sites, and increasingly influential customer review sites, such as Yelp.[xix]

---

[4] This apparent contradiction actually makes complete sense. As we see with the New Small, there's no universal "right" way of doing things. There is only a "right" way to do something *for each company*.

Note that the future of sites such as Yelp is beyond bright. In December of 2009, *The New York Times* reported that the company turned down a $500M acquisition offer from Google.[xx] Some in the know expect the company to go public in the near future.[xxi]

The Erosion of the Employee-Employer Social Compact

For decades, most large American companies offered very secure jobs, if not the permanent or lifetime employment of their counterparts in countries such as Japan. For a variety of reasons, including global advances in technology and some degree of Wall Street greed, this situation began to change in the mid-1980s, when even many highly profitable companies laid off employees to boost profits even more. To some extent, these types of guaranteed jobs still exist in the public sector, although the U.S. national debt and annual deficits mean that, at some point, severe cutbacks are inevitable. Today, the employee-employer relationship is fundamentally different from 25 years ago—and it has been for some time.

Perhaps nothing crystallized this difference more than the dot.com boom of the late 1990s and early 2000s. Rather than feeling any loyalty to their employers, many employees—particularly those with highly desirable technical skills—frequently jumped from job to job, often receiving 20 percent raises in the process. Although those halcyon days (at least for employees) are long gone, that attitude has not entirely disappeared. Even during the Great Recession, many people have kept their eyes and ears open to new employment opportunities, making strategic moves if circumstances warranted.

Any myths of the benevolent employer have long been shattered. Today, the American worker knows that companies will always do what's in their best interest. By the same token, many people are reciprocating. "What's in it for me?" is never far from most workers' minds. If they are not getting the right experience, exposure, compensation, or training, many of them won't hesitate to switch jobs. Foolish is the company that expects its employees—especially its key ones—to remain motivated by sheer loyalty and a sense of obligation. That ship has sailed.

The Increased Use of Contractors

For years now, many organizations have increased their reliance upon *non-employees*: temps, contractors, consultants, and others not hired on a

W-2[5] basis. I first became aware of this trend in 1995 when I began my graduate studies at Cornell University's School of Industrial and Labor Relations (ILR). In the last 15 years, this trend has hardly abated; if anything, it has intensified.

In a May 2010 MSNBC article entitled "Need a Job? Contract Work Could Be New Normal," Eve Tahmincioglu confirms what many have long suspected. She writes about the "vanguard of an emerging new contingent workforce. For some businesses, these contingent workers could become a permanent solution, eliminating a huge swath of full-time jobs with benefits, say labor and business experts." Tahmincioglu continues:

> Garry Mathiason, senior managing shareholder at Littler Mendelson, said it (the prevalent use of contractors) is the new normal.
>
> "As the economy gets moving faster, there will be more opportunities, and many of those will be in contingent jobs," he said. Such free-agent work has gone far beyond low-skilled jobs and the construction sector, he said, where contract work long has been prevalent.
>
> Mathiason expects to see a rise in the use of contingent workers in highly skilled positions—including scientists, engineers, professionals, and managers—as companies aim to do more project-based work with small groups of professionals they can bring in as needed. He compares it to making a movie, where producers bring in the crew needed to get the job done.
>
> "The business model has definitely arrived," he said. "It was starting to arrive, but the recession caused an acceleration in the process."

Although arguably inimical to the typical American worker, this trend has yielded some unexpected consequences. Specifically, many people are getting their feet wet working for themselves *before* starting proper businesses. This certainly was the case with Laura Schoppe, whose company, Fuentek, is profiled in Chapter 13. Labor market trends have blurred the definition between salaried, secure, full-time jobs and working for oneself. It's not as if working for someone else is that much more risky than

---

[5] Form W-2, Wage and Tax Statement, is used in the United States income tax system as an information return to report wages paid to employees and the taxes withheld from them. W-2 employees typically receive proper benefits from their employers and, with some exceptions, are covered under most U.S. labor legislation, including OSHA, EEOC, FLSA, and FMLA. Contractors are not. See http://en.wikipedia.org/wiki/W-2#W-2.

self-employment. Today, many people are their own *de facto* bosses whether they've incorporated or not. Many have their own clients or secondary clients through consulting firms or temp agencies. They discover that they:

- Enjoy the benefits of self-employment
- Can handle the considerable risks of doing so

To be sure, many people still fear working for themselves; it's folly to claim otherwise. However, the explosion of content and the social nature of today's web mean that it's easy to find stories and advice about how to do your own thing. Many people are doing just that.

The War for Talent

For years, we've been hearing about the increasingly competitive global workforce. In their 2001 book, *The War for Talent*, authors Ed Michaels, Helen Handfield-Jones, and Beth Axelrod predict a future in which many organizations compete for relatively few high-performing employees with scarce skills. That future has arrived.

The authors write about the types of companies that are most likely to win this war:

> The better companies differentiate the pay, opportunities, and other investments that they make in people. They reward their best performers with fast-track growth and pay them substantially more than their average performers. They develop and affirm the solidly contributing middle performers, helping them raise their game. They remove weak players—believing that "blinking" on these hard decisions is unfair to the people working under that manager, to the organization at large, and even to the underperformers themselves. These companies have a very different ethic about what it means to manage their people.

How many large organizations actually match this description? From my experience, very few—and I've seen more than my fair share as a technology consultant over the last 10 years. Small businesses in general—and the New Small in particular—are in a unique position to attract and retain top-tier talent. Along with the erosion of the social compact discussed in the previous section, these companies can pounce on highly skilled employees who, perhaps even 15 years ago, would have considered working at a small business beneath them—or at least lacking sufficient prestige.

Many people are doing what Ray Wang did. After more than two decades of product management, consulting, and marketing roles in large corporate environments, he started looking for something different. He served his time in highly regarded big organizations, including Forrester Research,[xxii] Deloitte Consulting,[xxiii] and Oracle Software.[xxiv] In 2010, he finally started his own "star analyst" firm. Wang and several like-minded folks formed The Altimeter Group,[xxv] a research-based advisory firm. Wang—and his partners and employees—are among increasing numbers of people leaving the big corporate world to work in the greener pastures of the New Small. And Wang is hardly alone. Whether by choice or necessity, many talented individuals are joining small businesses or starting their own.

You don't need to be as senior as Wang to realize the benefits of working for the New Small. In fact, more junior employees are seeing the light. "Relative to large organizations, small businesses offer employees opportunities sooner," says Professor Peter Cappelli, professor of management at the Wharton School at the University of Pennsylvania and author of *Talent on Demand: Managing Talent in an Age of Uncertainty*. "An entry-level marketing analyst may be able do things at a small company only available to employees at larger companies toward the end of their careers. Of course, there's a downside. At small companies, employees are often forced to learn by doing. They may lack the formal support or training provided by larger firms. This may make learning harder."[xxvi]

The inherent conflict and inertia of many big companies have driven some of their most talented and ambitious employees away. What's more, it gives many other people ideas about starting their own shops. Certain personality types—and I firmly put myself in this group—generally do better in smaller settings in which problem solving trumps politics. As you see throughout the book, New Small owners and founders are either former corporate folks or serial entrepreneurs who never bought into the big corporate life. The people running these companies have no intention of leaving anytime soon for the formerly safe havens of "working for the man."

Roles have switched. Now the big companies are having increasing difficulty attracting and retaining the top talent. The New Small often is more appealing than large organizations with greater brand recognition.

Differentiating the New Small: Valuing Employees through True Workplace Flexibility

People are our most valuable asset. Sound familiar? Just about every company claims as much on its website, annual report, or marketing literature. It has become cliché. Whether or not companies practice what they preach is a separate discussion.

At this point, it's fair to ask several questions. What makes the New Small different? Do these companies *really* value their employees? How do we know that this is not mere lip service? To these questions, three answers come to mind:

- Workplace policies
- The liberal use of technology
- A pragmatic style of management

The New Small gets more out of its employees by effectively using these levers. And for their part, employees get more out of their jobs, perform better, and are less likely to leave. Let's look at each in more detail.

Workplace Policies

At the New Small, formal and informal workplace policies codify the mutually beneficial relationships between employees and employer. These companies offer flex hours. They permit employees to work from home—or wherever, in many cases. They don't micromanage. Part II will provide a cauldron of specific examples. Now, I'm hardly the first to claim that "pro-employee" policies allow people to better manage their personal lives. But policies alone do not create better workplaces; they need to exist in the real world. Many companies' ostensibly employee-friendly policies lack teeth. When employees with personal issues cannot take time to deal with them, the policy becomes a sham, employees become even more upset, and workplace morale suffers.

The Liberal Use of Technology

Technology plays an essential role in the New Small. (Chapter 3 will have a great deal more to say about that.) Employees can be only as productive as their company's tools let them be. Even the hardest working person who requires zero sleep cannot move heaven and earth. Many New Small founders know from their previous jobs the frustration of having to make do with outdated technology. As such, they do not want their employees to struggle using inadequate tools. The New Small wants—*and needs*—their employees to be as productive as possible. Emerging technologies are crucial in this regard, especially collaborative ones (discussed at length in Chapter 17).

For example, consider a company that lacks a basic screen-sharing application. As a result, employees must be in the same physical office to work on a project together—or slug it out over e-mail. The company just does not provide another (read: better) way for its employees to get the job done. Although the company saves a little bit of money on technology, what are the costs to productivity and employee morale? Think of the employee disaffection when a company is too cheap to spring for a pretty common tool, especially on those snowy winter days and two-hour commutes. This is just pennywise and pound foolish.

A Pragmatic Style of Management

Much like company policies, technology does not exist in a vacuum. The New Small offers productive, flexible, practical, and employee-friendly workplaces *not* merely because they employ the latest technologies. Management at these companies is more mature and practical, especially when compared to most of their larger counterparts. Many big companies cannot break free of old-fashioned habits, including the tendency to emphasize face time over results, politics over productivity. Unfortunately, this is true even in jobs that lend themselves to flexible work arrangements.[6] The rigid and often nonsensical policies of bloated, bureaucratic companies often offset any potential efficiency gains to be made by deploying the Five Enablers.[7] Emerging technologies ultimately disappoint at many organizations because corporate edicts, internal politics, bad data, cultural issues, and their ilk never give them a realistic shot at succeeding.

The New Small operates under a different mindset. These companies understand several essential things about the world of work:

- Technology does not exist in a vacuum. Bad management can kill the most promising initiatives.
- Productivity trumps hours worked; results matter more than the time required to achieve them.
- Under most circumstances, where employees work ultimately doesn't really matter.

In a June 2010 article in *BusinessWeek* entitled "Working on the Waterfront,"[xxvii] Joel Stein writes about how technology is enabling a newfound flexibility, particularly in small businesses:

> Aided by technology, pioneers are now converting the beach into a fully functional office. People who work from the beach in non-hotel, non-burger-stand, non-pot-dealer capacities are still rare enough that no agency tracks the phenomenon. Brooks Brothers does not yet make a three-piece bathing suit; Herman Miller (MLHR) doesn't sell an Aeron chaise.

---

[6] Does the following situation sound familiar? John worked until 7 P.M. but took a two-hour lunch and frequent smoking breaks. He actually didn't do a whole lot today. Yet management holds him in higher esteem than his counterpart, Jordan. He arrived early, worked through lunch, and left at around 5 P.M. He actually accomplished a great deal in the office, but it was in relative isolation.

[7] To quote Dennis Miller, "I don't want to get off on a rant here, but...." Trust me. I could go on for hours about this.

It's not like these beach workers are slackers; they just don't like being controlled. It's the same reason why we TiVo shows or e-mail and text more than call. When you can work from wherever you want to be—especially if it's the place where everyone wants to be—work isn't so bad.

Bill Kilburg, 48, is the chairman and chief executive of Scottsdale (Ariz.)-based Hospitality Performance Network Global, a broker of group meetings. For six weeks each summer, he and his co-founder rent houses five blocks apart in Mission Beach, San Diego, and work from there. "My CFO gets my parking space, so she's happy," Kilburg says. He generally works from the shore on his BlackBerry until 1 p.m., then cracks a beer and heads into the ocean. He's philosophical about his ability to lead the 170-person company from the beach. "My job is the strategic growth of the company," he says. "It's not like I have to be sitting in my office to do that."

Again, think about it. How many people working for large outfits provide their employees with anywhere near this degree of flexibility? How many of your friends would trade the ostensible prestige of working for a big company for the ability to work at the beach?

And this is no gimmick. As stories like Kilburg's become more common, others ask themselves how they can sign up—and more small businesses are offering the chance to do just that. This open-mindedness provides an enormous advantage for the New Small in the war for talent.

SUMMARY

A confluence of events has allowed the New Small not only to exist, but to thrive. These companies have astutely taken advantage of both labor market and technology trends to create nimble environments with productive, largely satisfied, and happy employees. Although technology is important in this regard, it is no silver bullet for obsolete processes and management styles rooted in nineteenth-century theories. In other words, technology is a necessary but not sufficient condition for the existence and success of the New Small.

The next chapter delves into more detail about the specific technologies used by the New Small.

Endnotes

i   http://avc.blogs.com/a_vc/2006/03/my_favorite_bus.html

ii   http://www.nytimes.com/2009/05/25/technology/start-ups/25startup.html?_r=1

iii   http://www.ning.com/

iv   http://tinyurl.com/ning123-x

v   http://mike2.openmethodology.org/blogs/information-development/2010/06/07/freemium/

vi   http://www.godaddy.com/

vii   http://macronimous.com/

viii   http://www.tatumllc.com/

ix   http://www.consultyourcfo.com

x   http://drupal.org

xi   http://www.wordpress.com

xii   http://www.joomla.org

xiii   http://dev.twitter.com/pages/api_faq

xiv   http://the56group.typepad.com/pgreenblog/2009/07/time-to-put-a-stake-in-the-ground-on-social-crm.html

xv   http://mike2.openmethodology.org/blogs/information-development/2010/08/02/charlie-rose-customer-service-and-the-master-twitter-record/

xvi   http://www.5anhour.com/

xvii   http://www.nimble.com/

xviii   http://www.mashable.com/2010/05/21/social-crm/

xix   http://www.yelp.com

xx   http://tinyurl.com/yelp-google-x

xxi   http://paul.kedrosky.com/archives/2009/12/netscape_yelp_a.html

xxii   http://www.forrester.com/rb/research

xxiii   http://www.deloitte.com

xxiv   http://www.oracle.com/index.html

[xxv] http://www.altimetergroup.com
[xxvi] Personal conversation, 07/14/2010
[xxvii] http://www.businessweek.com/magazine/content/10_27/b4185073587611.htm

Chapter **3**

THE FIVE ENABLERS

All truth, in the long run, is only common sense clarified.

—Thomas Huxley

As discussed in Chapter 2, emerging technologies have been collectively a mixed blessing for many companies. On one hand, opportunities abound. On the other, compared to years past, organizations of all sizes seem to be having more difficulty keeping up with advances in applications, platforms, and systems. No doubt, this trouble arises in part from economic conditions. In many companies, cutbacks have resulted in fewer employees doing more work.

To be sure, *emerging technologies* is a broad term, meaning different things to different people. What's more, not all are created equal. In this book, I focus on five emerging technologies and what the New Small is doing with them. I call these "the Five Enablers," and they are the following:

- Cloud computing
- SaaS (software as a service)
- Free and open source software (FOSS)
- Mobility
- Social technologies (social media and social networking)[1]

---

[1] Note the term *social technologies* includes social media and networks. I do this for the sake of simplicity. Although they technically are different things, they seem blurrier to me every day. Also, I have a problem with collectively calling them *social*. Call me cantankerous, but these days too many people take adjectives and make them nouns or verbs.

This chapter provides definitions, benefits, risks, and limitations on each of the Five Enablers. Although a comprehensive look at each is outside the scope of the book, a brief overview of each provides the requisite background for the company profiles in Part II. The chapter then examines the cost ramifications of the Five Enablers within the context of current economic conditions. It concludes with a high-level look at the relationships among these individual technologies.

Business Need: To Adopt or Not To Adopt?

Before beginning the discussion of the Five Enablers, it's important to establish some common ground. This chapter discusses many emerging technologies adopted by the New Small. Although the specific reasons, vendors, tools, and methodologies often vary, the underlying business rationale does not. As you read this chapter, keep the following in mind with respect to the New Small:

- **Not all technologies are created equal**—On many levels, the adoption of a new platform such as cloud computing is fundamentally different from experimenting with a new social media site. The former is a measured decision involving considerable time, money, and expense that no company should take lightly. The latter is very different.

- **Sense of purpose**—The adoption of a technology is often a nascent attempt to solve a problem or address a core business need. New Small companies don't play "keeping up with the Joneses." These specific technologies need to increase communications, reduce costs, increase revenue, improve productivity, or offer some type of other significant benefit.

- **The ability to walk away**—The technology will ultimately be replaced if, for whatever reason, it doesn't work out.

Cloud Computing

Cloud computing is one hot technology, and for good reason. The National Institute for Standards and Technology (NIST) defines cloud computing as "a model for enabling ubiquitous, convenient, on-demand network access to a shared pool of configurable computing resources (e.g., networks, servers, storage, applications, and services) that can be rapidly provisioned and released with minimal management effort or service provider interaction."¹ Note that there are many definitions of cloud computing from many reputable sources. I can't tell you that the one from NIST is the right one.

At a high level, cloud-based applications allow employees to access company information from wherever they are. Data and applications in the clouds are simply more accessible than those stored in a single location. Although there are security implications related to de-perimeterizing the enterprise, cloud applications are gaining momentum as organizations try to improve accessibility of information—and reduce the cost of getting it.

Although the term *cloud computing* came into vogue in 2007, its origins are much older. Formerly called *utility* or *grid computing*, the concept originated in Douglas Parkhill's 1966 book, *The Challenge of the Computer Utility*. Cloud computing has become both more possible and popular because of three factors:

- The massive explosion of bandwidth
- The decline in the cost of storage
- Mobile devices

Even as recently as the early 2000s, most people accessed their data and documents via a desktop or laptop, the latter typically at dial-up speeds. That has all changed. Forget the fact that virtually no one uses a dial-up modem anymore.[2] Everyone seems to connect via high-speed broadband. The devices that people use to connect to the Internet have exploded. Mobile devices such as Google's Droid, Apple's iPhone, RIM's BlackBerry, and countless others are effectively mini-computers. Although their popularity is waning, many people still go online via netbooks. In short, we can get to data anywhere now because we can now use computers anywhere.

Advantages

Among the benefits of clouds are these:

- **Reduced cost**—Cloud technology is purchased incrementally, saving organizations money.

- **Increased storage**—Small companies typically can store more data on cloud servers than on their private networks.

- **High degree of automation**—Companies and their employees no longer need to worry about manually keeping software up to date. They can focus on more important matters, such as innovating and running things.[ii]

- **Flexibility**—Cloud computing offers much more flexibility than past computing methods.

---

[2] And who really misses those annoying dial-up sounds, anyway?

■ **Increased mobility**—Employees and customers can access information wherever they are, rather than having to remain at their desks.

With benefits like these, it's no surprise that the New Small has embraced cloud computing. Perhaps the greatest advantage of cloud computing for the New Small relates to software development. On its eponymous website, cloud and SaaS stalwart Salesforce.com espouses the benefits of clouds:

> Enterprise application development with traditional software has always been too complex, too slow, and too expensive. A new model called cloud computing has emerged over the last decade to address these problems. Applications that run in the "cloud" are delivered as a service so companies don't have to buy and maintain hardware and software to run them—or huge IT teams to manage and maintain complicated deployments.[III]

Sure, there's more than a little self-interest at work with claims like these. Salesforce.com benefits from those that embrace this mindset—and purchase its products. However, that fact doesn't make its criticisms of traditional software deployment any less valid. Consider Salesforce.com's record second quarter revenue of nearly $400M USD.[iv] Part II of the book shows that many of the New Small are betting their futures on cloud computing.

Major Risks and Limitations

All technologies present risks, and cloud computing is no exception. In the case of cloud computing, most of its risks are, in fact, closely related to its benefits. Putting applications and data out there to be accessed anywhere is simultaneously beneficial and inimical. With regard to the latter, clouds introduce increased potential security and privacy concerns.[3] Organizations' traditional approach of using on-premises applications behind a virtual private network (VPN) *may* be more secure than cloud computing. However, the only way to keep data and applications *completely* secure is to leave them offline altogether. For obvious reasons, that's hardly a viable option for most organizations these days.

Beyond security and privacy, clouds present for many companies a core familiarity, process, and control issue. This should not be understated. Consider the current state of IT support at many organizations, especially large ones:

---

[3] This is a far cry from saying that clouds are inherently insecure.

- End users discover and report technology issues to the IT manager or department. *Can someone say support ticket?*

- IT works with employees, individual vendors, and sometimes external consultants to find bugs, tweak settings, apply patches, test their efficacy, and so on.

- IT decides if and when to take down the application, network, or system.

- Depending on the skill of the IT folks involved, the complexity of the problem, and other factors, the problem is ultimately resolved.

This process changes with clouds. End users still report problems, but an external vendor such as Rackspace[v]—not internal IT—is tasked with fixing them. In a very real sense, a company is no longer directly responsible for handling its own network disruptions and issues, for example. (Let me make two observations here. First, relying on a third party is certainly not a bad thing on some absolute level. Nowhere is it written that companies have to handle these things themselves. Second, I certainly don't want to overstate these types of problems; reliable and reputable cloud vendors operate professional-grade data centers that are typically up and running at least 99.9 percent of the time.)

"The control issue" is not a problem for *all* organizations. However, today relatively few organizations are used to relying on third-party vendors in this manner; most are accustomed to owning and controlling their data and applications—or at least thinking as much. Letting go represents a fundamental process change to many businesses. Relinquishing control can be difficult, although this is less of an issue at the New Small.

The Bottom Line with Clouds

Cloud computing is gaining traction because people no longer access information only at their desks via big gray boxes. The ubiquity of mobile devices and laptops has in fact made clouds more than just convenient. We live in an impatient, 24-7 world. Speed kills. We want what we want *now*, not when we return to the office. As a result, many professionals need access to their documents, data, and applications everywhere and at any time. Cloud computing enables this immediate access to information. This is why we are hearing so much about clouds these days.

Consider Amazon.com for a moment. Aside from selling books, CDs, and electronics, it is now an accidental cloud vendor. The company has discovered that selling excess compute power[4] is a very profitable endeavor. Although prescient, it's doubtful that CEO Jeff Bezos had this in

---

[4] Note that this is usually referred to as *computing power*.

mind as a revenue stream when he founded the company in 1994. In fact, Amazon.com "has made so much headway in cloud technology that this area of their business will generate, according to an estimate recently published by UBS, something in the order of $750 million in 2011."[vi]

To be sure, there are significant risks associated with clouds.[vii] Many of them apply to larger organizations with strict regulatory requirements. For small businesses and the New Small in particular, the pros of cloud computing far exceed the cons. Chapter 6 shows how Skjold-Barthel embraced clouds and has never looked back.

The Second Enabler: SaaS

SaaS is kind of a cousin to cloud computing. In fact, the latter enables the former. To be sure, there are many definitions of SaaS. The following one is particularly beneficial because it contrasts SaaS with traditional on-premises software:

> SaaS is a software distribution model in which applications are hosted by a vendor or service provider and made available to customers over a network, typically the Internet.
>
> SaaS is becoming an increasingly prevalent delivery model as underlying technologies that support web services and service-oriented architecture (SOA) mature and new developmental approaches, such as Ajax, become popular. Meanwhile, broadband service has become increasingly available to support user access from more areas around the world.
>
> SaaS is closely related to the ASP (application service provider) and On Demand Computing software delivery models. IT research firm IDC[5] identifies two slightly different delivery models for SaaS. The hosted application management (hosted AM) model is similar to ASP: a provider hosts commercially available software for customers and delivers it over the web. In the software on demand model, the provider gives customers network-based access to a single copy of an application created specifically for SaaS distribution.
>
> The traditional model of software distribution, in which software is purchased for and installed on personal computers, is sometimes referred to as *software as a product*.[viii]

---

[5] International Data Corporation (IDC) is the premier global provider of market intelligence, advisory services, and events for the information technology, telecommunications, and consumer technology markets. See http://www.idc.com/about/about.jsp.

In short, SaaS applications are rented, not purchased in the traditional sense. For any type of business, this is probably a net positive. I always like to use a real estate analogy. If you're in a bad lease, it's easier to break or wait until it expires. If you've purchased a house, however, it can be very difficult to sell, especially if the housing market tanks and nobody's buying.

Advantages

For small businesses, the considerable advantages of SaaS include:

- **Cost**—SaaS applications typically cost less on an annual basis than on-premises alternatives.

- **Ease**— Saas enables easier software administration via automatic updates and patch management.

- **Consistency**—All users have the same version of the software, ensuring compatibility throughout the organization.

- **Ubiquity**—SaaS applications can be accessed anywhere from any computer or connected device.

- **Reduced IT burden**—Organizations need not rely upon internal IT for application management to the same extent.

- **Security**—Security is typically stronger than many on-premises applications, especially for small businesses.

- **Trials**—Companies have the ability to "date before getting married." Companies can typically try an application before making a purchase decision.

- **Speed of deployment**—Companies typically deploy SaaS applications in less time than their on-premises equivalents. Applications with standard functionality are already available and ready to be configured to reflect a company's needs.

Major Risks and Limitations

These may include the following:

- **Trust**—Like clouds, SaaS often presents a trust issue. Some organizations find it very difficult to relinquish control. They don't trust third parties to manage their applications and data. Of course, small businesses tend not to have these issues to the same extent that large organizations do.

- **Application availability**—Depending on the industry, there may not be a valid SaaS alternative. Remember that SaaS is a relatively new phenomenon. Although broadly used and mature applications for CRM exist, the same might not be true for a niche application.

- ◼ **No panacea**—Companies with major problems will find that SaaS is no silver bullet. The same issues that plague a company using an on-premises solution exist, regardless of who hosts the application. SaaS does not circumvent problems like bad data, inconsistent business practices, poorly trained end users, cultural resistance to change, and so on.

- ◼ **Cost**—Depending on the vendor's pricing model, the cost of using SaaS may in fact exceed that of a purchased, self-hosted application.

The Bottom Line with SaaS

Small businesses and the New Small have embraced SaaS in many forms, as you see in Part II of the book. Not only is it easy to get up and running, it's easy to walk away if a particular application or technology doesn't pan out. SaaS is here to stay.

The Third Enabler: FOSS

FOSS alternatives to traditional (read: paid) offerings have been gaining acceptance for years. For those who doubt the penetration of open source software in ordinary life, consider that it is now penetrating even the hallowed—and traditionally conservative—halls of academia.

> Over the last few years, groups nationwide have adopted the open-source mantra of the software world and started financing open-source books. Experts—often retired teachers or groups of teachers—write these books and allow anyone to distribute them in digital, printed or audio formats. Schools can rearrange the contents of the books to suit their needs and requirements.[ix]

Note that I'm grouping free and open source software together under the category of FOSS. Technically, these are in fact two separate groups of software. For our purposes, however, covering these two software types together is just simpler. There really isn't a point in making overly technical distinctions throughout this book.

Advantages

At a high level, the six major advantages to using FOSS relative to proprietary or closed-source software[6] are:

---

[6] For more on these advantages, see http://open-source.gbdirect.co.uk/migration/benefit.html.

- **Increased reliability**—A large group of volunteer developers often creates a more reliable application (read: one with fewer defects) than a small, paid group of developers does.

- **Increased stability**—A large group of volunteer developers often creates a more stable application (read: one less prone to crashing) than a small, paid group of developers does.

- **Increased auditability**—In a nutshell, developers can investigate a software vendor's claims about system performance, functionality, and so on because that code is available for all to see.

- **Reduced cost**—Obviously, small businesses can save a great deal of money on software licenses by using FOSS, although support for applications may not be free.

- **Increased flexibility and freedom**—This can be broken into two dimensions: freedom from a single vendor and freedom to modify software.

- **Increased support and accountability**—Again, support of any application tends not to be free. However, the notion that closed-source applications provide superior support is often a myth. Proprietary software licenses are intended to absolve the vendor of liability for almost any problem incurred by a client. Most large software vendors employ large legal teams tasked with preventing the vendor from being liable for anything.

Note here that these are *general* and *relative* benefits. They may not apply to any one particular application in comparison to its paid counterpart. In other words, don't take this as gospel. You may think that OpenOffice[x] is more reliable than Microsoft Office, for example. (It certainly is cheaper.) You might find more bugs in Excel than Google Spreadsheets. However, the better alternative is largely a matter of opinion. In fact, many small businesses continue to use proprietary software for completely valid business reasons. In other words, there's just no one right answer for a particular company. Despite this disclaimer, one thing's clear: in general, the New Small has embraced FOSS in many forms, as the companies profiled in Part II of the book manifest.

Major Risks and Limitations

Although the following list isn't definitive, companies encounter different risks and limitations when using FOSS applications. These may include:

- **Legal**—Depending on the particular application, organizations that use FOSS *may* face legal issues related to infringement and intellectual property (IP).[xi]

- **Availability**—Don't assume that there's a free version of every closed-source equivalent. There isn't.

- **Quality**—In some cases, the quality of a FOSS alternative doesn't measure up to its paid counterpart.

- **Security**—If "the community" is responsible for updating an application against malware, viruses, and other threats, then is any single person, group, or individual responsible?

- **Support**—As mentioned above, free support is either nonexistent or of dubious quality.

- **The ticking clock of free apps**—Many vendors make their apps available for a limited time—or with limited functionality—under a freemium model.

The Bottom Line with FOSS

FOSS has arrived, and the New Small has embraced it in many interesting ways. What's more, this isn't abating anytime soon. As Si Chen, project manager at opentaps,[xii] a provider of open source CRM and enterprise resource planning (ERP) software, says:

> FOSS has not only leveled the playing field between small and large businesses, in many cases it has helped propel small businesses ahead of their larger counterparts. Today, open source infrastructure software such as Apache, MySQL, and PHP help small businesses get online quickly and cost-effectively. Open source blogging and content management software such as WordPress, Drupal, and Joomla! are at the forefront of their fields. They are also helping small businesses create unique brand identities online. Finally, open source ERP and CRM software now give small businesses enterprise-class management software, but with the flexibility to tailor it to their particular market niches.

> In contrast, larger companies in traditional industries have often been mired with expensive but outdated commercial software, and it has slowed their progress in the growing online marketplace. This is why many of today's most successful online businesses, including Facebook and Google, flew straight

past their traditional competitors. They all started as small but nimble companies powered by open source.

Looking ahead, I see FOSS empowering many smaller, niche-oriented businesses with unique product offerings and per-sonalities. Together these smaller businesses will take an in-creasingly larger chunk out of the online marketplace.[xiii]

Consider the pros and cons before going the FOSS route; it doesn't meet every business need. Don't let anyone tell you otherwise. In some cas-es, proprietary software is still the way to go. As a group, however, the New Small knows that the benefits of FOSS are too large to unilaterally ignore.

The Fourth Enabler: Mobility

Mobile technologies extend the capabilities of certain applications, particularly in retail, manufacturing, and inventory-related environments. The number and variety of consumer-oriented applications are absolutely astounding. Beyond the consumer space, many software vendors have in-troduced Mobile Supply Chain Management (MSCM) applications that al-low end users to access their systems via cell phones and other portable devices. The bottom line with mobility is this: people no longer need to be chained to desktops or laptops to access or receive information.

The potential of mobility is simply massive. Collectively, the New Small has embraced the use of smartphones and productivity-enhancing apps. Mobility is unquestionably useful. Unfortunately, many companies are too scared to embrace a mobile world. Others are intrigued by its possibilities but, for whatever reason, cannot make headway.

Advantages

It's simply impossible to succinctly list all of the benefits of mobility. There are just too many different mobile apps, frameworks, types of com-panies, and industries. At a high level, the *general* benefits of mobility typi-cally include these:

- **Cost**—Operational costs are reduced.

- **Improved employee productivity**—Although mobile devices are not full-fledged computers, employees can be productive away from the office. For example, meetings can continue if someone leaves to catch a plane.

- **Increased reach**—You can reach customers and employees any-where. (Although some people may consider the latter a hin-drance.)

- **Customization**—People have greater flexibility in customizing devices via themes, sounds, settings, and apps. Employees can personalize their experiences.

Mobility can be a huge asset to just about any business, something the New Small has already figured out.

Major Risks and Limitations

General risks of mobility include these:

- **Loss or theft of a device**—Either could cause extensive damage to an organization. People misplace smartphones much more often than they do desktop computers.

- **Security and privacy concerns**—If you think that mobile networks are entirely secure, think again.

- **The mobile medium**—Mobile devices, including the recently released iPad, impose some limitations on work. As many have pointed out, including *New York Times* technology columnist David Pogue,[xiv] they are not replacements for more powerful devices such as laptops. I'd argue that they're better for consuming content than producing it.

Additional risks apply to organizations moving to a mobile framework for the first time from a traditional one. As my friend and prolific author Bhuvan Unhelkar writes in *Mobile Enterprise Transition and Management*, risks of migrating from a traditional framework to a mobile one include these hazards:

- Failing to adopt a formal methodology to achieve mobile transition, which can potentially confuse the employees and customers of the organization; it can also prove to be expensive if unsuitable mobile applications and technologies are procured.

- Utilizing an *ad hoc* approach to mobile transition, which can lead to failure in adopting mobility, and as a result, damage the image of an organization, particularly in the view of its stakeholders and customers.

- Failing to consider organizational culture.

- Organizational structures, and the goals and objectives that can be affected by a change in the business processes. Not understanding the business processes that need to be transformed.

- Failing to adequately plan for coexistence of mobile business processes. What are the business processes that could be transformed?

- Jumping in without a leveled and phased approach to transition.
- Failing to consider the direct impact on customers and employees once the new technology is fully implemented.[7]

The Bottom Line with Mobility

Not all small businesses have to deal with lofty transitional issues stemming from moving from traditional platforms to mobile ones. In fact, because of their size and newness, the New Small often lacks many of the traditional barriers to going mobile faced by large organizations. Ask the questions ahead of time to ensure a successful deployment. But ignore mobility at your own peril.

The Fifth Enabler: Social Technologies

Social networking and media are piping hot topics these days. Many people at least partially understand how to use social networking tools on a personal level. However, fewer are sure about what—if anything—these tools can do at work. Many people wonder whether they should even be on Facebook, Twitter, or LinkedIn while on company time.

Benefits

At a high level, social technologies allow organizations to improve communication and productivity among employees. Collaboration is one word that we're hearing quite a bit—and there's a chapter in this book about it. More efficient platforms allow for information to be disseminated among disparate groups of employees. Communication with vendors and suppliers is also enhanced.

Social technologies help organizations and their end users by enabling the following:

- **Reduced clutter**—These tools can prevent overloaded e-mail inboxes.

- **Superior communication and diffusion of knowledge**—Collaborative applications allow for more open communication, filtered by relevance. This leads to people learning what they need to know faster. Employees can easily discuss ideas, post news, ask questions, and share links with one another—as they do with more formal suites of collaborative tools.

- **Superior search**—These tools allow employees to review previously answered questions—and search for those answers.

[7] Excerpted from *Mobile Enterprise Transition and Management*.

But social technologies can yield additional benefits. Chapter 11 shows how DODOcase used social media—not marketing dollars—to reach $1M in sales with four employees in a matter of months.

Major Risks and Limitations

The most comprehensive list of risks and limitations related to social technologies (at least that I could find) comes from ITBusinessEdge.[xv] Bogdan Dumitru lists these risks:

- **Data theft**—A social networking site is, basically, an enormous database that can be accessed by many individuals, increasing the risk that information could be exploited.

- **Involuntary information leakage**—Firms should be aware of the legal implications of data their employees post on social networking sites—for themselves or for the company. In the absence of a strong policy that sets clear lines between personal and corporate content, legal hazards are likely.

- **Targeted attacks**—Information on social networking sites could be used as preliminary reconnaissance, gathering information on size, structure, IT literacy degree, and more, for a more in-depth, targeted attack on the company.

- **Network vulnerability**—All social networking sites are subject to flaws and bugs, whether it concerns login issues, cross-site scripting potential, or Java vulnerabilities that intruders could exploit. This could, in turn, cause vulnerabilities in the company's network.

- **Spam and phishing**—If employees use their work e-mail addresses on a social networking site, there is a 98 percent chance they will receive spam and be targeted for phishing attacks, causing issues on the company's network.

- **Content alteration**—Without constant efforts to preserve the identity of the displayed content and in the absence of reinforced security measures, blogs, channels, groups, and profiles might be spoofed or hacked.

- **Malware dissemination**—Social networking sites provide an ideal and cost-efficient platform for the distribution of viruses, worms, bots, Trojans, spyware, and more. A company with a presence on these sites could be adversely affected.

- **Business reputation**—Attackers can distort information about companies and people on social networking sites, adversely impacting their reputation.

- **Infrastructure and maintenance costs**—Using social networking sites requires additional infrastructure and maintenance resources to ensure that appropriate defensive layers are in place to protect the company.

- **Productivity loss**—Companies should carefully monitor their employees' activities on the network to ensure that security is maintained and resources are not being wasted by social networking activities.

Aside from these, I would add a few more:

- **Lack of accountability**—Foolish is the manager who relies on a direct message via Twitter to communicate something at work that requires immediate action. The best way to ensure the completion of a task is to directly ask your employee to do something via phone or e-mail.

- **Information overload**—As mentioned in Chapter 1, no one can keep up with the interminable flow of information and new technologies. It takes time for people to digest and synthesize so much information.

Many small businesses have experimented with social technologies and, to varying degrees, have had some success. I liken using social technologies to learning how to play poker: you can do each in about 5 minutes, but it takes much longer to do well. Perhaps because it takes so little time to set up a Facebook page or Twitter account, many companies mistakenly think that they "get" social networks when nothing could be further from the truth.

The Bottom Line with Social Technologies

Social technologies are dynamic and expansive. One size certainly does not fit all. The New Small understands that the benefits of these technologies hinge on the following:

- The type of app deployed
- Specific features
- End users' familiarity with Web 2.0 tools
- The company's culture
- A host of other people-related factors

To be sure, many largely unanswered questions remain about social media and networking in the workplace. We are still in the early innings of the game. However, that uncertainty hasn't stopped the New Small from experimenting with them—and reaping major rewards, as Part II of the book shows.

The Five Enablers: Complements and Substitutes

Many of the Five Enablers complement each other, while others can be used as substitutes. For example, consider an area crucial to any business of any size: customer relationship management (CRM). Part II shows how different New Small companies use different technologies based upon different business needs. Some might use a FOSS product such as SugarCRM,[xvi] deploying it either locally or via the cloud. Others use a SaaS-based application such as Salesforce.com. Still others go a different route. This may involve "forking"[8] an existing open source application or building a new application from scratch.

In any event, the New Small understands that no technology, application, or framework is perfect. Any number of solutions may suffice for a particular company. Armed with this knowledge, the New Small avoids making the following mistakes:

- Using several technologies (or types of technologies) to fulfill the same basic business need. To continue with the example above, a company wouldn't be wise to use Salesforce.com to manage some of its customers while concurrently using SugarCRM for other customers; the two applications do essentially the same thing.

- Delaying the deployment of an important application in search of the perfect one.

- Foolishly and irrevocably changing platforms because an ostensibly proven—but untested—alternative offers minor cost or functionality advantages.

The New Small, Cost, and the Recession

As this chapter has shown, the Five Enablers offer companies many different advantages and opportunities. These technologies can do so much more than merely save companies money. To some people, however, cash is—and always will be—king. In the 1987 classic film *Wall Street*, Michael Douglas's Gordon Gekko quips, "It's all about bucks, kid. The rest is conversation."[xvii] Although I don't entirely agree with this sentiment, I certainly understand it.

---

8 In the software development world, this is slang for taking a legal copy of source code from one software package and starting independent development on it, creating a distinct piece of software.

At this point, it's completely fair for the reader to be asking questions such as.

- How much do these technologies cost?

- How can I justify major technology costs in this economy?

- If I adopt these technologies, exactly what kinds of savings can I expect to see?

This final section of the chapter addresses questions like these.

The Great Recession has not affected all companies equally. Some, like Chaotic Moon (profiled in Chapter 15), actually *started* during the economic malaise. Let's consider the contrast between the New Small and large organizations with respect to the ability of each to withstand the downturn.

Big companies have dramatically reduced their IT budgets, in many cases to 2005 levels.[xviii] Some cuts have been much deeper than that. These days, rare is the large organization undertaking a major technology initiative, at least company-wide. Many are struggling to survive and carry out basic operations, trying to do more work with fewer employees. Many big companies are feeling pain primarily because many of their costs are fixed: they have purchased expensive software licenses from enterprise software vendors and have signed multiyear deals to support those applications.

Example: The Five Enablers in Action

Let's say that a large organization decides to replace its legacy system[9] with a new on-premises application. To make this happen, it typically needs to spend:

- $400,000 in initial software license fees

- $400,000 in implementation consulting

- $100,000 for new hardware (servers and a new database)

And these are just the one-time costs. Under this traditional arrangement, companies also face the following *annual* costs:

- $88,000 in support[10]

- $30,000 in consulting (give or take)

- $150,000 in salary for two full-time IT personnel to support the system

---

[9] Legacy systems used to meet the needs of their companies but no longer do.
[10] 22 percent of the initial license fee is industry-standard.

In total, it's not uncommon for large organizations to spend over $300,000 annually on basic IT. First-year costs can *easily* exceed $1M. Many big companies surpass these numbers by considerable amounts.

Although these numbers are estimates, they are probably understated; they may not reflect an organization's total IT budget. Many organizations use different applications for CRM, ERP, and other mission-critical areas. More licenses mean more money just to make things work—to say nothing about working *well*.

Many of these IT costs have historically been givens. Many CIOs have considered them table stakes; few organizations would have looked at these costs as optional. There just were no realistic alternatives. These have been *fixed* costs incurred by the organization whether it sold $10M worth of widgets or $1. Try calling Oracle—one of the biggest software vendors on the planet—to return an unused license.[xix] To lessen IT expenses, organizations have traditionally had to wait until their contracts expired. Only then could they try to negotiate better terms. In fact, some enterprise software vendors have fought attempts by their clients to resell unused licenses to other companies.

There's another problem with purchasing and deploying on-premises applications. Getting a new system installed and working is no small endeavor. For all sorts of reasons, the entire process is perilous, a topic discussed at length in *Why New Systems Fail*. For now, suffice it to say that success is hardly guaranteed. I have personally seen $1M budgets *doubled* while key stakeholders remained disappointed in the outcomes of the projects.

Types of Savings

For several reasons, the New Small has not faced the same recession-related problems as large organizations—or at least to the same degree. IT budgets at the New Small were never bloated to begin with. Moreover, to a much greater extent than large organizations, the New Small has replaced many fixed costs with variable ones in three key areas:

- **Payroll**—The New Small uses contractors strategically and extensively to augment permanent staff.

- **Office space**—In some cases, people work exclusively from their homes. The New Small often rents space on an as-needed basis. It isn't about to lock itself into expensive multiyear leases that may be more than the business requires.

- **Technology budgets**—The New Small saves a great deal of money by using the Five Enablers. By deploying emerging technologies, these companies spend fewer dollars on traditional software and hardware—and fewer dollars altogether. As Part II shows, the net savings have been considerable.

Should things not turn out as expected, the New Small just scales back, purchasing—and paying—less. Of course, there are always risks to this type of approach. For instance, a company can have a breakout year and actually pay more for contractors than it would have in employee salaries. Alternatively, it might write a bigger check to Salesforce.com, based on additional licenses or transactions.

The New Small is more than willing to accept these risks. "All you can eat" typically doesn't make sense for a start-up or small company, no matter how promising its business model, product, or value proposition. By embracing largely variable cost structures, the New Small can weather storms and maximize financial flexibility. When these companies need increased capacity of any sort, they simply pay for it. What's more, the New Small applies these same principles to all types of costs. Finding more human resources is approached in the same manner as renting more office space or purchasing additional bandwidth.

SUMMARY

This chapter introduced the Five Enablers. These are the key emerging technologies used by the New Small: cloud computing, SaaS, FOSS, mobility, and social technologies. They are, quite simply, essential to the New Small.

To be sure, companies using the Five Enablers face risks. However, the New Small realizes any and every technology—new or established—presents risks. The fundamental question is: are the rewards of these technologies worth their risks? By and large, these small businesses have generally answered in the affirmative. The New Small uses the Five Enablers to slash costs, improve efficiency, and increase the availability of critical applications and information.

The next chapter switches gears. It examines what these technologies mean as we search for meaning at work.

Endnotes

i   http://csrc.nist.gov/groups/SNS/cloud-computing/

ii   http://web2.sys-con.com/node/640237

iii   http://www.salesforce.com/platform/

iv   http://www.techcrunchit.com/2010/08/19/salesforce-posts-record-revenue-in-q2-net-income-drops/

v   http://www.rackspace.com/apps

vi   http://www.businessweek.com/technology/content/aug2010/tc20100810_440259.htm

vii   http://www.infoworld.com/d/security-central/gartner-seven-cloud-computing-security-risks-853?page=0,1

viii   http://searchcloudcomputing.techtarget.com/sDefinition/0,,sid201_gci1170781,00.html

ix   http://www.nytimes.com/2010/08/01/technology/01ping.html

x   http://www.openoffice.org

xi   http://library.findlaw.com/2004/May/11/133415.html

xii   http://www.opentaps.org

xiii   Personal conversation with Si Chen, 08/12/2010

xiv   http://www.nytimes.com/2010/04/01/technology/personaltech/01pogue.html

xv   http://www.itbusinessedge.com/cm/community/features/guestopinions/blog/the-risks-of-social-networking-and-the-corporate-network/?cs=33877

xvi   http://www.sugarcrm.com/crm

xvii   http://www.imdb.com/title/tt0094291/quotes

xviii   http://www.net-security.org/secworld.php?id=8723

xix   http://blog.softwareinsider.org

Chapter 4

THE CONTINUING SEARCH FOR MEANING AT WORK

The unexamined life is not worth living.

—Socrates

So, how have all of these trends and technologies affected life in the American workplace? It's an important question without a simple or definitive answer. This chapter looks at the resources, opportunities, and challenges that face employees and employers as we enter the second decade of the new millennium. As we saw in the last chapter, from a technology standpoint, there are at least some reasons for optimism. Compared to years past, small businesses are using technology to do more for less. However, it's important to not overstate the importance of technology's role. Although tremendously important to just about every business, technology is only one part of the equation. This chapter is all about one of the other critical parts: the people.

Work-Life Imbalance

Remember the days of the punch in, punch out job? Before the Internet, voice mail, e-mail, smartphones, and instant messaging, offices were equipped with typewriters, ashtrays, secretaries, and interoffice memos. For those of you too young to remember those days, watch the AMC show *Mad Men*[i] to see a depiction of that bygone era.

Those days have long since passed. Relative to a few decades ago, fewer professionals can claim that their jobs are relatively stagnant environments in which technologies *occasionally* cause disruption. Today, most office employees are constantly bombarded with information, buzzwords, unfamiliar terms, and new technologies. To call the average workplace stressful is an understatement.

Let's consider more deeply the source of this increased workplace pressure—and often burnout. These days, many people lucky enough to have jobs feel an accompanying sense of anxiety. A recent *Harvard Business Review* study entitled "The Acceleration Trap" equates the status quo of the American workplace to sheer madness. Heike Bruch and Jochen Menge write:

> Faced with intense market pressures, corporations often take on more than they can handle: They increase the number and speed of their activities, raise performance goals, shorten innovation cycles, and introduce new management technologies or organizational systems. For a while, they succeed brilliantly, but too often the CEO tries to make this furious pace the new normal. What began as an exceptional burst of achievement becomes chronic overloading, with dire consequences. Not only does the frenetic pace sap employee motivation, but the company's focus is scattered in various directions, which can confuse customers and threaten the brand.
>
> Over-accelerated companies exhibit at least one of three patterns of destructive activity. The first is, simply, that employees are overloaded with too many activities. They don't have the time or the resources required to do their jobs. Some 35% of firms in our sample overloaded their employees. Bombardier Transportation, the Berlin-based global market leader for rail transportation technology, is one example. It had experienced success and enormous growth, but in the past few years, it was operating in a continual state of overload. To keep up with competitive pressures, it took measures to optimize efficiency and enlarge capacity. But as the value of its contracts more than doubled, its number of engineers grew only slightly. The company has since addressed the overload problem, but at the time, employee burnout was a serious threat.[ii]

Bruch and Menge are hardly the first to call attention to this trend. As books such as Juliet Schor's *The Overworked American* make clear, the delineation between work and leisure for many employees has always been blurry. Today, that line has arguably been obliterated in many workplaces.

For many employees, any semblance of work-life balance has disappeared, particularly for those who fear for their jobs.

Too Much Technology?

Interestingly, one can blame technological leashes such as laptops and mobile devices for at least some of this imbalance. In *The Rise of the Creative Class: And How It's Transforming Work, Leisure, Community, & Everyday Life*, Richard Florida makes the following important point about the world of work:

> With no big company to provide security, we bear much more risk than corporate and working classes of the organizational age did. We experience and often create high levels of mental and emotional stress, at work and at home. We crave flexibility but have less time to pursue the things we truly love. The technologies that were supposed to liberate us from work have invaded our lives.

Although it would be difficult to credibly argue that major advances in technology have not been a net positive, it would be equally foolish to ignore that they have not come at a cost—at least to some people and groups. Remember Kranzberg's first law from Chapter 1: technology is neither good nor bad; nor is it neutral.

Out of the Office?

At least we have our time off, right? Not really. Today, *out of the office* is a term with diminished meaning. Consider the following statistics:

- Some 88 percent of Americans carry electronic devices while on vacation to communicate with work, and 40 percent log on to check their work e-mail.

- A third of all Americans don't take their allotted vacation, and 37 percent never take more than a week at a time.

- Many employees have no choice because they are at the bottom of the pay scale and are forced to work to make ends meet. A third of all women and a quarter of all men receive no paid vacation. We've been globalized, downsized, and privatized until we are little more than production units.[iii]

- Four in 10 Americans say they haven't had a vacation in the past two years, according to a recently released survey commissioned by Mondial Assistance, an international travel insurance and assistance provider that has its U.S. headquarters in Henrico County, VA.

That's up six percentage points from the same survey conducted in 2009.[iv]

American companies provide less vacation time to their employees compared to companies in other industrialized countries. On her blog "The Society Pages," Lisa Wade, Ph.D., of Occidental College writes:

> The [U.S.] federal government dictates that employees are given exactly zero paid holiday and vacation days a year (that means, if you get such things, it is because your employer is being generous/in a benefits arms race with other employers). In every country included except Canada and Japan (and the U.S.), workers get at least 20 paid vacation days. In France and Finland, they get 30—six weeks off, paid, every year.[v]

A sense of imbalance can be particularly pronounced for employees of small businesses. Generally speaking, employees at smaller outfits are unlike employees of large companies: the former tend to have a harder time leaving work at the office.[1]

Foxconn Suicides

Carping about work is one thing—everybody does it. Killing yourself because you cannot deal with the repetition and utter meaninglessness of your job is quite another. This is exactly what happened at Foxconn Technology Group, perhaps the most gruesome modern-day work environment that I discovered in researching this book.

Founded in 1974, Foxconn has certainly come a long way from its inception. The Taiwan-based corporation is headquartered in Tucheng, Taiwan. Currently Foxconn employs a staggering 800,000 people in mainland China,[vi] including those living and working at the massive Shenzhen complex. It is now, at least according to its website, "the most dependable partner for joint-design, joint-development, manufacturing, assembly, and after-sales services to global Computer, Communication and Consumer-electronics ("3C") leaders."[vii] Foxconn also claims to be "the most trusted name in contract manufacturing services." To be sure, the company has benefitted from the concurrent rise in global demand for digital devices and cheap labor.

Foxconn counts as its clients major corporations:

- Apple Computer
- Intel Corp

---

[1] At least in my experience.

- Sony Electronics
- Dell
- Hewlett-Packard

But lately Foxconn has been in the news for all the wrong reasons. In the first six months of 2010, two Foxconn campuses in Shenzhen have seen 13 suicides or suicide attempts, including nine men and four women.[viii] Perhaps even more galling, according to Malcolm Moore, *The Telegraph's* Shanghai correspondent, "The company says it has prevented a further 30 people from trying to kill themselves in the past three weeks alone. Clearly, something out of the ordinary is going on."[ix] Moore goes on to note that most of the workers who have tried or committed suicide are from the same generation. "Usually better educated than their parents, they are prone to existential angst when confronted with 7-day weeks and 15-hour days of repetitive manufacturing. The nine Foxconn workers involved in suicide leaps this year were all under 25 years old and had worked for the company for less than six months."[x] For their part, human rights groups have taken notice of Foxconn's egregious labor law violations. Pay stubs of deceased workers have confirmed that they worked obscene hours with minimal—if any—overtime pay.

Clearly, most contemporary workplaces aren't nearly as oppressive as Foxconn seems to be. Although U.S. labor law might not be perfect, it's certainly far better than that of China, a country with an absolutely deplorable history of employee and human rights. In this vein, China stands in stark contrast to most countries in Europe and North America. But, in a way, the sense of dissatisfaction, disillusionment, and depression felt by those unfortunate souls at Foxconn isn't entirely dissimilar to the disenchantment felt by many people at their jobs. I'm no expert on Chinese culture, but it seems to me that most people—whether in China, the United States, or Timbuktu—want simple things from their employers: meaningful work, a fair wage, and balanced lives. The drastic steps taken by those Foxconn employees clearly reflect a disturbing—but possibly accurate—belief that basic human wants and needs cannot be met in an oppressive factory.

Employee Wants and Needs

As examples such as Foxconn graphically illustrate, few employees want to do the same thing repeatedly for obscene hours at little pay. Whether they have a reasonable alternative, however, is a separate matter far beyond the scope of this book. At this point, let's consider questions surrounding employee wants and needs such as:

- What do people ultimately want from their jobs?

- In which types of jobs are employees more likely to find what they are searching for?
- Can people find fulfillment at work?

Linchpin Mentality: Godin and Maslow

In his 1943 paper, "A Theory of Human Motivation," American psychologist Abraham Maslow posited an ambitious theory of human needs. After carefully researching a number of "exemplary people," he theorized that all needs can be placed into one of the following five categories: physiological, safety, love/belonging, esteem, and self-actualization. Visually, they can be represented as follows:

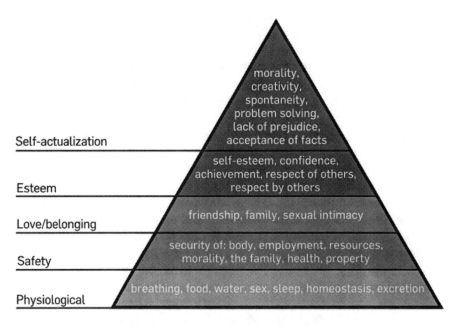

Figure 4.1: Maslow's Hierarchy of Needs[xi]

Although hardly universally accepted, Maslow's work has been a bedrock of many organizational behavior classes ever since. Many scientists from a variety of fields have studied applications of Maslow's theory in the workplace, examining possible causal links between employee satisfaction and performance. Researchers for years have wondered whether a happier worker is a more productive worker. Despite many attempts to prove causality, however, a great deal of doubt remains about whether such a relationship truly exists. Many other factors are at play.

Of course, many laypersons are not remotely interested in all of this theory. Pragmatists could not care less about the existence of a scientific link between satisfaction and performance. Although many employees choose to leave their brains at home, others simply enjoy—and are on the lookout for—challenging and rewarding jobs, whether they've heard of Abraham Maslow or not. This is especially true of Millenials or Generation Y.[xii]

Indeed, more than 70 years after Maslow, Seth Godin tapped into this sentiment in his best-selling book *Linchpin: Are You Indispensable?* Godin writes about the need for people to make themselves invaluable and irreplaceable in the workplace. He argues that, for two reasons, employees should strive to be essential while on the clock. First, there's the basic job security argument: those who are mere cogs in the machine are much more likely to lose their jobs—or compete with workers in low-wage countries. Faced with pressure to contain costs, organizations cannot resist replacing incumbents with people willing to work for substantially lower salaries. In fact, technology enables this. Second, becoming a linchpin is about more than mere self-preservation in a global economy: it allows people to fulfill deeper needs beyond food, money, and shelter. Linchpins can move up Maslow's hierarchy and derive greater satisfaction from their work, ultimately reaching a state of self-actualization. They're inclined to think less about *work* and their *jobs;* they're more likely to enjoy their *careers.* But how exactly does one become a linchpin?

An Example

Consider James, a fictitious employee in an entry-level position for a large corporation. He is 27 years old, and he graduated from a very good college. He's paid relatively well for his services. Maybe he's a customer service rep or a junior financial analyst. James is a talented guy, and over beers, tells his friends that he feels underutilized in his current role, which requires him to do only one thing well. Such is life in a big company, he supposes.

James reads *Linchpin* and is suddenly inspired. He wants a job in which he's indispensable. Rather than just give notice to his current employer, he asks himself a few tough questions:

- If I remain in my current position, will I become indispensable to my company?
- Do I have any real job security in a large company?
- Can I redefine my current role to make myself more valuable?
- Are the benefits of staying in such a limited job worth their long-term costs?
- If I stay in my current job, will I enjoy a slightly modified version of this job in five years?

If James is honest with himself, the answers to these questions are probably no. In all likelihood, he will need to change jobs if he wants to be indispensable. Although not impossible in his current job, it will be much easier for him to become a linchpin at a small business. Making the jump will allow him to use more of his talents and skills. He will learn more on the job—and may well be able to even define his new job to some extent. He can take on multiple responsibilities and wear multiple hats. He'll face more ambiguity, his decisions will have greater impact, and he'll get to use exciting technologies such as the Five Enablers. Most important, although nothing is guaranteed, James stands a better chance of enjoying what he does every day, and he'll probably be more successful.

Bitsmiths and Employee Value Creation

No employee exists in a vacuum. Much like the NFL quarterback who just doesn't fit in his coach's offensive system, some people and cultures just don't jibe. This has always been the case, although some people are just figuring this out. Many companies are only now discovering that, given the vast technological changes taking place these days, they cannot plug just any employee into a predefined role and expect successful results. Context matters.

On his *Harvard Business Review* blog,[xiii] John Sviokla writes about the importance of employees who can put ideas into action:

> In our work so far, we've discovered the primary difference in how they do work is that they have the power to shape their work environment—which means that they can customize, upgrade, and even create new information technology to propel their productivity.
>
> If one looks throughout history, workers' productivity has always been proportional to the quality of the tools they use. In physical work, a man with a backhoe is much more productive than one with a shovel. Yet many firms—in their desire to save money by creating "standard" information environments—actually hamper the potential productivity of their knowledge workers. It's the knowledge work equivalent of outlawing backhoes.
>
> Our research at investment banking, asset-management, insurance, and computer-software firms found that they empowered their high-EBITDA[2] employees to buy the non-standard

---

[2] EBITDA stands for "earnings before interest, taxes, depreciation, and amortization."

tools they think they need to improve their performance. An easy test of whether your firm is doing the same is to analyze how hard it is for someone to get an additional computer screen, a known productivity-booster. Given how cheap screens are these days, if it's hard, your restrictions are probably too tough.

Who does all this fancy design and integration? Many of the high-performance teams that we studied had a member we christened the "bitsmith." Bitsmiths are people who have deep knowledge of both the work content and the tools used to support the work. In other words, they are almost as expert in derivatives or computer design as they are in computer-programming languages. Because they understand both the domain and the tools, bitsmiths can take an idea from concept to implementation quickly.

Of course, it's folly to assume that all organizations are equally adept at enabling bitsmiths, linchpins, or any other empowering term that describes critical employees. They're not. As Part II shows, the New Small has a fundamental advantage over its larger brethren in this regard. These companies have a leg up in creating meaningful jobs, challenging cultures, and satisfied employees due to two things:

- **Acts of commission**—The New Small has embraced the Five Enablers, true workplace flexibility, etc. (See Chapter 3)

- **Acts of omission**—The New Small lacks many of the antiquated policies, politics, and problems that continue to plague many large organizations.

Why is this important? The most talented and valuable employees are increasingly attracted to the best jobs—and not to the companies with the glitziest names. For these folks, things like quality of life and work trump salary, title, fancy offices, and other traditional carrots offered by big companies. Against this backdrop, the New Small is now in a unique position to attract and retain top-flight performers.

The Politics of Job Creation

Andrew Grove is a smart guy. He's the former chairman and CEO of tech giant Intel and the author of several books. It's an understatement to call his career distinguished. Grove also has some strong opinions about job creation. In a recent piece in *BusinessWeek* entitled "How America Can Create Jobs" Grove argues that the United States needs to reestablish its manufacturing base. Small companies are simply not capable of creating the number of jobs required to resurrect the ailing U.S. economy:

> Startups are a wonderful thing, but they cannot by themselves increase tech employment. Equally important is what comes after that mythical moment of creation in the garage, as technology goes from prototype to mass production. This is the phase where companies scale up. They work out design details, figure out how to make things affordably, build factories, and hire people by the thousands. Scaling is hard work but necessary to make innovation matter.

> The scaling process is no longer happening in the U.S. And as long as that's the case, plowing capital into young companies that build their factories elsewhere will continue to yield a bad return in terms of American jobs.[xiv]

Grove is right from at least one standpoint: it's easier for large manufacturers to add jobs *en masse* compared to small businesses. I have never heard of any type of company with 10 employees adding another 500 in a month—or even a year.[3] Delving a bit deeper, Grove's article raises fundamental questions about future job creation, such as these:

▨ Are manufacturing jobs likely to remain in the United States?

▨ Are these *good* jobs—and what exactly is a good job anyway?

▨ What kinds of companies are mostly likely to create meaningful jobs?

▨ Can technology make for better jobs? If so, how?

▨ What role should government play in all of this?

Now, I don't profess to have all of the answers to these admittedly lofty questions. Much depends on your point of view. Some argue that individual people and companies ultimately need to take responsibility for creating jobs, not the government. Others believe that government and the business community at large have a fundamental obligation to create meaningful jobs—and try to keep them in the United States. And there are those with entirely different thoughts on these matters. Discussions and political debates such as these are hardly new, and it's unlikely that they'll end anytime soon.

Regardless of your political bent, however, it's hard to argue with the following assertions. First, all else being equal, most rational folks would prefer to enjoy what they do for a living—or at least not despise their

---

[3] Customers, of course, are another matter.

colleagues, jobs, companies, and bosses. Whether they ultimately do, however, is a separate question—and really always has been. Second, even during the economic downturn, many small businesses have continued to create meaningful, relatively secure jobs. This is either by choice or by necessity, although ultimately that distinction doesn't matter. Although no one would mistake any workplace for utopia, most New Small employees actually enjoy coming to work each day. There's something to be said for that.

SUMMARY

This chapter has examined the state of the American workplace. Hit by massive economic, societal, and technological change over the last 25 years, it has evolved considerably. The traditional notion of job security now seems quaint. Employees lacking critical skills and knowledge can be replaced with ostensible ease, particularly at big companies.

Beyond job security, there is a growing chasm between many small and large companies in another important area: employee job satisfaction. Particularly at many large organizations, survival and earning a paycheck often come at the expense of personal fulfillment. At the same time, the opposite is happening at New Small companies: employees genuinely and generally like their jobs, a topic addressed extensively in Part II.

Endnotes

i   http://www.amctv.com/originals/madmen
ii   http://hbr.org/2010/04/the-acceleration-trap/ar/1
iii http://www.alternet.org/economy/61122
iv   http://www2.wsls.com/sls/news/state_regional/article/survey_finds_40_of_americans_havent_taken_a_vacation_in_2_years/108927
v   http://thesocietypages.org/socimages/2010/01/31/paid-holidaysvacation-days-in-the-u-s-versus-other-oecd-countries
vi   http://news.xinhuanet.com/english2010/china/2010-05/25/c_13313857.htm
vii http://www.foxconn.com
viii http://www.nytimes.com/2010/06/07/business/global/07suicide.html
ix   http://blogs.telegraph.co.uk/news/malcolmmoore/100039883/what-has-triggered-the-suicide-cluster-at-foxconn/
x   *Ibid.*

xi http://honolulu.hawaii.edu/intranet/committees/FacDevCom/guidebk/teachtip/maslow.htm
xii http://humanresources.about.com/od/managementtips/a/millenials_2.htm
xiii http://blogs.hbr.org/sviokla/2010/04/do_your_knowledge_workers.html
xiv http://www.businessweek.com/magazine/content/10_28/b4186048358596.htm

Part II

THE NEW SMALL

This section details the New Small. After an introductory chapter, we'll meet 11 fascinating companies—and the people behind them.

As you'll read in the following pages, the New Small is many things. Perhaps first and foremost, however, it is a pragmatic bunch. This is a group with a plan. Common sense, reason, and long-term considerations drive their decisions, from which employees to hire to which technologies to use—and when.

The New Small adapts well—and often. These companies are not beholden to 50 years of corporate tradition; they don't cling to policies that no longer make sense in this day and age. At a high level, this sense of pragmatism and adaptability takes on several forms:

- Knowing what to do—and what *not* to do
- Knowing when to act—and when *not* to act

The New Small consistently exhibits a kind of emotional intelligence combined with acumen and savvy developed over the years.

Chapters

Chapter 5

DEFINING THE
NEW SMALL

It always seems impossible until it's done.

—Nelson Mandela

ew Small companies tend to exhibit similar characteristics. This occurs despite the fact that they are in different industries and are in many ways very different companies. Before telling their stories, let's first get to know them as a group. This chapter examines why these companies are different—and special. Such an examination is essential. Simply put, not every company is wired to embrace uncertainty, innovation, and emerging technologies. We need to know what sets the New Small apart from other companies.

Part I of this book laid the groundwork for the New Small, examining important technologies and trends. Up until this point, I have largely contrasted the New Small against big companies. This begs the question: are *all* small businesses part of the New Small?

In a word, no. Many old-guard small businesses refuse to embrace emerging technologies—or mature technologies, for that matter.[1] As such, they cannot take advantage of new and exciting opportunities. These established, risk-averse companies are typically rooted in their ways. Often, they have successfully carved out niches for themselves and just don't want

---

[1] A friend of mine recently left a job at a small local government agency in which the employees didn't believe in voice mail. All messages needed to be hand-written. You just can't make this stuff up.

to rock the boat. This mentality is best described as "If it ain't broke, don't fix it."

In a way, as we saw with my friend Tim in the Preface, these companies are often victims of their own success. Although they are small, they act big—and not in a good way. They resemble bloated and conservative organizations struggling to survive or dying on the vine. Small business owners like these often claim that they don't have the time to learn about emerging technologies, much less use them.[2] Perhaps they don't fully understand cloud computing or social technologies. Now, on some level, this is understandable; not everyone is comfortable learning new things, especially when their jobs already require so much of their time and effort. By the same token, however, change is imperative. To quote Charles Darwin, "It is not the strongest of the species that survive, nor the most intelligent, but the one most responsive to change."

An Overview of the New Small

At this point, it's natural to ask, what are the major characteristics that separate the New Small from their peers? In doing the research for this book, I discovered that these companies are remarkably similar in the following 11 ways:[3]

- Their founders and owners share similar backgrounds.
- They have been formed relatively recently.
- They are comfortable with change and new technologies.
- They are willing to experiment.
- They are unwilling to reinvent the wheel.
- They convert technology to a variable cost.
- They understand the importance of social CRM.
- They are "long-term greedy."
- They want something else out of work.
- They are very cautious about future growth.
- They recognize the importance of user-friendly and content-laden websites.

[2] This is one of the primary reasons that I wrote this book.
[3] Note that this isn't a recipe. Rather, these are general attributes inherent to the New Small.

Similar Backgrounds of Founders and Owners

New Small owners and founders are rarely recent college or MBA graduates. They are not idealists with dubious business plans scrawled on the back of a napkin. What's more, they typically fall into one of the following categories:

- They got their chops in the big corporate world before starting their own companies.
- They are serial entrepreneurs who have always worked for themselves.

Relatively Recent Formation

Almost all of the New Small has been formed relatively recently—many of them in the last few years. Only NSI Partners (Chapter 10) and Fuentek (Chapter 13) have been in existence for longer than five years. As a result, most of them didn't have to rid themselves of systems or technologies that no longer met their needs. (Not coincidentally, the same two companies had to successfully replace major internal systems that had outlived their usefulness).

Comfort with Change and New Technologies

As a corollary of being relatively new, the New Small realizes enormous advantages in terms of embracing change and adopting new technologies. From the start, these companies have intelligently selected, deployed, and implemented technologies that made sense. As a result, they have become very comfortable with change and new technologies. By way of comparison, larger, more mature companies typically struggle with new technologies and organizational change. This is not the case at the New Small; company culture and tradition do not get in the way of making needed improvements.

A Willingness to Experiment

The owners of the New Small are usually energetic—even fidgety. They often experiment with new technologies, business directions, vendor relationships, or business processes. For example, if a collaboration tool or suite of productivity tools isn't working for the company, they try another sooner rather than later. They believe that, as a general rule, the costs of inaction exceed the costs of action. Of course, this willingness to experiment is not solely a function of a free-spirited business owner. The New Small understands the following:

- Companies today can deploy a wide variety of applications, software, and technology options, especially compared to 10 years ago.
- Many of these offerings are available on a freemium basis, allowing companies to try them out before they commit to anything.
- Prices on many applications have dropped considerably. No longer does a company have a financial incentive to stay with a tool that just isn't meeting the business's needs.

In other words, it's not terribly expensive to kick the tires on a new tool.

An Unwillingness to Reinvent the Wheel

Perhaps nowhere is the contrast between the New Small and many old-guard companies more stark than here. Experimentation with new technologies is all fine and dandy, but there's just no reason to spend time, money, and resources trying to build a marginally better mousetrap from scratch. Unlike many larger companies, the New Small never mistakes "Can it be done?" with "*Should* it be done?"

Allow me to tell two personal stories here, as they are particularly germane. In 1998, I started working at Merck & Co., Inc., the venerable pharmaceutical company and one of the original 100 companies listed on the New York Stock Exchange (NYSE). Of course, at that time, only nine were still around in their original forms, certainly a credit to Merck's success as a company.

I was absolutely astonished to learn that Merck had built the vast majority of its own internal IT applications. This was analogous to IBM manufacturing its own aspirin. Merck management honestly believed that it could—and should—create superior enterprise systems than it could buy. Although I worked with some competent IT folks at Merck, it's fair to say that the world's best programmers and software developers don't go to work at pharmaceutical giants.

Second, a few years later, I worked at a small marketing company. The company built its own customer relationship management (CRM) system via the Microsoft .NET Framework, ostensibly allowing employees to track sales of college loans—the company's chief product and source of revenue.

Lamentably, the CRM system was fraught with gaping holes. Collectively, they made simple questions such as "How many sales have our reps made today?" impossible to answer. In addition to deficient technology, there was a fundamental management issue: employees incurred no penalties for cheating the system. They would book sales multiple times, something that the company's homegrown system couldn't prevent.

In both cases, the companies would have been justified in building new systems had there been no viable—and affordable—alternatives. However, this was hardly the case. In fact, each company spent vastly more money building deficient applications themselves than they would have buying and implementing a custom off the shelf (COTS) application. New Small companies would never dream of building these types of applications and systems themselves; there's just no need, and there are too many other things to do.

Converting Technology to a Variable Cost

From their inceptions, nearly all small businesses attempt to minimize their fixed costs. This isn't rocket science. However, few are as successful at doing this as the New Small, for one main reason. These small companies have been able to transform many technology costs into variable ones (see Chapter 3). They have adopted the Five Enablers in large part to minimize their IT expenditures.[4] Wherever possible, they don't lock themselves into large annual expenses.

Understanding the Importance of Social CRM

Chapter 3 demonstrated how the social web has empowered customers like never before—especially dissatisfied ones. Tech-savvy consumers are hardly shy about airing their grievances over the Internet. Their negative experiences with behemoths such as Verizon, Comcast, and Dell Computer become fodder on a wide variety of sites.[5] Big companies 1-800 numbers, labyrinth Interactive Voice Response (IVR) menus, and long hold times tend to frustrate many folks. *They're mad as hell, and they're not gonna take it anymore.*

ZDNet blogger Dion Hinchcliffe discusses how traditional CRM has become more social. Hinchcliffe writes that "traditional methods for staying in touch with customers don't hold a candle to true social engagement."[i] The New Small understands the true power of social CRM; it is a two-way communication requiring new applications and technologies. Many CRM systems were conceived years ago and haven't kept up with the times. Today many are insufficient on three levels:

---

[4] As a result of these wise decisions, many of these companies do not even employ a full-time IT manager. There just is no need for this expense.

[5] While many people vent on Facebook and Twitter, others have created specific sites to air their grievances. Check out http://www.verizarape.com and http://www.dell-hell.net.

- They allow companies to handle different types of communication with customers , such as e-mail , mobility, geolocation, social technologies, and texting.

- They allow companies to store, access, and analyze much of the unstructured data[6] that this two-way communication generates.

- They cannot be easily integrated with other critical client-facing applications.

For these very reasons, NSI Partners replaced an older CRM application (Goldmine) with a much more robust one—Salesforce.com (Chapter 10).

A Mentality of "Long-Term Greedy"

As a group and on many levels, the New Small is fundamentally different from large companies. The former understands the need—and just as important, has the ability—to maintain a long-term focus. Admittedly, this is easier at smaller companies. Because these companies are privately held, they are not beholden to quarterly earnings and shareholders.

Again, allow me to tell a personal story here. In mid-2010, I was approached by a large health care organization (call it YYZ[7] here) about doing some potential report development work. I'll omit the details of the work itself; it isn't terribly interesting to the average person. I will, however, briefly provide a high level overview of YYZ's current report distribution process:

- Super user runs report.

- Super user prints report.

- Admins segregate reports by customer.

- Admins scan individual reports as separate Adobe PDF files.

- Admins e-mail PDFs to customers.

Obviously, this is not the acme of efficiency. After years of doing it this way, YYZ finally realized that the money spent on automating its report distribution process would more than pay for itself. YYZ asked me whether I wanted to do the work, but I passed on it.

Why? Let me rule out three reasons:

---

[6] Unstructured data resides in blogs, chats, comments, tweets, and the like. Structured data typically resides in database tables and spreadsheets. Examples include employee, order, and customer lists.

[7] Yes, this is an intentional reference to the classic Rush song of the same name from the amazing 1981 album *Moving Pictures*. It's also the acronym for the Toronto Pearson International Airport.

- **I couldn't do the job**—Although I may not be the world's greatest report writer, I assure you that I can more than hold my own. I have very little doubt that I could have done what the client wanted.
- **I don't have the time**—I could have fit the work into my schedule.
- **I don't need the money**—Property taxes in NJ (where I live) remain the highest in the nation, at least according to *The Wall Street Journal.*[ii]

I turned down the work because YYZ really didn't need my help after all. They only thought they did.

After doing five minutes of research, I discovered a little and relatively obscure product called PDF-eXPLODE[iii] that should allow YYZ to send reports with a few mouse clicks. What's more, buying this product would, in all likelihood, cost the company much less than hiring me to do the same thing.

Like most people on the planet, my contact at YYZ was not aware of PDF-eXPLODE, much less the fact that it is available for free as a trial version. (As discussed in Chapter 1, this is true of many products these days.) Rather than keeping this information to myself and taking the gig, I passed this information on to YYZ.

Some people might call me crazy to turn down work, especially in this economy. In the short term, perhaps I am. Many large consulting firms would never have done what I did. In fact, had I worked for such a company, my boss would have left me a grave message, no doubt starting with those dreaded words, "We need to talk."

In the Preface, I wrote about the time I worked for a large consulting outfit that vigorously pursued every lead. Anyone who asked, "Does the client really need this?" would have been in hot water. By constantly selling as many products and services as its clients could stomach, the company frequently made awful decisions. Project failures were common.

So, why does the New Small sometimes turn down work? In short, because it is long-term greedy.

Long-term greedy[8] is a powerful and evocative phrase coined by Gus Levy of Goldman Sachs, a company that has been in the news a great deal these days for all of the wrong reasons. The once-distinguished firm has been plagued by a scandal stemming from some ethically questionable financial activity during the housing meltdown.[iv] But the company's recent problems are, in a way, moot to this discussion. As a business strategy, being

---

[8] As initially conceived by Levy, the phrase means that, as long as the firm makes money over the long term, mild short-term trading losses are not a cause for concern.

long-term greedy is just plain smart. Returning to the preceding example of YYZ, consider the following:

- If PDF-eXPLODE doesn't meet YYZ's needs for report distribution, I'll bet you a Coke that my contact will reach out to me.

- If I had taken the job and done the work, what would have happened if YYZ found out about PDF-eXPLODE? I doubt that they would have asked for a refund, but they'd naturally wonder, "What else is this supposed reporting expert not telling us?"

- YYZ probably has other report development or consulting needs, and because of my honesty, I'm probably at or near the top of their list.

- People talk. Word of mouth is huge. The goodwill that I built up with YYZ may very well translate into additional clients for me.

The New Small understands this notion of long-term greedy. This is not to say that these companies are a collection of saints. They are not inherently benevolent. They have bills to pay just like the largest corporations. However, their size, freedom from answering to myopic stockholders, flexible costs, and pragmatism allow these companies to make decisions in the long-term best interests of their employees, partners, customers, and *themselves*.

A Desire for Something Else

Owners, founders, and employees of the New Small have, for the most part, made conscious choices to reject traditional corporate life. No one was conscripted to work at these companies. Many people intentionally left traditional jobs at large organizations for typical reasons. Others were laid off, and instead of trying to return to the rat race, used the experience as an opportunity to start anew. Entrepreneurial sorts knew the downsides—and decreasing upsides—of working for corporate behemoths. They never wanted to go down that road.

Cautious Growth

The New Small is not interested in growth at all costs. These companies know that getting big runs the risk of undermining the cultures and jobs that they have worked so hard to create. Although they don't shun growth altogether, the New Small is much more cautious than organizations that emphasize growth at any expense. New Small employees enjoy having different and multifaceted jobs. They promote workplace flexibility and friendly cultures. To these ends, recklessly pursuing growth just doesn't make sense.

Small Giants **and the New Small**

There's a well-worn and still-relevant old adage: So many books, so little time. About halfway through writing the initial manuscript for this book, I spoke to Marisa Smith, head of The Whole Brain Group,[v] a social media and web design company. We'll meet her in Chapter 12. I clicked with her immediately and in much the same way I did with the other people interviewed for this book. In the midst of our exciting initial conversation about the advantages of being small, Smith mentioned the book *Small Giants: Companies That Choose to Be Great Instead of Big* by Bo Burlingham. I immediately ordered it and devoured it in two days. I also gave it a glowing review on my site.[vi]

It turns out that *Small Giants* is much more than a great book; there's an entire community of people and companies that embraces its tenets. It has become a way of life for some people. According to the Small Giants' website, these people strive to "move beyond the pressure of endless growth to define success by not only their bottom line, but by their contributions to the community, dedication to great customer service and creation and preservation of workplace cultures of excellence."[vii] The group's delightful *raison d'être* is: "It's not what we do. It's who we are."

This begs the question: is there overlap between *The New Small* and *Small Giants*? The answer is an unequivocal yes, and I'm unabashedly proud of that fact. However, the focus of each book is different. *The New Small* is primarily about emerging technologies used by progressive small businesses. To be sure, *Small Giants* does not ignore technology. However, technology hardly represents a major emphasis of Burlingham's book; it is more tangential. This isn't a criticism. In any event, the sentiments that underlie *The New Small* and *Small Giants* are more similar than dissimilar.[9]

Books like these make me realize one thing: evidently, I'm not the only one out there who understands "the power of small." We will return to *Small Giants* in Chapter 18 in the context of small companies using consultants.

The Importance of Websites

When it comes to technology, there are many opinions on which ones companies absolutely need to use—and plenty more on how they ought to use them. My years as a consultant have at least taught me that much. As discussed in Part I, today companies are using technologies in a multitude

---

[9] In fact, while I'm playing Oprah and telling you what you should read, I might as well add another recent discovery to your growing reading list. Check out Paul Spiegelman's book, *Why Is Everyone Smiling? The Secret Behind Passion, Productivity, and Profit.*

of ways to (try to) achieve very different things. Contrast that with the 1990s, a period of relative technological uniformity.

These days, just about every company uses at least one common technology: a website. However, saying that all websites are equally effective at reaching their intended audiences—and maintaining their interest—could not be further from the truth. And this is hardly new. For years now, a website has been a company's primary window to the world. Many a business relationship began with someone discovering a website—and countless others were never consummated because of an unprofessional web presence.

90s Sites

Today, many companies' websites are still glorified brochures. I call these relics "90s Sites," and they usually consist of only the following pages:

- Home
- Products and/or Services
- Contact
- News
- Testimonials
- About

Now, there's nothing inherently *wrong* with 90s Sites *per se*. It's just that they could be more—so much more. The New Small understands this. They know that creating a robust and content-laden website can pay serious dividends, including these:

- Increased Alexa and Google Page rankings[10]
- Increased traffic and quite possibly inquiries for products and services
- Increased information about your customer base
- Increased stickiness of—and customer time on—the site
- Increased buzz
- Decreased bounce rate[11]
- Increased *probability* of additional business

---

[10] These are good proxies for gauging site popularity. This is art more than science, though.
[11] While precise definitions vary, *bounce* or *exit rates* represent the percentage of people who quickly leave a site soon after visiting it.

The New Small understands that prospective and actual employees, customers, suppliers, and the public at large can tell a great deal about a company by merely perusing its website. Although what you see and read on a website is important, so too is what *you can't see*. In other words, many sites are notable for what they are missing. At a high level, 90s Sites lack three critical things:

- Meaningful content
- Style
- Interactivity

Meaningful Content

There's rarely a compelling reason for people to return to 90s Sites. Yes, they are informative on a basic level: you can learn about what a company does and how to contact it. However, these sites provide little in the way of meaningful content. The New Small understands that these days, whether the company sells mortgages or legal services, its site should contain the following:

- An insightful and well-written blog.[12] This doesn't mean that a lawyer should divulge the details of her case on her blog. Nor should a mortgage company explain specifically why it rejected less-than-credit-worthy prospects in a podcast. I'm talking about general tips, pieces of advice, or articles well stocked with valuable information and examples (even if names are changed).

- Written content other than blog posts, such as white papers and eBooks. No one is going to read a 4,000 word blog post.

- The ability for readers to subscribe to comments.

- Powerful search capability. If people cannot find something, they'll simply go away.

- Social media icons for Facebook, LinkedIn, Twitter, and other sites that enable easy link and information sharing. Adding social media integration takes minutes on content management systems (CMSs) such as WordPress. These plug-ins and widgets are not terribly difficult to install and manage.

- Ways to subscribe to content.[13] Examples include the ability to subscribe via e-mail and a really simple syndication (RSS) feed.

[12] Blogs should be integrated with a company's main site. Why you'd send someone away from your main site to a separate blog is beyond me.

[13] This is a bit irrelevant to 90s Sites because there's really no reason to subscribe.

- Multimedia content, such as videos, webinars, and podcasts. Not everyone wants to read a blog. Plus, hearing voices and seeing videos can be more powerful than mere text.

Think about it. As social media expert and author Chris Brogan recently pointed out on ABC News,[viii] people don't buy magazines for the ads. They don't watch TV for the commercials. New Small companies give people a reason to return to their sites—and tell others about them. Note that companies need not create daily content, but monthly updates are not often enough; greater frequency is required to truly engage customers in meaningful dialogue.

Style

Even many sites with loads of content suffer from poor layouts, missing features such as search bars, superfluous aesthetics, and generally bad design. Consider four very different types of websites:

- **Site A**—A pretty brochure lacking meaningful content
- **Site B**—An overly busy site with tons of poorly arranged content
- **Site C**—A bare bones site with valuable content (see previous section)
- **Site D**—A simple yet well-designed site with a trove of interesting information logically organized

All else equal, which site is best? For most people, the answer is Site D. Next up, they'll take Site C. New Small companies understand the importance of creating user-friendly sites. Although substance may matter *more* than style, style still matters.

Interactivity

Finally, many of the New Small's sites are interactive; they are not merely one-way vehicles for these companies to communicate *to* the outside world. By and large, their sites don't just *allow* comments from readers, viewers, and listeners; these things are *encouraged*.

Roadblocks to Change

So, what's preventing old-guard small businesses from polishing their sites—and adding valuable content? The usual reasons (read: excuses) are the following:

- "I don't understand social media and blogging."
- "Social media is a waste of time."
- "These technologies are just fads."

- "I don't have time."
- "I don't know where to begin."
- "It's not my job to do social media."
- "It probably costs a great deal of money to redo a website."

These objections are ultimately a function of time, money, and willingness to learn something new. Many small business owners think—or, perhaps more accurately, *hope*—that the web is going away.[14] It's not.

The New Small knows that, despite the time involved, developing their websites—and regularly adding *meaningful* content to them—pays enormous dividends. It's not that these companies—and their employees—aren't already busy doing other important things. Nothing could be further from the truth, especially since they are relatively leanly staffed. But these efforts will pay significant dividends, and as a result, they *make* the time. These people ask themselves a critical question: would potential customers come to our site and stick around? Even if the answer is yes, they keep working on—and adding to—their sites.

SUMMARY

This chapter described the common characteristics of the New Small. Although these companies are hardly perfect and face many of the same challenges that other companies face, they are fundamentally different. They readily admit mistakes. They intelligently adopt new technologies and experiment with others. They identify areas of improvement—and then put their plans into action. They are flexible, pragmatic, and logical. Not coincidentally, they are also very successful.

That's enough of the broad strokes. In the following 11 chapters, we get to know the New Small and the companies and people behind them. These chapters describe what they're doing and not doing, how they're doing it, and what makes them great.

---

[14] If you think so too, then I have some old pagers that I'd like to sell you.

Endnotes

[i] http://blogs.zdnet.com/Hinchcliffe/?p=1194&tag=trunk;content

[ii] http://blogs.wsj.com/developments/2008/10/08/new-jersey-has-the-highest-property-taxes-in-the-nation/

[iii] https://secure.softwarekey.com/solo/products/Product.aspx?ProductID=145168&DistributorID=50299

[iv] http://money.cnn.com/2010/06/10/news/companies/goldman_sachs

[v] http://www.thewholebraingroup.com

[vi] http://www.philsimonsystems.com/blog/writing/book-reviews/small-giants

[vii] http://www.smallgiants.org/home.php

[viii] http://abcnews.go.com/Business/video/make-money-blogging-10487402

Chapter 6

THE BIG SWITCH
IN ACTION

The basis of optimism is sheer terror.

—Oscar Wilde

A hundred years ago, manufacturers created their own power via windmills and waterwheels. There were no power companies as we know them today. This wasn't entirely efficient, and most companies eventually realized that this was just plain silly. Why should they spend the time and expense building their own, independent power sources when plugging into electric grids would serve the same purpose—at a fraction of the cost?

Fast forward to today. No organization—no matter how large—even remotely considers making its own electricity. (Well, other than the power companies.) There's a similar transition taking place right now in the world of computing.

In *The Big Switch: Rewiring the World, from Edison to Google*, Nicholas Carr writes about the contemporary parallels between electricity and computing power. Carr describes how organizations, formerly used to maintaining their own servers, databases, networks, storage, and servers, are realizing the benefits of an entirely different model: cloud computing. In other words, compute power is going the way of a power utility. Personal computers (PCs) and mobile devices are supplanting hard drives as access portals to data.

As prominent technologist and author Amy Wohl wrote in *The Next Wave of Technologies*:

In the past few years, as the cost of a unit of compute power has continued to decrease—but the cost of humans with the skills to implement and manage computer systems has not—the vision of centralized computing has returned. It has taken several turns. Some computer scientists have suggested (and experimented with) a vast grid of computers, attached via the Internet, whose power can be combined for large-scale tasks when needed. In some cases, very large computing systems can be part of these grids for specialized tasks. Others have suggested a computing utility that would provide just as much computing power as an organization needed, on an on-demand basis, much like electricity.

Carr and Wohl are hardly alone in espousing the benefits of cloud computing (as described in Chapter 3). Many organizations have been quick to embrace the clouds, as have many people.

Ben Skjold was one of them.

The Switch

At first glance, Skjold-Barthel seems like your typical small law firm. Founded in September of 2006 and based in Minneapolis, MN, the seven-attorney firm provides a range of legal services to its clients, typically small and midsize businesses. According to its website,[i] the firm stresses practical advice and innovative solutions ahead of firm politics or finances. Of course, many law firms make similar claims. Claims like these hardly make Skjold-Barthel special. As we'll soon see, however, Skjold-Barthel is actually a different type of law firm.

Of course, it wasn't always this way. Like many law firms and small businesses, Skjold-Barthel had been plagued by common technology issues, some of which were:

- Lost documents
- Network performance
- Decreased productivity

By 2009, the company's server was unable to handle its massive volume of digital documents. What's worse, the growth in the number of those documents showed no signs of abating. This nearly crippled the company. Employees were unable to handle their existing workloads, let alone scale to meet litigation caseloads.

The company also felt the sting from periodic network slowdowns. This problem often led to a "hurry up and wait" mentality among the firm's employees. Slow response exacerbated employee frustration, resulting in lost time and lower productivity. The firm also found it costly and disruptive to implement, maintain, and upgrade multiple applications. Version control issues and software licensing headaches more than occasionally prevented attorneys from concentrating on practicing law.

This was tough for Ben Skjold, one of the firm's principals, to swallow. Skjold is a self-admitted technologist. Whereas many of his contemporaries are content to maintain the status quo, Skjold is always trying to push the envelope and do things faster, better, and cheaper. In other words, he's just like the rest of the New Small founders. He doesn't merely understand emerging technologies; he embraces them.

Impetus for Change

Many small businesses—and law firms in particular—live with subop-timal technology. They consider it a cost of doing business, erroneously be-lieving that the cost of change exceeds its benefits. Perhaps Skjold-Barthel would have done the same, but an incident in 2009 served as a tipping point and pushed the company to adopt emerging technologies. An employee accidentally deleted one portion of a single client file. The firm scrambled to restore the file, a process that ultimately took 10 days.

For Skjold, enough was enough. He asked himself, "Does continuing on the same path and consistently expanding our internal infrastructure make sense?" The answer was no. It was time to fundamentally change the way that the firm used technology. Doing so would not only prevent future disasters; it would allow the firm to build a scalable model. It could concurrently scale up or down as needed, handling cases of all sizes in the process.

Attorneys are revenue producers. By Skjold's estimates, suboptimal technology was hurting the bottom line. Employees were losing roughly 15 percent of their productivity because of system issues. Quite simply, the firm wasn't making as much money as it could expect to because of defi-cient and unreliable technology. Skjold felt that technology should be a solution and an enabler, not a problem or hindrance.

In making the business case for change, Skjold asked himself a funda-mental question: what kind of business are we? The answer was simple: a service organization. More services meant more revenue and profits. The company's technology had to enable the business, not inhibit it. "I wanted the technology to let us do what we do best: practice law," Skjold says.

Vision and Specific Changes

Skjold believes that we are entering a new age of law firms. Many industries and companies have discovered that technology is going to lead the way to increased flexibility and, ultimately, profitability.

But in addition to the aforementioned downtime, Skjold noted another problem: the firm's systems and applications did not allow for detailed client reporting. He has company here. Many law firms are still stuck in the old days, with line items on invoices exceptionally vague, even for large blocks of hours and thousands of dollars of work.

Skjold's vision entailed the following:

- Lowering both capital expenditures (CAPEX) and operational expenditures (OPEX)
- Saving money on power and electricity
- Increasing the firm's agility
- Enhancing the firm's billing systems
- Continuing to foster a culture conducive to flexible work
- Building a platform for collaboration and innovation

Embracing Clouds and a Different Type of Software Licensing

To effect his vision, Skjold first decided to change how the company procures much of its software. The company used to license Microsoft software on a per-user basis. It now pays on a per-month basis. The company still licenses other software products in more traditional ways, but those applications are managed centrally (SaaS). Additional users are added and upgraded easily. The firms' attorneys never need to update their software.

Through the cloud, all of this just happens behind the scenes; it's invisible to the firm's employees. Skjold doesn't have to manage that process— nor do any of the firms' attorneys. Skjold simply makes a telephone call to purchase inexpensive server space. The firm benefits from additional flexibility on the litigation side to scale up and scale down.

To be clear, the firm did *not* absolutely need to move most of its data and applications to the cloud to handle traditional client work. Indeed, the firm still does a great deal of business representing small to midsize companies, drafting contracts, and reviewing leases, non-competes, and executive contracts. For this kind of work, cloud computing might have been nice to have, but certainly not imperative.

Skjold-Barthel embraced the clouds because it wanted the ability to easily and effectively represent companies on larger litigation matters. For this, cloud computing is perfect. Although Skjold is more tech-savvy than most attorneys, he certainly did not attempt this transition on his own. The risks of failure were simply too great. Although you may not need a degree in computer science to implement the Five Enablers, moving from a traditional architecture to the cloud is not as simple as downloading a file and walking through an installation wizard—at least not yet.

Skjold knew that he would need a partner to help his company seamlessly make the transition to the clouds. He found one in the form of Paragon Solutions Group.[ii] Again, as you see throughout this section and the rest of the book, the New Small knows its limitations and is not afraid to contract partners—both for short-term projects as well as long-term support and maintenance. Although they are very often independent and extremely capable, these companies know their limitations, particularly with respect to doing it yourself (DIY).

Networking

The firm addressed its bandwidth issue by adopting a peer-to-peer (P2P[1]) network. Skjold did not do this alone. He would be the first to tell you that he's no expert on P2P networks. To his credit, though, he realizes the limits of his knowledge and set up a contract with the firm's chief technology partner to deploy and maintain the network.

The results have been striking. No longer is a centralized network the source of many bottlenecks—and frustrated attorneys and clients. Rather, the new network distributes processing power, disk storage, and network bandwidth across multiple nodes.[2] This switch has paid major dividends: the network is always directly accessible by the users at speeds averaging 10 megabytes of data per second.[3]

Effective Change Management: The Move to the Clouds

For reasons discussed in Chapter 3, many companies struggle with the idea of cloud computing. Fortunately, Skjold-Barthel faced very few technological barriers to making its move to the cloud. Reasons for the relative ease include these:

- The firm's size.
- The firm's structure.

---

[1] Short for *peer to peer*. Computers in peer to peer networks connect to each other without a centralized infrastructure.
[2] Microsoft Encarta defines this type of node as "an active electronic device that is attached to a network, and is capable of sending, receiving, or forwarding information over a communications channel."
[3] While not the fastest on earth, this is a very good speed for most companies.

■ The relative sophistication of its employees. Most attorneys are relatively savvy concerning basic applications and computers these days.

In fact, as you see throughout this section, major and relatively painless moves are typical for the New Small. These companies—and their end users—are able to handle major shifts in technology much better than their larger brethren.

According to Skjold, perhaps the largest challenge was his colleagues' uncertainty about the change itself—they feared that they would lose the control and personalization to which they had become accustomed. However, attorneys and staff soon realized that the benefits of cloud computing outweighed any temporary discomfort.

Of course, smooth does not imply perfect. Skjold notes that data migration was a delicate process because of the poor shape of the firm's existing server. This challenge is important for two reasons. First, the migration would have been trickier if the firm had undertaken it independently. Skjold knew that Paragon would be there if and when issues arose. He was willing to pay for support in the event that the firm needed it. Second, the New Small does not let relatively minor issues derail its goals. Companies looking for the perfect technology will never make critical changes that will enable other parts of their business. Skjold kept his eye on the ball, knowing that the long-term benefits more than justified any short-term pains.

Future, Results, and Challenges

In the future, Skjold-Barthel will continue increasing its use of the Five Enablers.[4] The company has shown that it doesn't operate like a typical law firm. And absent a technology-related disaster, they don't expect their willingness to adopt new technologies to abate anytime soon. They have had a great deal of success so far.

By embracing the cloud, the firm has drastically reduced its technology infrastructure costs. Applications now quickly and easily scale as attorney caseloads increase. Although formerly a challenge, remote access from anywhere is a given for the firm's attorneys. What's more, "We have levels of security, backup, redundancy, and performance that go far beyond those found at the typical law firm," Skjold says. "And we save money in the process."

The firm has successfully converted its technology spending into a monthly service fee for which it can easily budget. The firm estimates that

---

[4] Note that there are legal reasons for law firms' relative caution to blogging and other forms of social media. Some people might interpret a blog as legal advice, even with clearly visible disclaimers.

it will save 16 percent in overall technology expenditures its first year in the cloud, with up to 85 percent annual savings in capital expenditures going forward. Skjold states that they also will realize an additional 20K annual savings moving their Voice over Internet Protocol (VoIP) service to the cloud in early 2011. Moreover, Skjold views the cloud environment as a revenue enhancer—projections show the efficiencies of the new model will enable the firm to generate an additional 17 to 21 percent in revenue annually. "If we get 100,000 pages of documents, I just call Paragon and rent additional space during the period of the case," Skjold continues. "Compare this with five years ago. We would have had to purchase and roll out a more expensive and powerful server."

Because of the switch to the clouds, the firm no longer experiences significant downtime—and related issues. At the same time, it has increased its level of data protection. This certainly reassures the firm's current and prospective clients. Employees couldn't be happier. Attorneys can now work anywhere; they are not tied to a geographic location.

New billing applications provide itemized breakdowns of all attorneys' invoices. Now, even a bill of several thousand dollars may contain 10 to 15 entries on it. Clients appreciate increased accountability and specificity, and the attorneys need not spend their time painstakingly and manually accounting for every minute worked.

SUMMARY

Even traditionally conservative companies— such as law firms—can benefit greatly from the Five Enablers. In this case, Skjold-Barthel's use of cloud computing has paid enormous dividends. Those who believe that clouds aren't ready for prime time take note: clouds have arrived and can make a world of difference right now.

The Five Enablers—and cloud computing in particular—have allowed Skjold-Barthel to make its traditional legal practice more scalable, cost-effective, and secure. Employee satisfaction has also increased. Skjold-Barthel has embraced the cloud—and has no plans to abandon it.

Chapter 6: The Big Switch in Action

Endnotes

i   http://www.skjold-barthel.com
ii   http://www.paragonsg.com/

Chapter 7

THE HIGH-TECH
DENTIST

Truth is not what is, but what others can be brought to believe.

—Michel de Montaigne

O n one level, Holly Lewis and Drew Zima are unlike the other founders profiled in this book: they spend all of their time working with teeth. Yet, on many other levels, they are just like the other owners and founders of New Small companies, especially with regard to their use of the Five Enablers.

Lewis and Zima each wanted to start dental practices. For her part, Dr. Lewis began making concrete plans in the spring of 2008, after working four years in the field. "While I had the educational background," Dr. Lewis says, "I needed to learn the ins and outs of the business before I could open my own shop."

Drs. Lewis and Zima met at the Virginia Commonwealth University School of Dentistry.[i] Dr. Lewis was an assistant professor and Dr. Zima a resident in the Pediatric Dentistry department. In December of 2009, the two ultimately formed Hanover Pediatric Dentistry (HPD),[ii] located in Mechanicsville, VA—not far from Richmond. The practice employs seven people when fully staffed. As you see later in the chapter, finding the right employees has been a challenge.

Necessity and the Mother of Invention

Of course, becoming a dentist isn't easy—or inexpensive. Both Drs. Lewis and Zima know that from personal experience. Consider some numbers from the site Dental Compare:

> The vast majority of today's dental students are graduating with significant debt. Most new graduates ultimately desire to own a practice—and that's where smart financial decision-making comes in. Everyone knows of that person in dental school who bought a new car or went on expensive vacations courtesy of their student loans. But the reality is that generally student debt is rising right in step with tuition and fees.
>
> According to the American Dental Education Association (ADEA) Survey of Dental School Seniors, in 2005, the graduating class averaged educational debt at graduation of $129,639. Only 8.4% of new graduates were able to finance their dental education without taking on debt. That means that 91.6% of graduates have student debt.[iii]

Saddled with significant debt from dental school, many new dentists are loath to start their own practices—at least immediately. They'll often join established practices to both learn the ropes and to avoid—or at least minimize—many of the following costs:

- Office purchase and construction (around $1 million)[1]
- Dental equipment (more than $100,000)
- Purchase of computers and software (more than $10,000)
- Dental supplies (thousands of dollars per month)
- Insurance (more than $1,000 per month)
- Utilities and fees (more than $1,000 per month)
- Marketing and advertising (more than $1,000 per month)

Against this financial backdrop—not to mention the current political climate—the prospects for opening a new dental practice these days can look pretty dim. Although the failure rate of new dental offices may not approximate that of new restaurants, success is hardly a lock. The odds are better if a new practice can significantly reduce technology-related expenses.

---

[1] Of course, not all dentists build their own offices, but it is common for dentists to own their own buildings. The $1 million represented the price of the building, along with related construction costs.

HPD is an interesting case study for many reasons. As has become painfully obvious throughout the national health care debate, few hospitals and doctors' offices have been able to digitize their medical records, despite the significant benefits of doing so. Electronic medical records (EMRs) help coordinate a patient's care, eliminate duplicate testing and conflicting prescriptions, provide backup, and generally cut costs. At present, a mere 15 to 18 percent of U.S. physicians have adopted electronic health records.[iv]

Strategic Use of FOSS

To be sure, neither Dr. Lewis nor Dr. Zima is a technophobe. The two are able to successfully navigate the web and handle personal matters, like most young professionals. That's a far cry, though, from being able to do the following:

- Set up an internal network

- Configure personal computers (PCs) and different software applications

- Deploy and maintain a server that runs a shared database

- Schedule automated nightly remote backups of server data

- Link X-ray machines to networks and servers

- Train staff to use the new practice management and X-ray software

- Monitor and maintain the software, computers, and internal networks

When it comes to technology, many dentists who open their own shops simply don't know where to start. Their business revolves around the mouth, not the computer. Dentists know a great deal about teeth—and much less about configuring servers and networks.

To this end, it's entirely logical for newly minted dentists to hire technology specialists to get their practices off on the right foot. Consulting firms such as Athena Consulting[v] exist to address the IT needs of dentists. Since purchasing and deploying expensive hardware and software has its own special set of challenges, these outfits can be particularly valuable.

Of course, nothing is guaranteed. Consultants can be expensive, and there are risks in using any vendor, no matter how ostensibly qualified. Not everyone is sold on the value of these specialists. On his website, Dr. Lorne Levine (aka "The Digital Dentist") writes:

It just amazes me how unreliable and unqualified many computer technicians still are today. When you call them for help, you end up talking to their voicemail. Then when you finally get them on the phone, they make you wait for hours—even days—before they can actually come out to see or guide your staff. Even at that, they still cannot fix the problem because the new $30,000 digital X-ray machine and the $15,000 digital pano[2] you just purchased are not "compatible enough" for your current computer to handle. No wonder why this process could be seen as a huge financial risk![vi]

For HPD, the question about hiring consultants was moot. The practice had an ace up their sleeve in the form of Dr. Lewis's husband, Ben, a seasoned and extremely knowledgeable IT professional at a Fortune 500 company.[3] Although not an expert on technology for dental practices, Mr. Lewis could at least get things started on this front. At a minimum, he could do the following for HPD:

- Do much of the setup work usually performed by consultants
- Assess the true benefits of hiring consultants for more involved technical issues
- Offer valuable insight regarding technology-related expenses, such as purchasing software and hardware
- Oversee technology decisions
- Serve as HPD's *de facto* head of technology

Drs. Lewis and Zima took advantage of Mr. Lewis's extensive IT experience. However, Mr. Lewis is the first to admit that he doesn't know everything about technology. He certainly had never connected an X-ray machine to an internal network before. To that end, he enlisted a colleague to help with the more technical pieces. All of this came at a relatively low cost to HPD. As it turns out, enabling EMRs for a small dental office is a surprisingly simple process, especially when the company has these advantages:

- A population willing to embrace EMRs
- Knowledgeable technology personnel
- The right hardware and software

Lest I understate its complexity, the process of enabling EMRs for an individual dental office is far easier than integrating those records with other dental offices, hospitals, insurance carriers, and other organizations. Still, HPD's deployment of EMRs exemplifies how the New Small is often able to successfully tackle problems that large organizations find so vexing.

---

[2]   These are digital X-ray machines for dentists.
[3]   He has also been a personal friend of mine for nearly 15 years.

Other Recommendations

HPD wisely adopted Mr. Lewis's other technology recommendations. The first was deploying OpenDental,[vii] a robust open source practice management application on par with—if not better than—proprietary and expensive applications such as Dentrix[viii] and Easy Dental.[ix] OpenDental handles patient records, billing, electronic medical records, charts, and other features essential to running a dental practice. OpenDental comes bundled with the popular open source (free) database MySQL for maintaining the practice's data reliably and securely.

Second, Mr. Lewis suggested that HPD forgo traditional licenses of Microsoft Office, preferring instead to make OpenOffice[x] the standard throughout the company. Although the savings don't approximate what HPD saved on consulting and proprietary dental software, for small businesses such as HPD, every little bit helps. Finally, he recommended that the company use Carbonite[xi] to handle backup and disaster recovery. Too many small businesses don't worry about document retrieval until it's too late.

Benefits of a Greenfield Site

Many businesses of all types and sizes suffer as they attempt to replace one technology with another. End users accustomed to doing things one way often struggle as they try to learn a new one. Data is sometimes lost or compromised in the migration process, particularly in *brownfield* sites.[4] As a general rule, the New Small typically avoids or minimizes these thorny conversion issues.

HPD successfully rolled out several major technologies in approximately two weeks: OpenDental and EMRs. There are two reasons for such rapid and successful deployments. First, from a business perspective, Drs. Lewis and Zima understood the benefits and requirements of both technologies. Although the deployment of each was not seamless, the founders didn't resist either technology or change.

Contrast HPD with Hospice Buffalo,[xii] a larger, more mature organization with hundreds of employees.[5] Although Hospice Buffalo eventually implemented EMRs, the entire process was exceedingly difficult, primarily because its doctors and nurses had long been accustomed to paper records. Used to writing on charts for 20 years, many of its doctors often questioned the benefits of going digital. To its credit, Hospice Buffalo overcame these obstacles and finally adopted EMRs. Compared to HPD, Hospice Buffalo required considerably more time, resources, and effort.

---

4   I use this term to refer to companies that have previously moved from one application to another.
5   I spoke with employees from Hospice Buffalo in doing research for this book.

Dr. Lewis's openness to new ideas and lack of existing infrastructure allowed HPD to adopt current and powerful technologies, all while saving a considerable amount of money. As a direct result, the company is well positioned for the future. More broadly, HPD shows that the New Small quickly and easily adopts new systems and applications, especially compared to large companies tied to dated technologies.

Future, Results, and Challenges

By using the Five Enablers and Mr. Lewis's expertise, HPD avoided having to purchase conventional software and pay for IT support. In the process, it saved over $15,000 in up-front costs. What's more, with Mr. Lewis's help, the practice saves nearly $2,000 per month in ongoing support.

The savings from OpenDental alone allowed HPD to purchase the following:

- Two video gaming systems
- Several LCD TVs for its waiting area
- An LCD TV to place above each dental station

Young patients and their parents appreciate these diversions as they wait for something that few like: having their teeth cleaned.

Looking toward the future, HPD's top priority is staffing the office with the right folks. "Ultimately, I want to focus on the dentistry, not on the administrative side of running a practice," Dr. Lewis says. "I want to know what's going on without having to check up on everyone." This is characteristic of the New Small. The owners of these companies don't micromanage their employees, although they are not afraid to take on extra roles in the event of a crisis or major issue.

With its technology backbone now firmly in place, HPD will begin to shift focus. The company plans to grow its practice through the following:

- Establishing a better online presence through an improved website. Admittedly, HPD's site could use some work.
- Continuing to use traditional marketing and advertising approaches, including e-mail newsletters.
- Experimenting with different social technologies.

HPD knows that it has yet to fully harness the power of many of the Five Enablers—and social technologies in particular. Although the company has established a rudimentary Facebook page,[xiii] it's hardly the community that it can be. Twitter and other social networks represent additional opportunities for HPD to foster a sense of community and engage in conversations.

To the company's credit, however, Drs. Lewis and Zima recognize this vast and untapped potential. This open-mindedness is hardly unique for the New Small. These companies don't claim that a technology isn't important without fully investigating it. Rather, they remain curious.

For HPD, the increased use of social media makes perfect sense. Lacking a massive marketing budget, it will benefit from simple word of mouth—just like any small business. Word of mouth is still the best form of advertising available, something that social technologies have not changed. Drs. Lewis and Zima recognize this and will surely use social technologies to a greater extent in the future. Perhaps they will take a cue from social media wizard Chef Tony, profiled in Chapter 16.

Staffing

Like many of the New Small, HPD has faced considerable challenges, particularly with regard to finding suitable staff. Although the unemployment rate has meant that 100 or more people apply for a single opening, Dr. Lewis admits that it has been difficult to find people with appropriate skills, experience, and reasonable salary demands. Several ostensibly qualified individuals interviewed well but did not work out. "We've struggled with trying to find affordable people with the right combination of knowledge and attitudes," Dr. Lewis says. The company pays competitive wages for its front desk, office manager, and assistant positions. "We are not a six-office practice that can offer massive pay and benefits," Dr. Lewis notes.

To HPD's credit, it quickly severs ties with problematic employees. The New Small knows full well that every person in a small business has the ability to help or hurt the bottom line. "Hiring good staff continues to be our biggest challenge," Dr. Lewis notes. "The hardest thing about owning and running a business is managing people."

SUMMARY

All businesses are cost-conscious, especially these days. By saving money on technology expenditures and embracing the Five Enablers, the New Small increases funds available for other key areas. HPD is a case in point. The benefits of technology are most pronounced when combined with an open-minded and intelligent approach to management. Of course, technology does not exist in a vacuum. Technology makes things easier, but it does not eliminate the day-to-day challenges of running a small business. For example, even for the New Small, it can be difficult to find good people in an economy with high unemployment.

Endnotes

[i]   http://www.dentistry.vcu.edu
[ii]   http://www.hanoverpediatricdentistry.com
[iii] http://www.dentalcompare.com/featuredarticle.asp?articleid=108
[iv]   http://www.technologyreview.com/biotech/21428/#afteradbody
[v]   http://www.athenaezell.com/services/new-practice-startup-consulting
[vi]   http://www.thedigitaldentist.com/website/article.asp?id=7&title=Home
[vii] http://www.opendental.com
[viii] http://www.dentrix.com
[ix]   http://www.easydental.com
[x]   http://www.openoffice.org
[xi]   http://www.carbonite.com
[xii] http://www.hospicebuffalo.org
[xiii] http://www.facebook.com/pages/Hanover-Pediatric-Dentistry/105539849481151?v=desc

Chapter 8

RESTRAINED CREATIVITY

Distrust any enterprise that requires new clothes.

—Henry David Thoreau

Like many people profiled in this book, David Ciccarelli is a serial entrepreneur. He attended the Ontario Institute of Audio Technology (OIART), where he studied the ins and outs of audio recording. There Ciccarelli learned the operations side of audio production studios. Upon graduating in 1999, he decided to start his own studio that focused on mobile recording[1] and digital technologies. He recorded many independent bands and had some success, although he realized that his time with this part of the music business was finite. He decided to move to more commercial music and voice-over work.

This decision led Ciccarelli to start a company with his wife, Stephanie. At the time, the company focused on corporate and commercial audio production. He started a small eponymous website that attracted more visitors than expected. After a few tweaks to the business model, Ciccarelli built a self-serve platform in which he charged artists to post their profiles on his site. "I was convinced that there would always be more talent than openings," Ciccarelli said.

Buoyed by early success, Ciccarelli decided to go all-in. In 2004, he sold his physical recording equipment to raise $50,000 CAN. He hired developers for his site and bought office equipment. The company targeted the

---

[1] Note that, back then, *mobile* meant laptops, not smartphones.

buyer side: specifically, marketing and advertising agencies that needed people for commercials. In November of that year, he and Stephanie formally cofounded Voices.com.

Fast forward to today. Voices.com is the world's largest online marketplace for voice talent. According to its website, the company is "the industry leading website that connects businesses with professional voice talents. Radio and television stations, advertising agencies, and Fortune 500 companies rely upon the Voices.com marketplace to search for, audition, and hire voice talents."[i]

Today, the 12-person company, based near Toronto, Canada, has amassed a global network of over 25,000 voice actors in over 100 languages. It currently serves more than 100,000 users online. Consider the company's *monthly* stats:

- Nearly 70,000 MP3 voice-over demos accessed
- More than 1,000,000 unique visitors
- An average of roughly 7,000 available job opportunities

Early Challenges

Of course, the company wasn't always this successful. Ciccarelli admits to making several key mistakes early on but, as is typical of the New Small, has learned a great deal from them. This chapter shows how Voices.com took a step backward only to take two steps forward.

Marketing Efforts

In 2005, the company spent $20,000 for a major marketing push to attract marketing and advertising agencies. The company hired a marketing agency to create jumbo-size postcards. Voices.com was giving away a few iPods to those who signed up on the site. Unfortunately, the response rate to this major campaign was practically zero. "Frankly, I think I got taken for a ride," Ciccarelli laments. "The firm was surprised that I had the ability to measure which people put in the codes and how many people responded."

The response rate was microscopic. In Ciccarelli's words, "The project was a complete disaster." He looked for a way to salvage at least a little value, asking himself, "What can we recoup from this?" A few things, as it turned out. For one, the company still possessed a list of people and companies for future marketing efforts. Second and arguably more important, the marketing agency had produced well-designed graphics. Ciccarelli realized that he had the makings of the company's visual brand. In fact, the company continues to use derivatives of those graphics to this day. By using them so prominently on its site, these "cartoonish" graphics have allowed the company to create a unique brand and identify. "We were able to avoid the stereotypical iconography," Ciccarelli says, noting that many voice-over companies tend to use the same types of stock photos to brand themselves.

Growth

Like many founders of the New Small, David and Stephanie Ciccarelli strongly complement one another. They recognize the other's strengths and limitations. Stephanie is more artistic and outgoing with customers. She's the champion of the business. On the other hand, David is the more technical of the two; he tends to focus on financial and technology matters.

Early on, the company struggled with the perception of being a mom-and-pop store. To overcome this perception, the company started at the University of Western Ontario Research Park (UWORP), one of dozens of incubation facilities in Canada. These research and innovation centers are typically located on university grounds. Their goal is to foster commercial knowledge and development. Through UWORP, the Ciccarellis were able to procure a proper office, expanding it as the company grew. This arrangement also allowed them to share the costs of common amenities, including cleaning services, photocopiers, and parking. Over the past five years, it has increased its office space from 100 to more than 2,000 square feet.

Voices.com is certainly not the only business taking advantage of alternative office space arrangements. Some companies use *coworking*, a cafe-like community and collaboration space for a wide variety of people. Roger Salazar, director of workspace management and promotions of ConvergeNJ,[ii] says:

> Technology has brought great change to the ways in which businesses are formed and operated. People can run successful businesses with little more than a laptop, Internet connection, and the will to do great things. They are no longer tied to traditional business structures. These individuals and businesses crave professional independence. Coworking meets the needs of these businesses, giving them structure, community, and a positive work environment—all at a lower cost. Coworking blends the benefits of traditional productivity with the modern concept of occupational freedom, which is why it's growing so fast.[iii]

Voices.com follows a consistent set of principles. Expanding physical office space is conceptually the same as expanding the use of a successful internal application. In each case, Voices.com increases its presence in the same flexible manner (see Chapter 5).

Management Philosophy

New Small companies realize the importance of fostering innovation and creating meaningful jobs for their employees. These companies realize that employees' ideas are often largely untapped resources: employees actually *like* making suggestions and seeing them put into practice. The New Small takes steps to ensure that employee feedback is given proper consideration. In the case of Voices.com, the company institutionalizes and reinforces this culture with seven guiding principles. These are listed internally and on its website:[2]

- Innovation does not mean instant perfection.
- Share everything you can.
- Ideas come from everywhere.
- Work on special projects.
- Creativity loves restraint.
- Get users and usage.
- Don't kill projects: morph them.

Let's look at each in more detail.

Innovation Does Not Mean Instant Perfection

The company fervently believes in the benefits of launching new products and ideas early and often. Lessons from failures are more important than trying to perfect ideas behind closed doors—and only then releasing them to the public. Voices.com uses crowdsourcing, customer feedback, and polls to determine which projects are most successful.

Share Everything You Can

Small teams that communicate openly have proved the best results for Voices.com. The company insists upon transparency in the workplace; everyone knows what everyone else is working on. To this end, the company uses:

- Shared documents and shared calendars.
- Google Apps—which is tightly integrated with Salesforce.com.[iv] (This will be covered extensively later in the chapter.)
- The free version of Google Docs.

[2] The latter serves to inspire applicants.

Ciccarelli knows that technology alone doesn't guarantee collaboration. To that end, the company holds daily huddles: standing-only meetings of no more than 15 minutes.[3] During this time, people share facts, figures, ideas, and opportunities. The goal is, quite simply, to effectively act upon them as a team.

Ideas Come from Everywhere

Voices.com applies both critical thinking to generate ideas and crowd-sourcing by turning to the community of members for new ideas. The company uses Salesforce IdeaExchange,[v] an idea-capturing and voting application that lets team members add, organize, and discuss suggestions on how to improve the service. Colleagues vote for the best ideas, which, in turn, are assigned to the person who is in the best position to effect them. Does this sound like a hierarchical company with detailed job descriptions?

Work on Special Projects

Voices.com encourages employee creativity. Much like Google, the company allows employees to devote significant time and energy (10 percent of their time) to pursue their own high-risk/high-reward projects. The 10 Percent Rule has paid significant dividends for the company, including these:

- Enhancing the company's social media efforts, including increased presences on Facebook and Twitter,[vi] with over 5,000 followers as of this writing.

- Understanding the source of its web traffic and effectiveness of its keywords by using split testing with Google Website Optimizer.[vii]

- Allowing the company to understand why prospective customers leave its website via usertesting.com.[viii]

- Using fivesecondtest.com[ix] to refine its landing page. The tool allowed Ciccarelli to analyze the most prominent elements of the Voices.com site design and make important changes.

- Enabling employees to become Salesforce.com Level II Administrators.[4]

Voices.com lacks formal job descriptions with rigidly defined responsibilities. This is not to say that the work environment is chaotic. Rather, jobs

---

[3] There are those, like me, who believe that most meetings ought to be held in this way. People tend to get to the point much quicker while standing for one simple reason: they are not as comfortable as when they are sitting down.

[4] Employees have become experts in Salesforce.com, allowing the company to do much more with the platform than most. The training represented a massive investment by the company. Certifications cost $4,000 per employee, in addition to the travel and lodging expenses over a week in Toronto.

at the New Small probably won't appeal to people in search of highly structured and routine work.

Creativity Loves Restraint

Voices.com harnesses employee-generated ideas and focuses them on the company's goals. Although creativity is encouraged, it is not unfettered. Exploration and experimentation without boundaries is likely to be counterproductive. Employees aren't permitted to work on projects that, although interesting on some level, do not relate to the company's overall goals.

Get Users and Usage

The New Small recognizes the paramount importance of the website. This is especially true for companies such as Voices.com, whose sites require extensive customer interaction. Both form and function matter a great deal (see "90s Sites," discussed in Chapter 5). The company is constantly learning from its customers, regularly soliciting feedback. It has never introduced a feature on its site that its customers didn't request. The New Small knows that there's tremendous value in crowdsourcing: asking what customers want—and then putting those ideas into practice.

Contrast this with other companies unable to keep their eyes on the ball. Many want to build powerful, user-friendly sites. Yet, when faced with short-term pressures to minimize costs, they deviate from this principle. Some don't respond quickly to valuable customer feedback—or at all. The result: customers often feel alienated and are likely to take their business elsewhere.

Don't Kill Projects: Morph Them

Voices.com doesn't waste ideas. Instead, the company attempts to change and transform them into something useful. Aside from refining existing offerings and spawning new ones, this policy encourages more introverted employees to contribute. In this way, Voices.com gets valuable input from those who may doubt that their ideas are good ones.

Intelligent Use of the Five Enablers

For e-mail and personal information management, Voices.com had used Microsoft Entourage,[x] developed by Microsoft for Mac OS 8.5 and higher. In 2005, Ciccarelli realized that the company required an effective customer relationship management (CRM) solution to manage its rapidly growing business. It was evident that Entourage was not the best solution to handle its customer management processes.

Selecting a CRM System

Like the rest of the New Small, Ciccarelli firmly believes that problems need to be solved with a healthy mix of technology and people. The two need to be used in lockstep. Consider the following example. The company was handling its CRM very informally at first, using e-mail inboxes run on onsite servers. Ciccarelli realized the limitations of this approach and soon sought a proper application. He received a quote from IBM for a whopping $120,000 CAN. He sought a second opinion. Oracle's quote was also extremely expensive. Beyond cost, however, Ciccarelli simply didn't want to host servers to make the CRM application run. In deciding against offerings from Oracle and IBM, Ciccarelli wanted to run his business from anywhere at any time. At the time, NetSuite and Salesforce were the only two vendors that provided this functionality.

Voices.com ultimately purchased and deployed a solution from NetSuite,[xi] a company that makes integrated web-based business accounting, ERP, CRM, and e-commerce software. The reasons were twofold: NetSuite's product cost less and contained its own accounting system. At the time, Voices.com had no way of tracking its financials.

Soon after the product's launch, however, major usability issues emerged. They included these:

▨ NetSuite's shifting tabs and drop-downs confused the company's employees; the product did not provide a consistent graphical user interface (GUI) for those with different roles. As a result, nobody enjoyed using it.

▨ An outsourced accounting team found the application difficult to navigate.

Now, a new application or system always faces some resistance and a learning curve. These are to be expected. Ciccarelli knows this, but he sensed that there was something more at play. He suspected that the company's early difficulties with NetSuite weren't temporary. What's more, mass confusion could pose significant problems in the short-term—and hurt the company's long-term growth prospects. The New Small knows that it is better to light a candle than to curse the darkness, to quote a Chinese proverb. Voices.com sought an alternative.

Fortunately, Ciccarelli was prescient enough not to have signed a suffocating contract with NetSuite.[5] He quickly began to explore different CRM applications. He did not try to force-fit NetSuite to his company's culture or vice versa. By way of contrast, many large companies have no alternative when confronted with the same dilemma. They are essentially locked into

---

5 He originally signed a one-year contract with NetSuite.

long-term, expensive agreements with their software vendors. For financial, political, and/or legal reasons, they can't switch technologies or applications even if everyone agreed that doing so was advantageous—or even necessary.

SaaS, Clouds, and Salesforce.com

Voices.com sought an easy-to-use, cloud-based CRM replacement that could deliver whenever, wherever access and provide an end-to-end view of the business. Like many small businesses, Voices.com originally signed up for Salesforce.com—a software as a service (SaaS) CRM system—on a trial basis. (Salesforce.com makes its products available via the freemium model.) Ciccarelli wanted to take the system for a test drive.

Ciccarelli became familiar with Salesforce.com through its free trial. Before formally switching applications, however, Ciccarelli took advanced Salesforce.com training classes and ensured that he could import NetSuite data into Salesforce.com. General dissatisfaction with an application is one thing; not having any application at all is quite another. Further, Ciccarelli ensured that he would be able to extract, transfer, and load (ETL) critical data from NetSuite to Salesforce.com. Ciccarelli soon realized that data migration would not be a problem.

After investigating Salesforce.com, Voices.com purchased the Salesforce CRM Professional Edition, which includes Microsoft Outlook integration. Ciccarelli successfully migrated all data to the new application. In the end, the transition was smooth. Astonishingly, the company was live within one week with basic functionality. By contrast, many companies struggle for a long time adopting new systems, as I know all too well.

Building on Early Successes

After initial system activation, Voices.com began to roll out powerful reports to employees, allowing them to track important sales metrics and generate real-time reports on the fly. The company was able to easily deploy *free* additional apps and components from AppExchange,[xii] an online cloud-based marketplace for Salesforce.com. These extensions include the following:

- **Reports and dashboards**—For sales, service, and marketing.

- **Integrated Google Analytics and AdWords**—Allows the company to see who has opened a ticket, for example; the software links automatically with Salesforce.com.

- **VerticalResponse**[xiii]—An e-mail marketing application.

- **Employee Manager**—Allows employees to request time off via the web.

"It's important for us to keep the technology invisible," Ciccarelli says. "We want our employees to be able to create reports in 30 seconds, and they can—even if they're not that technical."

Consider the powerful reports that employees at Voices.com can run to understand and analyze sales. Now, contrast this with the difficulty that many end users in larger organizations have in answering simple questions such as "How many sales have we had this quarter from different referring sites?" Answering this simple question can be a major endeavor.

Ease of Customizations and Master Data

Through Salesforce.com, Voices.com employees can *individually* customize tabs and fields without breaking anything behind the scenes. Ciccarelli cites the example of easily hiding credit card information from employees who don't need to view it. Again, we see how the Five Enablers stand in stark contrast to traditional technologies that require proper programmers to make tweaks, many of which can either inadvertently break something else or disappear with an upgrade to the application.

Collectively, the suite of apps now allows for all employees to consistently enter and retrieve *the same* information. "If it's not in Salesforce, then it doesn't exist," Ciccarelli says.[6] This is a simple, yet powerful philosophy to data management. Employees and external parties can now easily find and enter the information required to do their jobs. Using Salesforce CRM Marketing, Voices.com created a form on its website to capture new leads that has a look and feel consistent with the other pages on the Voices.com site.

In addition to a more user-friendly front-end and enhanced reporting capability, the deployment of Salesforce.com has resulted in other tangible benefits. First, it has enabled Voices.com to minimize costs. Second, the company can now provide much better customer service than before. Salesforce augments the company's customer service with auto-response e-mails and searchable forums. Its knowledge base contains solutions to more than 500 issues. Without such technology, the company would have to employ at least two dedicated IT resources, as well as additional staff to manage the flow of information and customer inquiries.

All of this would have resulted in considerable cost, conservatively estimated at $200,000 per year. Salesforce.com allows customer inquiries to be captured, assigned, and answered with ease. As shown in Chapter 2, effectively engaging with social customers today is critical, something that Voices.com does exceptionally well.

---

6 Many large organizations struggle mightily with answering simple questions such as "How many customers do we have?" In many cases, these struggles emanate from having too many systems, databases, and applications. Voices.com proves that simplicity is king.

Finding the Right Technology

Do not mistake the decision to move to Salesfore.com as an indictment of NetSuite's products. By the same token, the change should not reflect poorly on employees of Voices.com. Sometimes a particular technology or application just doesn't jibe with a company's employees, culture, or business partners. For whatever reason, NetSuite simply wasn't the right tool for Voices.com, and it made the change.[7]

Voices.com shows how the New Small intelligently chooses among a wide array of different technologies. And this intelligence does not end with the initial selection of a specific application. New Small companies walk away from technologies that don't meet their needs much faster and more readily than other companies do. Of course, the reasons vary. At a general level, though, consider two reasons:

- The freemium model is extremely popular.

- These days, contracts with technology vendors are relatively short (read: monthly, not yearly). This allows companies to switch more easily from one offering to another.

Again, this isn't the 1990s, a period in which many organizations were essentially stuck with their software vendors for the foreseeable future. Few changed applications because, to paraphrase the old saying, the devil they knew was better than the devil they didn't.

Using Add On Tools

The delivered functionality provided by Salesforce.com met the majority of Voices.com's basic business needs (read: CRM). Based on its initial success, however, Ciccarelli was eager to extend the application's functionality to other areas. Specifically, he wanted to create an easy means for applicants to apply to jobs at the company.

For that, Voices.com looked to Force.com, a cloud computing platform that works in conjunction with Salesforce.com. Force.com allows developers to build multitenant[8] applications hosted on their servers. Ultimately, Voices.com built a custom jobs app via the Force.com[xiv] builder. The app

---

[7] If I did some research, I have no doubt that I could just as easily find a company that did the opposite: replaced Salesforce.com with NetSuite's offering. In all of my years consulting, I have never seen a software vendor with a 100 percent client satisfaction and retention rate.

[8] *Multitenancy* is an architecture in which a single instance of a software application serves multiple customers. Each customer is called a tenant. Tenants may be given the ability to customize some parts of the application, such as the color of the user interface (UI) or business rules, but they cannot customize the application's code. (http://whatis.techtarget.com/definition/multi-tenancy.html)

syncs with jobs that are posted directly to the Voices.com website and provides accurate data tracking and management within Salesforce.com. Most important, though, the company can generate detailed reports and display those reports as a series of visual charts in what's known as a *dashboard*—a single view of key performance indicators (KPIs). Dashboards allow managers to easily perform high-level analysis, spot trends, and take action. This is common at the New Small: business decisions are largely driven by data, not by policy or corporate edict.

Social Technologies

Of all of the companies profiled in this book, perhaps none uses social technologies better than Voices.com.[9] In addition to offering a trove of podcasts and videos on its site, the company maintains a number of well-written and useful blogs,[xv] each of which is tailored to a specific audience.

The New Small knows that, with respect to social technologies, one size certainly does not fit all. Many companies—and even some small—overtly and shamelessly use social media as just another marketing tool. They then wonder why it does not work, ultimately—and prematurely—dismissing it as a colossal waste of time. Ciccarelli knows that the best way to use social technologies involves providing a great deal of *meaningful* content. What's more, it's silly to expect results immediately. Social media takes time.

"We actually consider social media to be core to our marketing strategy," Ciccarelli says. The first numbers discussed during the company's daily huddles revolve around social media: specifically, the number of fans and followers on major sites such as Twitter, Facebook, and LinkedIn. The company has seen a constant upward trajectory in these numbers, reinforcing a virtuous cycle:

- Fans and followers mean website traffic.
- Traffic means users.
- Users mean customers.
- Customers mean revenue.

The company has been able to generate a decent amount of buzz via social networks, and winning a number of awards certainly hasn't hurt.

Where FOSS and Mobility Collide

Ciccarelli was quick to recognize the power of mobility. "Mobile applications are kind of like building websites in 1999," he says. "They are really mobile websites. The cost to develop an iPhone app might exceed

---

[9] Chef Tony's (profiled in Chapter 16) is also high on the list.

$100,000. We could spend the time and money on it, and there would be no guarantee that it would get into the AppStore."

In 2010, Ciccarelli recognized that his company would benefit from a mobile app. However, it lacked the funds required to hire proper software developers. Being relatively technical in nature, he took the DIY approach. He started doing research and downloaded iWebKit,[xvi] an open source software development kit. Ciccarelli created a Voices.com mobile site using the tools, ultimately putting it together over a weekend. "I was really in a flow that weekend," he says. "I would make changes and test them on an iPhone simulator." Although developing a mobile website over a weekend might be exceptional for even the New Small, this sense of intense concentration during critical projects certainly is not. Later chapters will show how this temporary and intense singularity of purpose is common among New Small owners and employees.

Today, the Voices.com Mobile App[xvii] is available for the iPod, iPad, and BlackBerry for mobile users in North America and Europe. It allows people to find a complete listing of audio samples organized by specific categories and includes features such as:

- Optimized browsing experience with smooth screen rotation
- Audio samples available to play with the touch of a finger
- Click-to-call functionality to connect with a live Voices.com representative
- Integration with Google Maps to locate the company's head office
- Quick links to mobile versions of the company's Facebook and Twitter accounts

Future, Results, and Challenges

Although remarkably robust and customizable, Salesforce.com cannot meet every need for every company, and Voices.com is no exception. Yet once these small businesses get a taste of the Five Enablers, they want even more functionality, power, and integration. Along these lines, Voices.com plans to use eBridge[xviii] to integrate Intuit's QuickBooks[xix] with the rest of the company's core applications. By doing so, the company can quickly synchronize its financial data and remit invoices through Salesforce.com. In the early days, using standalone apps at Voices.com may have been acceptable. Not anymore. Although *every* business process probably cannot be automated, the New Small continues to identify new opportunities to use technology. This group seeks to automate as many processes as possible. It's just not a group content resting on its laurels. What's more, this ambition pays off.

It may not be possible or even necessary for Voices.com to calculate an exact return on investment (ROI) on its use of emerging technologies—and social technologies in particular. Still, it's hard to overstate how much the company has benefitted from effectively deploying the Five Enablers. For example, how do you quantify the precise benefits of having an accurate, 360-degree view of the business?[10] Employees can immediately view key sales, marketing, support, and billing data. Armed with this real-time information, Voices.com can make sound business decisions, especially compared to companies lacking similar data. Voices.com has also:

- Achieved a 62 percent increase in gross sales as a result of its Salesforce CRM deployment.

- Increased new business by 215 percent over three months.

- Realized an ROI of nearly 1,200 percent on its marketing campaigns.

- Successfully migrated to the new CRM system. That all employees immediately embraced Salesforce.com resulted in cleaner customer data and more streamlined business practices. That is, nary a single employee resisted Salesforce.com.[11]

- Significantly reduced operating costs and increased customer satisfaction via self-service and automated support features.

- Enabled collaboration across business departments via Google Apps and Google Docs. Employees start with a single version of a document and save it incrementally whenever team members make changes. Voices.com puts many key documents in the cloud, including sales and marketing strategies, event calendars, and so on. Avoiding Microsoft Office license fees saves the company about $3,000 per year.

- Saved significant money on file storage via cloud computing. The company switched from internally hosted, dedicated web servers to Amazon Elastic Compute Cloud.[xx] Remarkably, this change initially reduced monthly file storage costs from $1,000 to $2.10. Now, with several terabytes[12] of audio files, monthly costs run closer to $100. Voices.com could continue offering unlimited file storage for its users through additional cloud technologies such as Amazon Simple Storage Service (AS3).[xxi]

---

[10] This is exactly what Voices.com has.
[11] When confronted with new applications, employees at many companies refuse to get on board, pining for the "good old days." I have seen this many, many times.
[12] A terabyte is 1,000 gigabytes.

SUMMARY

Voices.com did not become the primary destination for professional voice talent by accident. Its success is a function of focusing on its customers, keeping an eye on the long term, and intelligently deploying emerging technologies. Like the rest of the New Small, Ciccarelli is not afraid to change, revert, and push the envelope as needed. The company's willingness to experiment with different technologies won't stop anytime soon. Change is deeply ingrained throughout the company, its employees, and its founders. Those who think that changes are permanent should take note.

Endnotes

i   http://www.voices.com/company/about
ii   http://www.convergenj.com
iii Personal conversation with Salazar, 08/24/2010.
iv   http://www.salesforce.com
v   http://sites.force.com/ideaexchange/ideaHome?c=09a30000000D9xt
vi   http://twitter.com/voicesdotcom
vii https://www.google.com/accounts/ServiceLogin?service=websiteoptimizer&continue=http://www.google.com/analytics/siteopt/%3Fet%3Dreset%26hl%3Den-US&hl=en-US
viii http://www.usertesting.com
ix   http://fivesecondtest.com
x   http://www.microsoft.com/mac/products/entourage2008/default.mspx#/interacting_entourage
xi   http://www.netsuite.com/portal/home.shtml
xii http://sites.force.com/appexchange/home
xiii http://www.verticalresponse.com
xiv http://www.salesforce.com/platform
xv   http://blogs.voices.com
xvi http://iwebkit.net
xvii http://m.voices.com
xviii http://www.ebridgeconnections.com/financial-systems-integration/intuit/quickbooks/overview-of-integration-with-intuit-quickbooks.html
xix http://quickbooks.intuit.com
xx   http://aws.amazon.com/ec2
xxi http://aws.amazon.com/s3

Chapter 9

FORGING THE RIGHT PATH

In the gray brain nothing is black or white.

—Eric Nelson

olin Hickey has served his time in stiff corporate cultures, specifically in the telecommunications and technology industries. It wasn't his cup of tea. Searching for a change, in 2008, he looked at the popularity of *mashups*—mixtures of content or elements. For example, an application that was built from routines from multiple sources or a website that combines content and/or scripts from multiple sources is said to be a mashup. The term became popular in the 2005 time frame.

Hickey also looked at the rise in the number of viable communication mechanisms. He began to think about how they could enable increased collaboration. Where many people saw chaos, Hickey saw opportunity. Why not offer a communication and collaboration mashup for small businesses? Having gone from the plush digs of AT&T to a small start-up, he knew from his own experience that many small companies were doing without many of the capabilities that large companies take for granted. This discrepancy might have been understandable in the past, but the proliferation of Internet-based communications applications has largely leveled the playing field. There's no reason that a smaller firm can't harness the power of *unified* communication and collaboration tools, including these:

- Instant messaging (IM) and chatting
- Threaded discussions

- Voice, web, and videoconferencing
- Document management

He and his business partner started PeerPort[i] in early 2008. The company's vision is to create an online collaboration and communications platform that enables virtual teams to work together more effectively. "The value chain has become much more virtualized than ever," Hickey says, reflecting on the now quaint old days in which different departments in the same company occupied adjacent floors of the same building. Communication was as simple as walking down a few flights of stairs or picking up the phone.

Hickey is hardly the first to note that many companies are structured in such a way that getting an answer no longer means going downstairs to talk to a single person. The company's product is an expert mashup that allows people to *easily* communicate and collaborate in real time across both geographic and company boundaries.

PeerPort's core product is a suite of highly integrated collaboration utilities, a term that Hickey describes as "predelivered glueware that fills in the gaps among applications." Each tool sports a user-friendly graphical user interface (GUI).

PeerPort started as—and remains today—an intentionally self-funded company. Hickey was no stranger to the start-up world and knew the strings attached to venture capital. Of course, with limited funds, it was imperative that PeerPort got three things right from the get-go:

- Selecting the right type of cloud
- Selecting the right development platform
- Selecting the right developers

Selecting the Right Type of Cloud

Because of capital restrictions, PeerPort never considered buying a server farm to deploy its offering. Also, creating *.exe* files seemed so, well, 1990s. Web-based deployment of its product is not only the future; it's the present. Cloud computing became the only logical alternative because it enabled rapid deployment and let the company easily add computing power as necessary. The clouds let PeerPort easily manage the supply of its offerings against client demand, a key part of the company's strategy from the first day. PeerPort needed to minimize fixed costs.

However, the question remained: what *type* of cloud offering? Although cloud computing enables many things simply not possible even five years ago, there's still a great deal of hype around it. He did some initial research on Amazon Elastic Compute Cloud (Amazon EC2), which is

> a web service that provides resizable compute capacity[1] in the cloud. It is designed to make web-scale computing easier for developers. Amazon EC2's simple web service interface allows you to obtain and configure capacity with minimal friction. It provides you with complete control of your computing resources and lets you run on Amazon's proven computing environment. Amazon EC2 reduces the time required to obtain and boot new server instances to minutes, allowing you to quickly scale capacity, both up and down, as your computing requirements change. Amazon EC2 changes the economics of computing by allowing you to pay only for capacity that you actually use. Amazon EC2 provides developers the tools to build failure resilient applications and isolate themselves from common failure scenarios.[ii]

Although EC2 appealed to him, Hickey knew that, for individual companies, mileage may vary. The telecom veteran suspected that operational management of EC2 might be a different story. As he did his research, he realized that this technology was in its infancy. Fully operational management and monitoring functions enable easy detection, troubleshooting, and resolution of issues.[2] Imagine a PeerPort client suffering from performance issues but unable to determine exactly the details of when, how, and why. The cloud, as Hickey soon discovered, was a collection of shared computing cycles, but it was nowhere near a mature service offering. In short, it wasn't ready for prime time yet.

What's more, at the time, Amazon had no viable pricing model. Amazon's sales reps asked Hickey how many computing cycles his product would need. Although hardly a technophobe, Hickey couldn't even begin to answer this question. "It was like going into a gas station and instead of paying by the gallon, you were suddenly asked how many wheel rotations your car would need," Hickey jests. "I had no idea. I don't think about compute cycles. I think about satisfying my customers."

For these reasons, EC2 wasn't a viable option back in early 2008, at least for PeerPort. The company contacted reliable but relatively inexpensive managed service providers (MSPs) who took advantage of cloud computing, but with several important distinctions:

---

[1] Again, this is typically called *computing capacity* or *computing power*.
[2] Note that this was true at the time that PeerPort made the decision to go with Amazon. As of July 2010, this is no longer the case. EC2 pricing and monitoring have evolved, as you might expect of the extremely dynamic nature of cloud computing.

- They could provide log files and a dedicated box to isolate, address, and resolve performance issues.
- They had transparent and viable pricing models.

PeerPort ultimately decided on Rackspace for its MSP.[iii] Rackspace and other emerging technologies allowed PeerPort—and the New Small in general—to compete with much larger, amply resourced organizations.

Selecting the Right Development Framework

After deciding to use cloud computing, PeerPort needed to select a development platform. When Hickey and his business partner created the company, they realized that platform-independence would be critical. If PeerPort's products worked only on Windows or in conjunction with Microsoft Office, for example, the company would have significantly limited its potential market. Remember, long gone are the days (the 1990s) in which everyone and every company use most of the same technologies. Because PeerPort targets other small businesses, easy deployment is imperative. Long, drawn-out implementations with excessive complications just won't fly in a small-business environment.

PeerPort could have chosen among many powerful and inexpensive frameworks, many of which fell under the umbrella of free and open source software (FOSS). PeerPort ultimately decided on Drupal, which, according to its website, is "a free software package that allows an individual, a community of users, or an enterprise to easily manage, organize, and publish a wide variety of content on a website." Hundreds of thousands of people and organizations are using Drupal to power a variety of websites, including these:

- Community web portals
- Discussion sites
- Corporate websites
- Intranet applications
- Personal websites or blogs
- Aficionado sites
- E-commerce applications
- Resource directories
- Social networking sites[iv]

So, why Drupal? Hickey did his homework. Like many major content management systems (CMSs), Drupal delivers robust functionality capable of being enhanced or customized. It supports electronic commerce, blogs, collaborative authoring environments, forums, peer-to-peer (P2P) networking, newsletters, podcasting, picture galleries, and file uploads and downloads. Finally and arguably most important, Drupal's development community is large and vibrant.

To create the PeerPort product, Hickey knew that he would need developers who could more than merely tweak existing Drupal code. They would have to go deeper, creating entirely new modules. To do this, the team would first have to assemble existing functional elements, starting with a robust e-mail program. Next, it would have to integrate each with the new code.

Choosing Drupal meant that PeerPort had a head start on development—something that the New Small attempts to do whenever possible. These companies never reinvent the wheel. PeerPort needed less than six months to release the first version of its offering. Had it started from scratch, development time may well have exceeded two years. What's more, development costs were one-tenth of what Hickey estimates he might have paid just five years earlier. Hickey knew that Drupal would allow him to increase the speed and reduce the cost of the PeerPort collaboration tool. "When it's your own money at stake," says Hickey, "you tend to do things a little more efficiently than the bigger firms out of pure necessity. That same efficiency also forces you to get it right the first time. As a result, we created a more robust solution, and at a fraction of what others might spend developing a lesser product."

Selecting the Right Developers

With the framework decision made, PeerPort moved onto the next step: finding developers to build the product. Although reasonably technical, Hickey was no Drupal programmer; DIY wasn't going to fly. He decided early on that hiring proficient developers on a full-time basis did not make sense. The company did not have the funds necessary. As an alternative, he considered contracting with a software development company. Unfortunately, that's hardly a risk-free proposition. Such companies often promise what they can't deliver or, in some cases, what doesn't exist—vaporware. Hickey knew that PeerPort needed to choose wisely; one wrong move could mean the death of the company before it really started.

During vendor selection, a software development company named Macronimous impressed PeerPort. Macronimous's salespeople asked logical questions about the business and customer needs; they did not just say "yes" when asked whether something was possible. In the end, PeerPort selected Macronimous specifically because it worked to understand the founders' vision, going to great lengths to help extend it even further.

Many New Small founders have worked with traditional software vendors and consulting firms. They know the perils of selecting the wrong partner. But Macronimous thought creatively and innovatively about different applications of the product. In other words, they did not just mechanically do what was asked.[3]

A month after PeerPort remitted the down payment, the basic product worked. However, as Hickey notes, "It looked terrible." The GUI, a key component to ensuring customer adoption and ease-of-use, needed significant retooling. Luckily, one of Hickey's friends, a graphic designer by training and a marketing wizard by profession, was between jobs. He worked with the two founders to better understand where and how the service would be used. His artistic background allowed him to conceive of a new vision for the GUI. Fast forward a few weeks: he generated an entire style guide complete with every screen, color, typeface, and layout the system would require. Using Adobe Illustrator, the artist's conception could be shared with the developers in real time, allowing them to better understand the required functionality and mirror the desired look and feel. This phase of the work completely overhauled the product's user interface, while retaining its core functionality.

This process was able to accomplish a number of key things:

- Expedite the development cycle
- Increase the progress of each iteration of the product
- Minimize confusion and rework
- Keep development costs to a minimum

In the end, the artist's depiction exactly matched the end-product. Hickey's vision had become a reality.

One Size Doesn't Fit All

Today, all employees face a "continuum of communication," as Hickey describes it. Long gone are the days in which everyone communicated via the phone and interoffice memos. The need to communicate—and receive—information is much more nuanced than even 15 years ago. In general, communication types can be broken down into the following categories:

- Not real time
- Nearly real time
- Real time

---

[3] This is often called *building to spec.*

People expecting real-time answers should *not* rely upon e-mail and really simple syndication (RSS) feeds; instant messaging (IM) tools and the phone are more appropriate. The New Small understands this and chooses its tools thoughtfully. PeerPort understood this when developing its platform and strove to bring these different forms of communication together in one place. Perhaps the chief benefits of PeerPort—and similar collaboration tools—are flexibility and simplicity.

By providing a range of tools, PeerPort allows employees to decide for themselves the best way to collaborate and communicate. Choice is a good thing; employees should not be forced to use inappropriate tools. Rather, the choice of applications should be a function of these constraints:

- The nature of the specific work or task
- The size and type of the information being handled
- The urgency with which it needs to be handled

These factors should dictate which form of communication and, by extension, which tool, is most appropriate. Many companies force-fit tools. The New Small doesn't.

The Benefits of Simplicity and Target Markets

The New Small is extremely cautious and deliberate in selecting its target markets. In the case of PeerPort, the company's sweet spot is small businesses—and this is by design. As we have seen throughout the book, smaller companies typically use technology in relatively simple ways, especially when compared to larger organizations. Also, as a general rule, big companies have much more complex applications, integration needs, systems, and architectures. Hickey is a realist; he knows that big companies are heavily invested in their current technologies. "These organizations may want our product but, for different reasons, might have a hard time implementing it because of internal technical issues," Hickey says. Technology aside, large companies typically suffer from internal politics, often unwieldy policies and procedures, and other cultural issues that might make the adoption of any new tool much harder than it needs to be.

The white whale can be a curse as well as a blessing, something that Hickey knows all too well. PeerPort avoids the problem of big. By focusing on small businesses, PeerPort faces fewer technology- and people-related hurdles. To be sure, small companies tend to have smaller budgets for technology endeavors compared to larger ones. However, the relative dearth of the types of thorny issues mentioned above means that technology projects stand a much better chance of success. PeerPort is more than willing to accept this trade-off. Hickey knows that it's better to have

10 small—and growing—businesses using his product well than one large, decaying organization struggling to implement his product. Especially in a social world, 10 little champions of your product can do wonders—as we'll see in Chapter 11 with DODOcase.

The romantic days in which all employees worked in the same building are gone; other structural changes have taken place in the workplace as well. Even within the same company, it's rare to find *everyone* using the same versions of the same software via the same operating system. Transcending companies, what are the odds that any one company's partners, suppliers, and vendors are all using the same applications? "Work is no longer a place but often a point in time and space, be it an employee working remotely or an independent contractor joining a virtual project team," remarks Hickey. "The tools that support work can no longer be tied to a specific software configuration, geographic location, or company affiliation."

Hickey is quick to point out that his customers could, if they had the time, money, and expertise, build tools similar to those that PeerPort offers. New Small companies don't reinvent the wheel, especially in this day and age. Smart small businesses typically don't have any of the requisite expertise—or desire, really—to reinvent the wheel. They want an easily deployable, powerful, and integrated collaboration suite. So that's just what the company provides.

Using Technology to Minimize Internal Costs

Like many of the New Small, PeerPort early on used free tools. Keeping costs down is important. At the same time, however, there are limits to the freemium model and free software. "Being a start-up business developing for other small businesses made us our own test bed,[4]" comments Hickey. The founders tried many of the same tools used by their target audience, such as Skype[v] for conferencing and Yahoo Messenger[vi] for IM. They experienced firsthand the shortcomings of a freeware approach, whether it was unpredictable Voice over Internet Protocol (VoIP) call performance or escort agency advertising on their chat client. In addition, none of the individual solutions worked with one another. "Just as the airlines have now made us baggage handlers and retailers have turned us into cashiers," Hickey says, "the software industry insists that we are all engineers. Therein lies the business opportunity."

While PeerPort was busy developing a better mousetrap, it began to notice solutions that could kill two birds with one stone:

---

[4] A *test bed* is "an environment that is created for testing purposes. A test bed may refer to software only or to both hardware and software." See http://www.pcmag.com/encyclopedia_term/0,2542,t=test+bed&i=52770,00.asp.

- Improve the development of the final product
- Improve the final product itself

For example, PeerPort relies heavily on conferencing tools to work with its development team, based in India. Hickey notes, "It was critically important, especially early on, that we embraced capabilities that extended beyond just e-mail. We needed both verbal and nonverbal communication to be incorporated." He tells the story of a developer who kept saying "OK" when asked questions, a response that he and his business partner mistakenly assumed implied acceptance and agreement. Hickey soon realized that, in India, "OK" typically means "message received—not 'yes and I accept.'" This is a critical distinction that could have caused major issues. Hickey continues:

> We incorporated P2P videoconferencing as a tool for dialog and project status review. Once we did that, we were able to quickly pick up on facial expressions that clued us in as to whether we were getting head-nods or real understanding of the issue. That drove our decision to incorporate affordable videoconferencing capability into our own system.

Think about how many development projects go awry based on fundamental misunderstandings about key design decisions. Hickey was able to nip this in the bud.

The company uses ConstantContact[vii] to communicate with its clients and prospects. PeerPort's other internal applications are fairly prosaic. QuickBooks handles its financials, and Microsoft Outlook is its e-mail client. Credit-card processing is handled by PayPal, which can be extensively customized and provides the added advantage of being PCI compliant. Companies such as Getty Images[viii] and iStockPhoto[ix] eliminate the need for a creative department, and Ring Central[x] keeps the business connected with the outside world.

Playing All Positions

Like many in the New Small, Hickey wears many hats daily, and no two days are ever the same. "I tell people that I play all positions in the infield and the outfield," Hickey says. "I'm a utility player." He and his business partner are part-time:

- Accountants
- Technologists and IT folks
- Systems designers and software developers

- Social media specialists
- Writers
- Marketers
- Salespeople
- Administrators
- Lawyers
- Managers

They love their jobs. Rather than feeling overwhelmed, they enjoy the challenges inherent in building a business from the ground up. They're wired to embrace the "greenfield" issues of growing a company, *their* company. They prefer these challenges to the political and cultural battles of *brownfield* or *blackfield* sites (read: large, bureaucratic companies).

Future, Results, and Challenges

Hickey surely won't forget the lessons learned as his company begins the next phase of its development. The same strategies that got them to this point will no doubt be integral to their future success. "There are so many things that enable an emerging business to ride the demand curve while enjoying scale economies," comments Hickey. Some of these include:

- Utility computing pricing models
- Third-party on-demand services accessible via common application programming interfaces (APIs)
- Network extensible technologies, such as Network Attached Storage (NAS) and Content Distribution Networks (CDNs)
- Search Engine Marketing (SEM) and Search Engine Optimization (SEO)
- Web-based sales lead generation tools and affiliate marketing programs

As a result, a company like PeerPort, which would have not been conceivable 15 or 20 years ago, now has the opportunity to compete with much larger companies, but with a much lower cost structure.

PeerPort has yet to turn cash positive. However, Hickey recognizes that the company couldn't have come this far this fast without the Five Enablers. And a little bit of good luck never hurts. Hickey describes the hurdles that every growing business faces in three distinct phases:

- Time to market

- Time to volume

- Time to profitability

"We made it through Phase I," Hickey says, "And we did it without deep pockets or a major financial backer. We leveraged tools, techniques, and talent that, until recently, were not available to a company of our size." But he also recognizes the challenges ahead. "Growing to scale takes money, and money is the purview of much larger partners, whether they are financial or strategic backers," remarks Hickey. "The good news is we've eliminated the business-building risk in the eyes of potential investors. Now their investment can instead be focused on eliminating scale issues, which makes us a much more attractive target." Although an exit strategy is not his primary goal, Hickey is emblematic of the New Small: these companies keep their options open.

Hickey is quick to note the difficulties often associated with wearing so many hats. But, he wouldn't have it any other way. He knows that working at a large organization just does not provide the same sense of ownership and accomplishment as running his own company. He's been there and done that. That doesn't mean that he's perfect. On the contrary, Hickey knows that he'll make mistakes; he just doesn't want a rigidly defined job with each day the same as the next. Like many New Small founders, he embraces uncertainty.

The Squeeze and the Juice

PeerPort is careful with its choice of clients, again refusing to embrace excessive complexity. Revenue is important, but not at any cost. New Small founders routinely ask themselves: for high-maintenance clients, is the squeeze really worth the juice? It makes little sense for most companies—especially New Small ones—to spend 90 percent of their time on 10 percent of their clients. "It's a constant balancing act of determining just how much complexity poison you can suck out of the wound of customer needs," as Hickey astutely points out. "Remove too little, and the customer has no incentive to buy. Take out too much, and you wind up killing your business, never mind yourself."

SUMMARY

Many large organizations that have dabbled with clouds and SaaS have yet to see the savings. Of course, they wonder why. Consider that these organizations are locked into traditional on-premises software licenses with attendant support agreements (typically classified as capital expenditures, or CAPEX. They then pay for additional cloud or SaaS services as operational expenditures (OPEX). As a result, their total IT costs are actually *higher* than before. CIOs will ask the question, where are our savings?

As PeerPort shows, the New Small isn't locked into expensive, long-term CAPEX commitments. These companies make use of the benefit of hindsight and to some extent can see where technology is going. This enables them to make intelligent and flexible choices while minimizing fixed IT costs.

Endnotes

i   http://www.peerport.us/introOne.html
ii   http://aws.amazon.com/ec2/
iii   http://www.rackspace.com/apps
iv   http://drupal.org/about
v   http://www.skype.com/intl/en-us/home
vi   http://messenger.yahoo.com
vii   http://www.constantcontact.com/index.jsp
viii   http://www.gettyimages.com/
ix   http://www.istockphoto.com
x   http://www.ringcentral.com

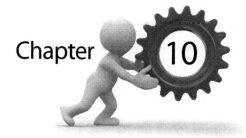

Chapter 10

REACHING THE TIPPING POINT

Leading is often a matter of changing question marks
into periods before they become exclamation points.

—Ed Klein

ounded in 1999 by Anthony Kirlew, NSI Partners offers marketing for technology services. NSI started out in the marketing problem-solving business, using emerging technologies to generate leads, increase sales and brand exposure, and improve internal processes and communications for its clients. The company helps its clients with traditional marketing, social media, and search engine optimization (SEO). Second, NSI offers a growing array of IT-related services. Today, the eight-person company with a base in Colorado is able to do much more than companies with more employees and resources. The NSI story is foremost about overcoming significant challenges.

A Better Way to Manage Customers

Along with ERP, perhaps no single application is as important to any business as its customer relationship management (CRM). Back in the mid-1990s, FrontRange's Goldmine[i] was widely considered to be one of the top

CRM system solutions in the marketplace.[1] NSI had long run Goldmine to handle its internal CRM after inheriting it *gratis* from COO Tom McClintock's previous employer. However, McClintock admits, "It was never easy." After years of struggles, NSI finally had ironed out the kinks in the application. The product finally worked reasonably well, despite the very tight budget allocated to its purchase and initial deployment. The company's employees were able to enter leads and sales into the system.

Often applications fall out of favor inside organizations. This happened with NSI and Goldmine. "Unfortunately, as the 2000s progressed, we became disenchanted with the direction that FrontRange was taking with Goldmine," McClintock laments. "We didn't have the resources to keep up with the product's changes. And we had to continue to work around the product's limitations."

And there were many limitations. First, Goldmine offered zero integration with Microsoft Outlook, the e-mail and calendar application of choice across NSI's client base. This proved to be cumbersome because contacts and appointments did not flow automatically from one application to another. Second, Goldmine didn't enable easy collaboration. Users needed to be at a traditional computer, connected to the network, to access any information or run reports. In the opinion of Matthew Frye, the company's IT manager, "These were poorly implemented, resource- and labor-intensive solutions to some pretty core problems." Finally, there was the big GUI[2] issue. NSI had grown weary of Goldmine's user interface. McClintock and other long-time employees knew Goldmine fairly well, but new users struggled to pick up the less-than-intuitive application.

But more than current limitations, Frye wondered about the direction of Goldmine and pondered the following questions:

- If it was already playing catch-up to other applications now, where would it be in five years?
- Would the gap between Goldmine and other CRM apps continue to widen?
- Had the Goldmine product reached a plateau?
- What were the costs to NSI of staying on a declining application so essential to its business?

[1] Like many large enterprise applications in the mid-1990s, Goldmine was based on a client-server architecture. In other words, there was no such thing as web-native back then. To access NSI's CRM data, one had to be at a computer with Goldmine installed. FrontRange's struggle to reinvent Goldmine is very typical of other software vendors' difficulties in transforming applications from a traditional platform to the web.

[2] GUI is shorthand for *graphical user interface*. This is basically the "front end" of the application, the screens that end users see while using it.

Despite these fundamental questions, McClintock had planned to continue using Goldmine, making do with a suboptimal system for the near-term. Perhaps Goldmine would improve in the future, as additional upgrades address some of the product's deficiencies. Also, NSI would stick with its preferred technology partner, Apropos Consulting.[ii] McClintock in particular was not a true Goldmine technical expert.

When asked about continuing with Goldmine, McClintock felt that he had no choice. "The idea of migrating to another CRM solution scared me," he candidly admits. "I didn't think that our little infrastructure would be able to handle that. We figured that we were stuck with Goldmine and its restrictions. We'd just have to make the best of it."

The Tipping Point

No business should take the decision to change major applications lightly—and CRM certainly qualifies as major. Although the upside can be considerable in the way of increased functionality and reduced costs, there are always significant risks, including these:

- Loss of key company data
- Disruptions in daily operations
- IT project failure
- Wasted time, money, and effort
- In extreme cases, dissolution of the business

In 2000, the original founders of Goldmine sold the application to an investor who ostensibly had no interest in developing the product, something that McClintock learned only after NSI had moved to Salesforce.com.

Also, in 2009, Salesforce.com significantly lowered its prices because it was making a push into the small-business market. Salesforce.com offered a significant discount to new clients as well. Frye did some informal calculations and determined that NSI should consider making the switch. Salesforce.com offered a number of advantages:

- Significantly increased functionality
- Lower licensing costs relative to Goldmine
- No requirement for its own dedicated internal server
- No need to rely upon Apropos for support

In the end, Salesforce.com was a cost-effective alternative, not to mention an overall easier one for NSI. Frye and McClintock determined that the migration was a no-brainer. "I went from thinking that we couldn't afford to switch off of Goldmine to thinking we can't afford not to," McClintock muses. "In the end, we're a better company for using Salesforce.com." The final blow for NSI's relationship with Goldmine came when Apropos was unable to produce a promised list of companies they claimed had migrated from Salesforce.com to Goldmine Premium. "We could find plenty that had gone the other way," McClintock says, "but Apropos' mysterious list never appeared."

The Migration

NSI knew that moving to Salesforce.com could present significant challenges; its user base was accustomed to Goldmine. NSI contracted a system integrator, ForceBrain,[iii] to assist with the migration. "It wasn't easy, and it was much harder than ForceBrain predicted," McClintock says. According to Frye, ForceBrain encountered major problems with the project, forcing NSI to bring in an independent, highly skilled external resource.

Note here how the New Small companies bring in the right resources to complete a project, even if they have to be creative and allocate additional funds. These companies understand that certain projects are simply too important to fail, even if that means exceeding a predetermined budget or chain of command.

"Looking back on it, I'm really glad that we did it," McClintock says. "I feel like it enabled us as a company to take a quantum leap forward. We wouldn't have been able to take our business to our current level under Goldmine." For his part, Frye says, "The cost was important but the technical differences between the two CRM applications really drove the decision." Frye and other NSI employees had much more important things to do with their time than worrying about Goldmine upgrades and performing regular server maintenance, something that Salesforce.com obviates. New Small companies have realized that the benefits of the software as a service (SaaS) model and increase in functionality are just too compelling to ignore.

Enabling Collaboration via Microsoft Online Services

Not many people associate Microsoft with small businesses, and arguably for good reason. To be sure, many of the company's traditional staples (Windows and Office) are found in just about every office in the United States, although that is changing—much to Steve Ballmer's chagrin. Many Microsoft products are simply too big, expensive, and powerful for small businesses. Consider two core Microsoft products: Dynamics for ERP and SQL Server, an industrial-size database. The cost of each is well beyond the reach of typical small businesses, and in my opinion, the functionality provided by each is just plain overkill.

This isn't a knock on Microsoft, though. No software company can be everything to everybody and every company; every tech company has its detractors, up to and including Google. To its credit, though, the Redmond-based behemoth has made great strides in recent years to meet the needs of small and midsize companies. Microsoft Online Services[iv] represents such an attempt. One such service, the Business Productivity Online Standard Suite (BPOS), delivers hosted communication and collaboration tools that provide high availability, comprehensive security, and simplified IT management.

Starting from $10 per user per month, the suite includes powerful applications such as these:

- Exchange Online for e-mail and calendar management
- SharePoint Online for collaboration and distribution of information
- Office Live Meeting for real-time meetings
- Office Communications Online for instant messaging (IM)

This array of tools addresses the concurrent needs of small businesses to effectively work together, but at a variable and easy-to-digest cost.[3] Microsoft Online Services (and competing products such as Zoho and Google Docs) would obviate the need for a small business to maintain its own server and handle patches and updates to key internal applications. In NSI's case, these were significant headaches in the Goldmine era.

Of course, McClintock had his hands full with NSI's daily operations. He wasn't about to make significant changes to the company's infrastructure by himself. To make better use of the company's technology, he would need someone to take charge. The timing of Frye's hiring was fortuitous because he joined NSI at the same time that Microsoft had ramped up its small-business offerings and related marketing efforts.

Frye researched Microsoft Business Productivity Online Standard Suite (BPOS). He was pleased to discover that NSI could take advantage of robust functionality previously available only to large Microsoft clients running enterprise-wide solutions. In short, BPOS allowed NSI to reap the benefits of Microsoft products without the traditional headaches and fixed costs.

---

3   For more on this, check out http://www.microsoft.com/cloud. Note that Microsoft's sudden embrace of cloud computing is a marked departure from its past position. Like other large, traditional software vendors (such as Oracle), Microsoft got cloud religion only after it realized that it had no other choice. Alternatives proliferated. A large enough number of its current and prospective clients demanded a cloud offering and, eventually, would have moved away from Microsoft products to the extent possible had the company not responded with a viable alternative.

"Once we realized this," Frye notes, "we no longer had to look for the 'next best' products." NSI is getting much of the bang for much less buck.

Additional Benefits of Staying a Microsoft Shop

But BPOS offered NSI other significant benefits. For one, at least for NSI's clients, Microsoft's file formats are still the *de facto* standards. Clients *expect* to receive presentations in PowerPoint, for example—not a comparable program. Frye stresses the importance of common denominators with NSI clients. McClintock tells the story of one of his clients who, back in the summer of 2009, didn't even know that there were alternatives to Microsoft Outlook. Had he told his client that NSI was "migrating to Outlook," she may have questioned the value of using NSI as a vendor. Of course, some individuals and people would have the opposite reaction. This merely underscores the point that there's no one right technology on an absolute level; there's only a right technology for a particular company.

What's more, BPOS also preserved the familiarity of core applications such as e-mail for NSI employees. Although hardly insurmountable, the move to another productivity suite would have invariably resulted in an end user learning curve. Staying a Microsoft shop eliminated that issue. Prior to moving to Salesforce.com,[4] NSI used different e-mail clients in different offices, including Goldmine's built-in e-mail module and Outlook Express.

NSI clients who call with specific application-related issues benefit from working with employees adroit at the very same tools; they are able to offer their clients tips and reduce the learning curve for new versions of familiar applications.

Finally, a close relationship with Microsoft buttressed NSI's future plans. The company has since branched out into website design and hosting. Frye used its connection with Microsoft to become a formal Registered Partner and reseller without having to hire a dedicated and certified Microsoft full-time employee. With this status, NSI received 10 advance *free*[5] licenses for Microsoft's Office 2010 product.[v] Aside from saving money earmarked for those licenses, NSI is now able to generate additional revenue through sales of Microsoft products to its existing client base.

The Migration

NSI chose to tie its future to Microsoft because it made sense. Both McClintock and Frye freely admit that, if theirs was a different business, the choice of chief technology vendor might have played out differently. Game developers, for example, tend to use Apple products much more than they do Microsoft products.

---

[4] At the time, Salesforce.com did not include a native e-mail application.
[5] Microsoft makes these available for free for one year to certain partners.

It's worth noting that Microsoft may not make "the best" collaboration software or "the best" content management application. BPOS offered NSI out-of-the-box integration among the different tools. NSI would not need to purchase best-of-breed applications and stitch them together with different interfaces and ETL[6] tools. Frye admits to the risks of a one-vendor solution but knows that for any technology, there are always points in favor and against.

Easier Backup and Storage

For service-oriented companies with distributed workforces (as is the case with many of the New Small), lost or damaged files can mean disaster. Businesses of all types need to be able to safely and reliably:

▩ Store and back up critical documents

▩ Share and manage content

The question becomes, which service or application should a company use?

In 2005, NSI began using Box.net,[vi] which the company used successfully until late 2009. NSI worked around a major limitation of Box.net: two people could concurrently work on the same file, with one person unintentionally overriding the changes made by another. Despite crafting detailed procedures to minimize the chances of this happening, occasionally NSI lost a considerable amount of work due to what was fundamentally a technology limitation. What's more, this problem inhibited collaboration. Eventually, NSI began the search for a replacement.

In early 2009, after a few months of research, NSI began using Egnyte[vii] as its backup system, although it also offered additional collaboration functionality. NSI did not attempt to make this change while migrating to Salesforce.com. That was a flat-out smart decision. The New Small recognizes that, even for relatively small applications, it makes very little sense to uproot more than one major piece of software or IT process at the same time.

Frye freely admits to not doing sufficient due diligence on Egnyte. Pressed for time and under pressure to generate revenue, he did not have time to properly kick the tires on Egnyte. The product demo looked good, and he signed the papers for NSI. The company also believed that Egnyte meant that it no longer needed to use the free version of Mozy,[viii] an online backup service.

---

[6] Extract, transform, and load (ETL) is a process in database usage and especially in data warehousing. At a high level, it means moving data from one system or platform to another via automated means.

After a relatively cursory review, Egnyte appeared capable of meeting NSI's needs. Upon implementation, however, Frye and some employees began experiencing a cauldron of errors when they attempted to access key files.

The decision to move to BPOS largely obviated the need to continue using Egnyte because Microsoft SharePoint provides practically identical functionality. Before moving to SharePoint, however, NSI kept Box.net up and running for six months in the event of a disaster or loss of key internal documents.

NSI has continually embraced the Microsoft suite. The company used to hold its meetings exclusively on the phone via Free Conference Calling.[ix] The company eventually switched to GoToMeeting[x] but, after making the move to Microsoft Online Services, quickly embraced LiveMeeting. NSI still uses GoToMeeting to interact with clients while continuing to test LiveMeeting, which, as of this writing, is still a work in progress.

Challenges and Striking the Right Balance

Although their work is often challenging, it's obvious that both Frye and McClintock love their jobs. The former performs a perennial balancing act, focusing on staying on top of trends in technologies while concurrently maintaining some degree of consistency throughout the organization, something facilitated by NSI's widespread use of Microsoft products. It's just not feasible to expect NSI—or any of the New Small, for that matter—to continually replace key applications simply because of a new feature. No company can function if end users constantly have to relearn how to do their jobs. At the same time, however, Frye knows that his work is never done. If Salesforce.com no longer meets NSI's needs, then it has to consider alternatives.

For his part, McClintock deeply appreciates Frye's role in managing all of these technologies. This frees the rest of the staff for project work and sales. McClintock says:

> I would never be a good IT manager because I have so little patience for trial and error, which is how I see that job breaking down. Once something stops working, you theorize any of a thousand different things that might have gone wrong and start testing your list one by one. As the clock ticks away, I get more and more frustrated. I suspect that Matthew, on the other hand, looks at all as an interesting, orderly puzzle to dive into. I just want to run in the other direction.

Effective Use of Social Technologies

NSI uses social technologies to communicate with clients and prospects in entirely new ways. What's more, this takes places without a substantial technology investment. "We already get clients through LinkedIn and Facebook," McClintock says. "Twitter helps us stay on top of trends we wouldn't otherwise know."

NSIs has designated Firefox as its official "social-media browser." By doing so, the company can tracks all the major social platforms in a single application with easily viewable tabs. As part of McClintock's morning routine, he launches Firefox with preloaded tabs for all of the major social media platforms. He can simply make his way through from left to right updating statuses, posts, and exchanges several times a day as part of his workflow. This is an example of how the New Small relies less upon manual contact-management tracking. Time savings can be considerable, while concurrently making relationships more productive.

Averting Disaster

NSI's reliance upon social media paid enormous dividends in the winter of 2009. After years of being on the outside looking in as a small but growing company, NSI was asked to make three presentations at the American Society of Association Executives' technical conference in Washington, DC. Although a great honor and a significant opportunity, it required months of research and a significant investment for a company with a tiny marketing budget.

Then disaster struck in the form of *force majeure*: a major snow storm blanketed the city, forcing the cancellation of the conference. McClintock was stranded in the Washington Marriott with seemingly no way to reach his audience. McClintock contacted NSI employee Don Baker, who was monitoring Twitter from NSI's relatively balmy Richmond office. Baker told McClintock that some of the conference leaders were planning to hold an impromptu UnTech[7] conference on the second floor of the hotel. Without social media, there was no way to contact them, other than to randomly knock on guestroom doors.

But Baker was able to use Twitter to successfully guide McClintock past one empty conference room after another until he finally hit the jackpot: a room full of social-media experts welcoming McClintock's presentation. With a seat at the table, NSI was able to help make UnTech10 a huge success, with online and live presentations to a national audience of 500 amid a snowstorm that had nearly paralyzed all other business in the region.

---

[7] This was the Unofficial Alternative to the Canceled Tech 2010. See http://untech10. conferencespot.org.

NSI and the other UnTech leaders are now busy planning next year's Un-Tech11.

Most important, though, is NSI's development of ReputationConnect,[xi] a listening platform.[8] This technology allows NSI to listen to and engage with online conversations using keywords important to its clients. "It has enabled us to stay ahead of, and even shape, trends affecting our clients' performance," says McClintock. "We can now understand and harness the thousands of conversations already taking place in our favor. It's quite the secret sauce and will be providing a lot of the interesting content for Un-Tech11."

Mobile Applications

Application compatibility does not stop at the computer: NSI has embraced mobility. The company has established a mobile marketing practice covering apps, .mobi sites,[9] text marketing, and bar-code marketing. But for NSI to sell a technology well, it has to use it well. Even for something as potentially mundane as e-mail, NSI needs to be sure that all employees can access their messages wherever they may be (read: via smartphones). Five years ago, such functionality might have been nice to have. Today, it's table stakes.

NSI had to face a fundamental issue around mobility: Does everyone get the same device? It's a nuanced issue. Supporting multiple devices through different providers takes more time, money, and resources. However, it provides increased depth of knowledge for NSI's clients. If different folks use BlackBerry smartphones, Droids, and iPhones, NSI can address just about any question about any device. On the other hand, enforcing standardization throughout the company saves on costs, but a client that happens to use a competing smartphone may have to go to another firm to have questions answered. NSI decided to diversify. It intentionally uses most of the mainstream smartphones. In NSI's view, the benefits of being able to support multiple products and platforms more than offset the resulting costs and integration issues.

Future, Results, and Challenges

The company is experimenting with the Microsoft Small Business Server line of products in two ways:

---

8   This is based on Alterian's highly successful SM2 platform.
9   The domain name *Mobi* is a top-level domain (TLD) in the Domain Name System of the Internet. Its name is derived from the adjective *mobile*, indicating its use by mobile devices for accessing Internet resources via the Mobile Web.

- To enhance its internal technologies and processes
- To add skill sets and technology service offerings to the small business market

NSI will also begin experimenting with server virtualization and the possibility of selling hosted services from these virtualized servers to small-business clients. It is also branching out into SMS-based marketing services for its marketing clients. It has developed iPad and iPhone apps. It continues to look into app development for smartphones as the new desktop.

New hires don't need to download 20 pieces of software to do their jobs. Nor do they have to manage multiple accounts. The services provided by BPOS make life much easier for NSI staff because they can focus more on growing the company and less on the plumbing.

Meanwhile, Salesforce.com has won everyone over internally in a way that Goldmine never could. What's more, its strong market share even provides collaboration opportunities across NSI and its strategic partners. NSI became very active in the Weber Street Marketing Association in the last year, an association representing the most cutting-edge marketing firms in its home state of Colorado. Because the association and many of its members use Salesforce, NSI is able to freely trade tips and tricks, and together the firms are building an impressive pipeline-reporting infrastructure.

Despite two recessions in the company's 10-year existence, NSI has done well, recently posting its best quarterly numbers. This is especially true given the fact that so many other marketing firms have had to recently close their doors. Both McClintock and Frye firmly believe that NSI's success would not have been possible without sage investments in the Five Enablers.

SUMMARY

NSI is typical of the New Small on several fronts. First, when NSI's technologies no longer met the company's needs, it took decisive actions. Second, much like DODOcase (Chapter 11) and Chef Tony's (Chapter 16), NSI's use of social technologies has increased awareness of its brand at minimal cost. Finally, the company's insistence that it use only technologies that it recommends to its customers minimizes any potential divide.

Endnotes

i   http://www.frontrange.com/goldmine.aspx
ii   http://www.aproposconsulting.com
iii http://www.forcebrain.com
iv   https://www.microsoft.com/online/default.mspx
v   http://office.microsoft.com/en-us/try/try-office-2010-FX101868838.aspx?WT.
     mc_id=MiG_Products
vi   http://box.net
vii http://www.egnyte.com
viii http://mozy.com
ix   http://www.freeconference.com
x   http://www.gotomeeting.com/fec/
xi   http://www.nsipartners.com/repconnect.html

Chapter 11

WHERE OLD AND NEW COLLIDE

We learn geology the morning after the earthquake.

—Ralph Waldo Emerson

I n 2005, Patrick Buckley and Craig Dalton had never met but, unbeknownst to them, had a few things in common: both were long-time entrepreneurs training for the IRONMAN Canada Triathlon. Buckley had created a Facebook app for high school rowers (Rowster[i]) and an iPhone app URL shortening service that allows for analytics on traffic sources and conversion (appsto.re[ii]). For his part, Dalton had worked on a number of mobile projects, including Proteus,[iii] I-play,[iv] and Mplayit.[v]

Upon meeting, the two hit it off immediately. In early 2010, they started a company, DODOcase,[vi] that has achieved a remarkable level of success. The founders named their flagship product as an ode to the bird that has been extinct since the mid-seventeenth century, knowing that physical books may be on that very path.[vii]

Not that Buckley and Dalton wanted the same fate for their business as befell the dodo—on the contrary. When founding the company, Buckley and Dalton had two goals:

- To make beautifully designed protective cases for the Apple iPad
- To preserve the art of book binding in San Francisco

"We wanted to help people to adapt to the latest technology," Buckley said, "It's really nice when you can provide the best of the digital and analog worlds."

Buckley explains the impetus for the product:

> We got the idea about halfway between when the iPad was initially announced and when it was launched. I started proto-typing maybe two and a half weeks before the launch and had one product by the time the launch came around. I threw it up on Shopify, didn't really know how I was going to make a lot of them but I figured if it was popular, I'd sort that out.[viii]

Of course, DODOcase was hardly the only company to (correctly) assume that the iPad case business would be huge. Apple products are extremely popular and not inexpensive. People would want to protect their investments, as they had with their iPhones and iPods. Although many people would purchase their cases in Apple stores, perhaps on their date of purchase, Buckley and Dalton sensed that there still existed a significant window of opportunity stemming from consumers' desire for different products.

DODOcase believed that it could compete on quality, not on price. Through Buckley's family connections, the two located a master crafts-man in San Francisco, CA, with more than 40 years of experience in binding books. Because each case is built from scratch and not mass produced, it takes approximately four to six weeks to create each one. Buckley and Dalton felt that their customers could live with this wait if they knew that they were ultimately receiving a high-quality product.

However, one major question remained: how would a company with a limited budget get its core product to its customers? The answer: Shopify.

Shopify: The Platform and the Contest

To bring DODOcase to the masses, Buckley and Dalton briefly considered Magento, an open source e-commerce platform,[ix] but ultimately decided against it. Instead, the two discovered and selected Shopify.[x] Shopify's core product is a web application that allows its clients—many of which are small businesses—to easily and quickly create online stores. Shopify uses the popular Ruby on Rails (RoR) open source web application framework.[xi] (In fact, RoR is the same framework initially used by Twitter before its massive growth forced the company to switch to a more powerful and propri-etary back end.) In March of 2010, DODOcase signed up for Shopify.

"We never would have started this company if it hadn't been for Shopify," Buckley says, "We knew that we could make a better case than Apple would." Interestingly, Buckley has a background in publishing. In 2008, he coauthored *The Hungry Scientist Handbook: Electric Birthday Cakes,*

Edible Origami, and Other DIY Projects for Techies, Tinkerers, and Foodies along with Lilly Binns.

In December of 2009, Shopify announced a contest on its blog in conjunction with one if its advisors—Tim Ferriss, author of the bestselling book *The 4-Hour Workweek*.[xii] Shopify would award a $100,000 USD prize to a company that used its product to generate the most sales in a six-month period. Other rules and bonuses included these:

- An additional $20,000 in prizes was available to other companies.
- Only new businesses were eligible to enter.
- The contest ran for six months, starting January 1, but people could register and start working on their businesses now.
- The best two months of sales were counted.
- Even if people didn't win prizes, they could end up with a viable business at the end of six months.
- The steps and details in the new, expanded edition of *The 4-Hour Workweek* would be used as ground-zero for instructions.
- The contest was open to U.S. businesses only. The tools and guidance were available to all entrants, though, so businesses were encouraged to enter no matter where they were.

The contest received a great deal of publicity, because media giants such as *The New York Times* covered it.[xiii] Ultimately, DODOcase won the grand prize of $100,000, with the largest gross revenue in its best two months. Other prize winners of the Shopify challenge included these:[xiv]

- **Nashville Flood Tees**[xv]—A company founded to raise money for flood relief in Nashville.
- **Buy Mafia**[xvi]—A company catering to the *Mafia Wars* masses.
- **Grove**[xvii]—A company selling bamboo iPhone cases. (Are you spotting a trend here?)
- **Vaporizers.com**[xviii]—A company selling twenty-first-century bongs.

Unexpected Growth via Social Technologies

To say that DODOcase used social technologies effectively is the acme of understatement. *The New York Times* recently profiled the company's unique marketing efforts:

To encourage early, positive buzz among Apple iPad buyers, Mr. Dalton hired street teams via Craigslist to "hang out with Apple fanboys, while they waited in line for hours, maybe even days, outside of Apple retail stores for a chance to buy the first edition iPad." The street teams, he said, hit Apple store locations in Boston, Chicago, Los Angeles, New York, and San Francisco.[xix]

Astonishingly, Buckley and Dalton spent a mere $500 USD on the street teams. The company has spent a fraction of what other companies have spent for marketing. The two posted ads on Craigslist sites in six different major cities, asking people if they enjoyed Apple products and wanted to be involved in the excitement of the launch of the iPad. They sent respondents marketing materials, offering to pay them for every case sold. The response was, in a word, strong.

Although atypical, viral responses to effective social media campaigns are not completely unexpected. Jason Baer, coauthor of the forthcoming book *The Now Revolution: 7 Shifts to Make Your Business Faster, Smarter, and More Social,* offers some insight into this:

> Overlooked in the social media discussion is that it's more about engagement than about audience. Ideally, you're winning hearts and minds a few at a time with authenticity and interaction, rather than splashing shallow messages to thousands of people at once via advertising. Consequently, small companies have a natural advantage.
>
> Social media allows big companies to act small again, and if you're already a small company, it should be even easier. You're closer to your customers, their needs, their problems, and it should be less of a stretch to humanize your operation.[xx]

Reviews

No person or organization can control social media—not even the New Small. Reviews, news, and stories take on a life of their own on the social web. The Engadget review got the ball rolling for DODOcase. According to its website, Engadget is an extremely "popular web magazine with obsessive daily coverage of everything new in gadgets and consumer electronics."[xxi] On May 3, 2010, it posted this particularly flattering review of DODOcase:

As far as we're concerned, this is the Rolls Royce of iPad cases. If it looks familiar, it should—it's patterned after the popular (and timeless) Moleskine notebook design. We were won over by the aesthetics of it right off the bat, but the functionality and quality of the build really put this over the top. The case itself is handmade and numbered—it even comes with a hand-written library card and sleeve, further helping to imbue it with an air of understated class. If you're a fan of the Moleskine journals, it will feel entirely natural in your hands (the faux-leather is identical, as is the binding), but the real magic is the construction of the "cradle" area. Instead of using straps or a slip, the tablet is surrounded by hand-carved bamboo (with notches in all the right spots for your headphone jack and buttons) and fits inside the case snuggly thanks to four rubber "stops" in the corners. At first we were worried the case could come popping right out, but it seems to be held firmly enough for our uses. Additionally, the shape of the case gives you an additional little slant when you've got the back folded over, so if you're looking to do some typing, you get a little more visibility (though it's not quite enough lift for heavy e-mail sessions or Great American Novel writing). Still, the DODOcase is [a] pure win as far as we're concerned—unless you're looking for something a little more rugged or packed with storage, you'll be hard pressed to find a better way to lose $49.99. One note—you may be in for a wait, as the company is currently slammed with orders for the case, so get in now, and try to be patient.[xxii]

And the hits just kept on coming. On July 14 of 2009, Evan Williams, then-CEO of Twitter, endorsed DODOcase on his Twitter feed: "Got my DODOcase. Sweet."[xxiii] Not bad, considering Williams had over 1.2M followers at the time. Additional reviews from popular sites such as The Unofficial Apple Weblog[xxiv] (TUAW) and Crunchgear[xxv] reinforced the perception that DODOcase was *the* iPad case to buy. All things considered, it's hard to imagine a less expensive—and more successful—marketing campaign.

Crowdsourcing and Social Technologies

After its initial buzz subsided, DODOcase kept the momentum going. It continues to use social technologies in innovative ways. A healthy cash flow means that the company now has sufficient funds for traditional marketing efforts. Despite this, it allocates exactly zero dollars to marketing. Instead, the company relies exclusively upon making a quality product and word of mouth to get the message out and raise awareness. Buckley and Dalton strongly believe that DODOcase's customers can evangelize its product much better than the company or expensive marketing agencies could. The company boasts nearly 5,000 fans on its Facebook page[xxvi] as of this writing and nearly as many followers on Twitter.[xxvii] It uses Facebook to keep its customers informed, most recently by having its fans vote on a new logo.

Although the New Small does not use crowdsourcing for every important business decision, promoting customer and fan involvement via social technologies is not only economical; it's just plain smart. "Before we invest a bunch of time and energy in developing new products, we want to poll fans to find out what they think," Buckley says. "They're the ones who make or break the company. People love being involved." By the same token, however, DODOcase is selective in soliciting customer feedback; it doesn't want to overwhelm people with too many requests. It also needs time to digest the feedback received. The New Small knows that crowdsourcing has its limits. A company can't throw *every* decision out there.

The company's use of video is particularly instructive. YouTube videos have been an important means of generating word of mouth for the company. The medium allows DODOcase to put a human face to what the company is doing. As a result of its effective use of video, its customers know exactly where their money is going—to a book binder in San Francisco. Buckley says. "We're helping preserve an art form." Videos on how a DODOcase is made have been exceptionally popular.

It also uses social networks like Facebook and Twitter to communicate with customers. Rather than waiting for customers to call or e-mail for updates, the company takes a proactive approach. Consider an update on August 26 to its Facebook page, "Today we'll be shipping into August 5th orders! Watch our back order list we might actually conquer you shortly!" How many companies reach out to their customers like this?

Outsourced Customer Service and Fulfillment

Without question, Shopify has been the single most critical element to DODOcase's success. Aside from the contest prize, the platform has provided user-friendly and powerful tools, enabling DODOcase to easily create coupon codes for both percentage and dollar discounts. These location-specific codes allow Buckley and Dalton to easily know where coupons are being redeemed. As a result, the company has a great deal of insight into its customer base.

Analytics such as these are commonplace at the New Small. They allow people to ask—and answer—valuable questions surrounding customer behavior, pricing, market segmentation, and the effectiveness of different sales channels.

Buckley describes the Shopify platform as "easy to get up and running." He notes that Shopify can support lots of different stock-keeping units (SKUs).[1] This may seem trivial for a new company with only one product (at this point), but the New Small is proactive and prescient. This is a case in point. Why would DODOcase tie itself to a limited platform that it may soon outgrow? The last thing that the company needs is a series of additional distribution and fulfillment problems, especially when it is already facing challenges satisfying enormous demand. These problems can kill a growing business, particularly when its customers are social and tech-savvy. iPad buyers certainly qualify on both fronts.

Buckley mentions some initial problems with merchant processing. Because DODOcase was such a new customer, without an established payment history, PayPal and Google Checkout were holding the company's funds for longer than normal. The former held funds for 45 days, causing cash flow to suffer.

Again, DODOcase looked to Shopify for the answer. Shopify forums provided a starting point, and the company's technical support helped them resolve this issue. In the end, Shopify worked with Buckley and Dalton to find a solution to the problem, expediting payment. What's more, because customers provide their e-mail addresses, Buckley and Dalton were able to easily contact customers whose orders had been delayed. Returning to Chapter 2 for a moment, note how DODOcase was able to use Shopify to proactively communicate with its customers and inform them of updates. Also note how few old-school companies would take such an approach.

Chapter 2 addressed, among other things, the importance of outsourcing. Returning to that theme for a moment, DODOcase outsourced two key elements of its business. First, it used Noonaco[xxviii] to handle product fulfillment. Noonaco is a shipping, storage, and fulfillment company that had effectively worked with Shopify clients. Second, the company quickly realized that roughly 80 percent of customer inquiries required a standard response. To that end, it outsourced customer service to 5 an hour.[xxix] Buckley and Dalton decided to hand them the other 20 percent—those whose answers required a personalized response.

Understanding the Social Customer

The New Small understands both the futility of trying to make everyone happy as well as the power of the social customer. We saw this in Chapter 8 with Voices.com. "We try to give the customers the benefit of the doubt all the time," Buckley says. "Sometimes we take it on the chin, but that's the

---

[1] Stock-keeping units (SKUs) uniquely identify each distinct product and service that can be purchased. They easily enable tracking inventory and product availability.

double-edged sword of social media. We ask the customer, 'How can we make you happy?'"

The company occasionally has shipping problems, particularly with international orders. Some shipments to Europe take four to six weeks to arrive because customs might hold the package. Coupled with the time to make each case, some international customers may wait up to three months for their DODOcases.

To minimize the potential impact of impatient customers, Dalton and Buckley share their frustration with their customers. Their message is, "I'm listening. Feel free to vent to me." This helps diffuse potentially tense situations and communicates that the company cares a great deal about customer satisfaction.

FOSS Extends Limited Budgets

As with most of the New Small, Buckley and Dalton did not have a massive budget prior to starting their company—and even after winning the Shopify contest. Although $100,000 is a great deal of money for many small businesses (not to mention the profits from having sold nearly 15,000 units as of this writing), Buckley and Dalton are typical New Small in the following regard: they are taking advantage of FOSS and low-cost alternatives to run their business. In the case of DODOcase, these include:

- E-mail with Google Apps
- Productivity with Google Docs for documents related to shipping
- Dropbox[xxx] for document storage
- SurveyMonkey[xxxi] to solicit customer feedback
- MailChimp[xxxii] for marketing and communications
- Skype for low-cost telecommunication
- Twitter for microblogging

By spending very little money on these applications and services, DODOcase has more money to spend on true essentials. "When Patrick and I started this business, we had no idea about what to expect," Dalton says. "It just wouldn't have made sense for us to purchase and implement expensive systems."

Quotes like this illustrate an important point: the New Small makes intelligent use of its finite financial and human resources. Why spend money on expensive proprietary technology when FOSS and low-cost alternatives suffice—at least for the time being?

Careful Selection of Tools and Platforms

As DODOcase illustrates, the New Small looks for platforms with three critical features when first launching their businesses. These include the ability to:

- Minimize costs.
- Allow for flexible and monthly pricing.
- Provide the complete range of tools necessary to bring their products to market. These include every element needed to run an online shop.

"Early on, bootstrapping where possible is a crucial practice," notes Harley Finkelstein, general counsel and director at Shopify. "Tools such as Shopify let entrepreneurs focus on what they do best within their trade. At the same time, they are providing small businesses with infrastructure needed to quickly and easily launch a strong and successful online shop."

New Small companies are reluctant to lock themselves into traditional multi-year contracts, something that Finkelstein certainly understands. To that end, Shopify offers scalable monthly plans—and it's hardly alone in doing so. As you saw in Chapter 1, long gone are the days in which small businesses needed to spend thousands of dollars for powerful software. Things just change too fast to attempt to predict the long term.

Future, Results, and Challenges

The New Small is quick to admit mistakes, and with DODOcase, Dalton thinks that his company should have outsourced customer service sooner. What's more, there have been some fulfillment issues stemming from such strong demand. Despite these challenges, Despite these challenges, the company has reached $1M USD in revenue after four months—despite employing only four full-time people and two contractors.

DODOcase plans to use the prize money mostly for product development. On the docket are these:

- Cases for new gadgets.
- Cases that accommodate gadgets equipped with the Square Inc. audio-jack mobile payments technology. Square Inc.[xxxiii] makes an audio jack that turns mobile devices[2] into a kind of digital register capable of accepting and tracking different types of payments.

[2] Including the iPhone, iPad, Nexus One, and Droid Smartphones.

In an interview on the site Mixergy,[xxxiv] Buckley describes his view of the world:

> I actually think that you shouldn't look at the world as software vs. hardware. If you can figure out a way to build a business that uses the power of the Internet as a communications tool to reach customers, and you have a really awesome physical product that people want to buy, then you should use one to leverage the other.

Clearly, Buckley does not want to create a typical company. "We enjoy working closely with our vendors and suppliers," Buckley says. "Even though they're not our employees, they have the drive to make their own business successful. For certain elements of our business, it's better to work with small companies than to hire employees. We have more meaningful relationships with them."

SUMMARY

DODOcase is instructive on a number of levels. Few do more than this company does with the Five Enablers. As other companies have shown, the New Small just plain gets social technologies. Beyond the social realm, DODOcase is a perfect example of how New Small companies quickly embrace opportunities when they present themselves. The company shows how, by using the Five Enablers, the New Small can go from idea to execution to massive sales in very little time.

Endnotes

i   http://rowster.org
ii http://appsto.com
iii http://www.proteus.com
iv http://www.iplay.com
v   http://www.mplayit.com
vi http://www.dodocase.com
vii BirdLife International (2004). Raphus cucullatus. 2006. IUCN Red List of Threatened Species. IUCN 2006. http://www.iucnredlist.org. Retrieved on 2006-12-07. Database entry includes justification for why this species is listed as extinct.
viii http://mixergy.com/dodocase-patrick-buckley-interview
ix http://developer.novell.com/wiki/index.php/Magellan/Roadmap
x   http://www.shopify.com/

[xi] http://weblog.rubyonrails.org/2006/6/5/shopify-is-open-for-business
[vii] http://blog.shopify.com/2009/12/10/win-100-000-with-shopify-s-build-a-business-competition
[xiii] http://boss.blogs.nytimes.com/2010/07/19/dodocase-top-shop
[xiv] http://www.wallstreetoasis.com/blog/dodocase-wins-shopify-challenge
[xv] http://nashvilleflood.myshopify.com
[xvi] http://www.buymafia.com
[xvii] http://www.materialicious.com/2010/05/ipad-case-from-grove.html
[xviii] http://www.vaporizers.com
[xix] http://boss.blogs.nytimes.com/2010/07/19/dodocase-top-shop
[xx] Personal conversation, 08/16/2010
[xxi] http://www.engadget.com/about
[xxii] http://www.engadget.com/2010/05/03/a-tale-of-two-ipad-cases-the-dodocase-and-m-edge-trip-jacket
[xxiii] http://twitter.com/ev/status/18569902591
[xxiv] http://www.tuaw.com/2010/05/04/tuaw-review-dodocase-for-ipad-makes-moleskines-weep
[xxv] http://www.crunchgear.com/2010/05/28/the-ipad-dodocase-wins-our-hearts-and-money
[xxvi] http://www.facebook.com/pages/dodocase/105269252845246?v=wall
[xxvii] http://twitter.com/dodosays
[xxviii] http://www.noonaco.com
[xxix] http://www.5anhour.com
[xxx] http://www.dropbox.com
[xxxi] http://www.surveymonkey.com
[xxxii] http://www.mailchimp.com
[xxxiii] https://squareup.com
[xxxiv] http://mixergy.com/dodocase-patrick-buckley-interview

Chapter 12

FLEXIBILITY PERSONIFIED

Don't count the days, make the days count.

—Muhammad Ali

I n *The 7 Habits of Highly Effective People*, Stephen Covey writes about the importance of beginning with the end in mind. For any business, this is much easier said than done, and lady luck plays its part. It is particularly pronounced in the software world because the incorrect choice of "platforms" can singlehandedly foil an otherwise promising business. The rewriting of code and subsequent testing can drain funds meant for new product development, expansion, marketing, infrastructure, and other key uses.

Of course, predicting the future of software or technology in general is anything but easy. Few people have the foresight to build a successful delivery model for their company's products and services that's ahead of its time. But Megan Torrance is one of them.

Torrance is justifiably proud of the little company she's created. After nearly a decade of working as an independent contractor with specific emphases on change management and business processes, in 2006 she founded the eponymous Torrance Learning. The now seven-employee company develops web-based courses for a wide range of organizations and is located outside of Ann Arbor, MI. At its core, hers is an e-learning design and development outfit whose projects have run the gamut. "We've learned about all sorts of interesting things from our clients—from how spray-dried cheese powder and organic soy crisps are made, to CRM software, to spinal cord injury assessment, to sustainable marketing…and whatever comes next," Torrance writes on her company's website.[i]

Ms. Torrance has always been comfortable with technology, something that she has imbued in her company's culture. This is especially critical for a largely virtual company such as hers; most of her employees never actually see their clients.

Embracing the Five Enablers from the Get-Go

Although technologically savvy, Ms. Torrance realized from the beginning that it made very little sense for her company to be in the traditional software development business. To that end, she uses several different SaaS-based learning management systems (LMSs) to deploy training courses to her clients. Because these LMSs are entirely web-based, Torrance Learning does not need to worry about messy deployment and integration issues. It can focus most of its energies on creating dynamic, interactive, and cost-effective courses for its clients.

The company uses a variety of web-based platforms to deploy new courses for its clients:

- The Via>Grapevine system by i3Logic[ii] connects employees from any location and at any time. It maximizes sharing and collaboration, both of which are critical because contributors are often geographically dispersed.

- Learnshare is an enterprise-scale, web-based LMS that can either interface with a company's HR system or support e-commerce.

- The Inquisiq[iii] system by ICS is an LMS that Torrance Learning recommends for its clients that need both e-commerce capabilities and the scalability to go from a handful of users to thousands of users. They pay on a per-user basis.

- Review by Rapid Intake[iv] allows for collaboration during the client review and acceptance process. It allows for tracking issues and tasks associated with multiple projects in a single, easy-to-use web-based tool.

These tools have allowed Ms. Torrance to put her vision for the company into practice. In addition to enabling collaborative-based course development, however, they allow her clients to easily provide essential feedback as courses are developed. The amount of rework required can be significant, and Ms. Torrance wants to make sure that her clients know what they're getting well before the final course is presented.

Platform Independence

Torrance Learning's clients benefit from the company's easy deployment of its courses. Because everything is web-based, no software installation is required. In other words, the courses are platform-independent; a client needs only a browser to take a course. This is important because it eliminates traditional problems associated with specific operating systems, hardware, browsers, and software installations. Clients can access Torrance Learning's training whether they use PCs or Macs, any version of Microsoft Windows or Apple's OSX, or any mainstream browser.[1]

Imagine the difficulties that Ms. Torrance would have experienced if she had not embraced the web as a delivery mechanism. At large organizations, it's commonplace to find outdated hardware, operating systems, applications, and browsers. By deploying its courses seamlessly and instantaneously via the web, Torrance Learning minimizes client headaches and angry phone calls from those unable to complete a course. In fact, tech support calls are exceptionally rare.

Minimizing the number of unhappy clients is only one benefit of SaaS-based deployment, however. Consider how Torrance Learning changed the whole notion of training at the American Spinal Injury Association (ASIA). In the 90s, ASIA took checks or credit cards over the phone and then sent out physical CD-ROMs with PDFs to course attendees—usually residents and therapists in spinal cord rehabilitation units. Today, ASIA sends nothing. Attendees can complete each of the six modules. Further, ASIA's system keeps track of who has enrolled and taken a course, whether they passed, and their test scores. At a micro level, the courses allow practitioners to enroll in courses, take them, track their progress, and print completion certificates. From a broader perspective, however, reporting is easier by an order of magnitude. ASIA—and the institutions that purchase group licenses—can very easily determine:

- Who has taken each course
- Who has *not* taken each course
- The results of each course's assessment test
- The success of specific test questions

ASIA doesn't have to keep track of progress, and it doesn't have to create and mail completion certificates after the fact.

---

[1] Of course, there were limits to Torrance Learning's prescience. Although no one could have possibly known it at the time, the immensely popular iPad doesn't support Flash-based programs (at least as of this writing). This decision has thrown the entire e-learning industry into a temporary state of chaos.

The power of online learning distribution and tracking came in handy after the Haiti earthquake in January of 2010. ASIA donated 50 course enrollments to the relief efforts in the ravaged country. Volunteer physicians on the ground in Haiti were able to get the training they needed to work in the spinal cord injury unit. Via the Internet, local administrators could easily track who had completed the course and who was ready for duty.

Ends and Means

The existence of industry-standard protocols for e-learning courses and learning management systems (LMSs) makes this platform-independent approach feasible, even commonplace, in the e-learning world. At Torrance Learning this is not so much the default, but rather the strategy. The company recommends that its clients use the standard e-learning protocols, even if they aren't immediately moving to an LMS solution. This allows them to change their approach in the future with minimal pain. By not locking into any one platform or provider, the company is free to recommend the best solution for each client's particular situation. As new tools become available, different members of the team download trial copies, try them out, and see if they're a good fit. "The big question is: does this solve a current problem better than our current solution?" says Ms. Torrance. "If the answer is yes, then we figure out a way to use it. Otherwise, we tuck it away in case we need it in the future." This willingness to experiment is characteristic of New Small companies, as we saw in the case of Voices.com, profiled in Chapter 8. Making a superior product trumps sticking to an antiquated technology, especially in the long term.

Consider how the company creates customized e-learning courses for its clients. Years ago, the company had used e-mail for handling the large files. Then Torrance Learning landed a new client—Dow Chemical Company—with a very restrictive e-mail policy that prevented any employee from receiving a file larger than three megabytes (MBs). Torrance Learning turned to YouSendIt,[v] a web-based file transfer site and, based on early successes, began using it with voice-over artists as well.

As the company grew, it began using professional voice-over artists with an assist from emerging technologies. Obviously, flying in professionals to do voice-over work in a studio is expensive. Technology came to the rescue. Each professional recorded files in his or her own studio and submitted them to Torrance Learning via YouSendIt. Today, during the recording process, if track-by-track direction is needed, Ms. Torrance listens in via Google Talk,[vi] chatting with the artists to provide real-time feedback.

Internal Applications and the Back Office

Like many small businesses, Torrance Learning uses QuickBooks for its financials and payroll, transmitting files to the company's accountant. It also uses Salesforce.com to handle its CRM. For internal project management (PM), Torrance Learning would never dream of using Microsoft Project,[2] a tool many consider to be bulky and dated. When coordinating projects with others in multiple companies, the company instead uses Basecamp, a PM tool made by the widely heralded company 37signals.[3] For example, Torrance Learning recently co-chaired an all-day women's business conference. She set up a Basecamp site for the project to easily track tasks, issues, milestones, team documents, agendas, and biographies for presenters. What's more, all the work was archived to give the next year's committee a head start on the conference.

Torrance Learning uses other tools commonly found in many small businesses. Although hardly high-tech, the company is a heavy user of instant messaging. Google Docs allows the company to work easily with its partners. It minimizes e-mail ping-pong and makes use of valuable built-in version control features. Unlike many small businesses, however, the company owns a Windows small business server to handle e-mail and internal scheduling.

An Innovative Partnership and Co-Employment

Companies with between 5 and 25 employees often find themselves at a crossroads. They are starting to see the need for more specialized full-time people, but they often lack the budget for them. Torrance Learning was no exception. It could not afford—and really didn't have the need—to hire a dedicated, full-time marketing and sales employee. At the same time, though, hiring a part-time employee would have posed its own challenges. Specifically, a skilled employee working 20 hours per week may well find a full-time position offering more hours, money, and benefits. No company wants to constantly backfill positions; it takes away from minding the store.

Torrance Learning addressed this challenge in an innovative way, deciding to coemploy[4] an administrative marketing and sales assistant with one of its partners, The Whole Brain Group,[vii] a Michigan-based web design and

---

[2] Of course, several larger clients still insist that project plans be presented in old standbys such as Microsoft Excel. Old habits die hard.

[3] 37signals is a privately held web application company based in Chicago, Illinois.

[4] *Coemployment* is a "situation in which two legally distinct employers have employer-employee relationship with the same person." See http://www.businessdictionary.com/definition/coemployment.html.

social media outfit. Each company uses this individual for approximately 20 hours per week. As New Small companies are well aware, technology can facilitate such effective coordination and collaboration. In this case, Google Calendar[viii] easily allows both co-employers and the employee to quickly determine schedules and tackle potential intercompany conflicts well in advance. Overbooking and double booking are easily avoided.

The entire arrangement works extremely well because the two companies—and their founders—have for years shared ideas, bid together on projects, and referred each other to potential clients. "It takes a village to raise a company" says Marisa Smith, head of The Whole Brain Group. Ms. Torrance agrees, saying, "The tools enable collaboration, and our regular face-to-face meetings smooth the way." Smith and Torrance work exceptionally well together, brainstorming ideas and using each other as sounding boards. The two are in the process of penning a book about female entrepreneurs.

Finding the Right Employees

Torrance Learning fosters an employee-friendly culture at her company. "We're committed to creating the kind of workplace that makes us *want* to come to work," she says. "That starts with hiring only the nicest, smartest, most fun people we can find. Then we let them work flexible schedules, feed them healthy snacks, and keep the coffee pot full. When we're happy, we're very creative. We happen to think that it shows."

The company emphasizes proficiency with various technologies during the hiring process. She has found that people who play with different applications and programs for fun are much more likely to be successful. "I ask employees to tell me about the last time that they learned how to use a new piece of software," Ms. Torrance says. She notes that "the best answers come from those who go to a software playground such as lynda.com,[5] figuring out how to use an application by just noodling with it."

Torrance Learning shows how New Small companies hire employees who enjoy experimentation and learn by doing. They avoid people who are intimidated by new technologies and change. Although roles vary, the need to find tech-savvy yet personable employees is fairly universal. Consider a staple question that Ms. Torrance asks her employees about candidates during the interview process: "Would I want to have lunch with this person, or would I use my lunchtime to escape this person?"

The company's open office floor plan allows for impromptu feedback and spontaneous collaboration. Google Talk chats erupt into actual

---

[5] http://www.lynda.com is a very cool e-learning site with many tutorials on how to use a wide array of different applications.

conversations during the day, or a client call sparks a brainstorming session. Everyone's in the game—and team members can pick up and help each other out to an astonishing degree.

All of this is just another way of saying that, although technology is important, it is not the sole criterion for employment. Team culture is just as important. "We're so small that we can't afford to have a bad egg in the group," Ms. Torrance remarks. No matter the skills, Torrance Learning passes on potentially problematic individuals. All Torrance Learning employees interact with clients—albeit to different degrees. There's just too much risk involved in hiring a technical wizard who doesn't play well with others.

Ms. Torrance tells the story of how one of the company's clients (who worked for a very large company) refused to move her e-mail archives from Outlook to Lotus Notes, for four years. "That would *never* fly here," Ms. Torrance says. "Here, on an individual and a company basis, it's keep up with the changing technologies … or get left in the dust."

Future, Results, and Challenges

Four years ago, Ms. Torrance worked by herself out of a spare bedroom in her house. Company revenues were just barely north of six figures. Back then, she could not imagine the company that exists today. In 2009, revenues were just under half a million dollars. The company is moving into its second professional office space in 2010. Ms. Torrance's vision for the future is all about controlled growth. Her philosophy reflects a careful, almost conservative approach, which is usual at the New Small. She wants to grow her company at a rate that allows the company to continue to effectively meet its clients' and employees' needs.

Ms. Torrance knows that things are going well, but at the same time, the company is anything but complacent. "We're constantly learning," she says. "Our goal is to make dramatic improvements in our work processes and products every year. When we look back on old projects, we want to think that we could significantly improve upon them if we started them today."

Going Agile

Torrance Learning has faced some obstacles with respect to project management. She is finding that boilerplate and Waterfall approaches don't seem to work as well anymore. Different clients often have very different needs, and it's just not easy to quickly and cost-effectively find the right solution for each client. Remember that Torrance Learning evolved from a one-person shop to a larger, more collaborative environment. It now employs instructional designers, course developers, and other creative types.

Ms. Torrance has discovered that traditional linear project management methods are no longer effective.

Aware of this issue, the company has integrated more agile approaches to software development, emphasizing:

- Collaborative teams
- A high level of interaction with clients
- An extreme focus on the needs of the end user
- Frequent iterations and inspections of the work

All this enables the company to work in a better, more iterative fashion, identifying issues and failing faster. Agile development and deployment methods find missteps earlier, allowing them to be corrected *before* they are wrapped into larger, downstream pieces of work.

Rather than hastily making the move to agile software development methods in a vacuum, the company is taking a more cautious approach, working with its more adventurous clients. These organizations are willing to experiment and take advantage of new development approaches, even if they encounter few problems along the way. As a testament to the company's upfront communication style, each client has had an opportunity to consider the approach and decide whether it wants to be an early adopter.

The company's willingness to adapt demonstrates several key points about the New Small. First, as these companies continue to evolve, their technologies and tools must evolve also. Second, each client has a different risk tolerance. There's no sense in trying to force a square peg into a round hole.

Finding the Right People

Despite trying to hire only the right employees and use the right contractors, not everyone has worked out. The culture at Torrance Learning emphasizes technology, change, and collaboration. Put simply, some people just didn't mesh. To the company's credit, though, Ms. Torrance recognized these mismatches early on. She continues to refine the hiring process to avoid repeating past mistakes.

Succession planning for key roles is a challenge in any small business, and Torrance Learning is no exception. The company will need to replace a valuable, long-time course developer who is soon moving with her family to Spain for four months. "It's a really great opportunity for her and the kids. They'll get the language immersion they really want, living with their Spanish relatives," said Ms. Torrance. "But we'll miss her terribly, and it's hard to lose someone with as much technical and historical knowledge as she has." Torrance plans to bring this employee back into the fold when she returns. In the meantime, however, she will again turn to technology to lend a helping hand. This is typical New Small. The employee will work a modified schedule from Spain, using the Internet to facilitate communication and bridge time zones. "Our multinational clients do this all the time. I just never thought we'd operate like a multinational with only seven employees," jokes Ms. Torrance.

SUMMARY

Torrance Learning is the very definition of the word *flexible*. Much like Fuentek (covered in the next chapter), the company makes extensive use of a dispersed workforce and the Five Enablers. Like other New Small companies, Torrance Learning willingly admits when something is not working—and quickly and decisively changes course.

Endnotes

i   http://www.torrancelearning.com
ii   http://www.i3logic.net
iii http://www.inquisiq.com
iv http://www.rapidintake.com
v   http://www.yousendit.com
vi http://www.google.com/talk
vii http://www.thewholebraingroup.com
viii http://www.google.com/calendar/renderOnline

Chapter 13

THE DISTRIBUTED COMPANY

Opportunities multiply as they are seized.

—Sun Tzu

These days, many employees work remotely—and even more would like to do the same. I have supported many of my clients without ever actually being on site, and I like to think everyone benefited. I didn't have to waste time in airports, and the client saved money on travel.

And then there's Laura Schoppe's company, Fuentek.[i] Telecommuting isn't just an option here. It's *required*. In fact, Schoppe has never even met some of her associates—and there are more than 40. (As a side note, I first discovered Fuentek after reading a *National Public Radio* [NPR] article about her innovative little company in early 2010.[ii])

Based in Apex, NC, near Research Triangle Park, Fuentek provides a range of customized intellectual property (IP) and technology management services for its clients, many of which are in the public sector. For example, consider an organization that has developed a technology for a particular purpose. Fuentek finds alternate uses—and revenue streams—for that technology. In a nutshell, it helps companies commercialize their innovations and identify potential partnerships.

Schoppe was always a techie. She attended Carnegie Mellon University[1] as well as Princeton University and the University of North Carolina.[2] After spending years working for large corporations, she reached a point of admitted burnout and began to do some independent consulting in 2001. She thought that maybe work could be fun and challenging again.

Perhaps a victim of her own success, she had to take on additional staff to meet her increasing workload. She reached out to friends and former colleagues who expressed interest in joining her, but there was a condition: these people did not want to forgo the flexibility of working at home. This wasn't a problem to Schoppe.

Schoppe founded her company in February of 2001 and embraced a virtual workforce from day one. The cost savings from not maintaining a proper office are self-evident.

Her staff consists of a variety of folks: pure techies, editors, and graphic designers. She hires only those with a keen sense of business as well as solid technical skills. These people are critical in assessing the commercial viability of a particular application and meeting her clients' needs. That is, Fuentek associates need to be able to recognize cool technologies and products that lack a market are just that: cool technologies.

Collaboration

Schoppe is the first to admit that collaboration can be a challenge at a company like hers. There are no water cooler conversations or impromptu discussions at the coffee machine at Fuentek. To address this potential problem—and real problem to some extent—Fuentek relies heavily on social technologies. Collaborating and sharing tools have matured and developed a great deal in the decade since Fuentek was founded. Schoppe dismisses concerns about a distributed workforce being unable to effectively work together. "Even if you were sitting under the same roof, you would be putting all of your documents on a common server," Schoppe notes. "We use many of the same tools that a brick-and-mortar business uses."

Of course, Fuentek is very different from most businesses.

The Move to SaaS

Collaborating on and sharing key company documents wasn't always so easy. In the early 2000s, Fuentek designed and implemented a now-dated web-based IP Asset Management System (IPAMS). Built by Schoppe herself, the tool was called COMmercialization MANagement Database

---

[1] As did I. Go Tartans—possibly the worst college team name ever conceived.
[2] I can tell you from personal experience that even the artists at CMU know their way around a computer.

(COMMAND). To her credit, Schoppe realized when her system had served its purpose. Io take her company to the next level, Schoppe would have to retire her baby. "To finally mothball it was tough," she admits, although she had conceived of the application in 1998 while getting her MBA.

The New Small often makes tough decisions like these—many companies do not. I personally have seen people who have built internal systems become very defensive and reluctant to even discuss replacing them. Many businesses have struggled because key individuals have refused to detach themselves from the applications and technologies they introduced.

Schoppe's willingness to change is rooted in her belief in the power of emerging technologies. "It just isn't logical to use technology today that was current 10 years ago," she notes. Although migrating systems is never easy, the new SaaS-based system (Sophia by Wellspring Worldwide[iii]) has paid enormous dividends. It is superior on many fronts, including system flexibility, reliability, and cost. In terms of the latter, the savings can be measured in the tens of thousands of dollars, no small number to a company of 40 associates in any economy, much less this one. "When the time came to swallow my pride, it wasn't that difficult," Schoppe notes.

What's more, the new system has functionality not remotely possible in its predecessor. Fuentek benefits a great deal from the following enhancements:

- Comprehensive search feature (data and documents)
- Customizable workflow capabilities
- Integration with intellectual property listing and exchange services

No longer do employees and contractors have to manually alert someone else that a document is ready—something that even the best of us occasionally forget to do, causing superfluous headaches and delays. The benefits of search cannot be overstated. Fuentek recognizes the significant time savings of being able to find one document among literally thousands. To facilitate this, documents are tagged by client, category, and keyword.

This kind of attention to time is very common at the New Small. These companies look for every opportunity to increase efficiency. Search alone saves Fuentek a great deal of money, minimizes frustration among team members, and facilitates knowledge transfer. Because so little time is wasted finding similar documents and doing other administrative tasks of little value, Fuentek's clients ultimately save a great deal of money. Hours billed—the core of the company's business—are rarely questioned because expectations are managed in advance—and they tend to be high-quality hours. In short, Fuentek's use of technology enables happy clients and employees. The New Small realizes that this is exactly what technology is supposed to do.

Wasted Opportunities

Many organizations miss key windows to upgrade their technologies. Many decide to stick with what they know, even though there are superior alternatives available. They refuse to overhaul—or replace—legacy systems and associated ways of doing things. Although Schoppe faced some of the same pressures with COMMAND, she kept her eye on the ball. Changing business needs made it impossible for her to keep updating and enhancing her company's primary application. Moreover, this continued maintenance took her away from her chief responsibilities: namely, growing Fuentek's business. She knew that the benefits of a long-term solution (like the IPAMS) more than justified their costs.

Today, Fuentek team members can easily upload all documentation prepared for clients into the IPAMS from any browser. Fuentek sets expectations with all employees that the IPAMS must be updated on a timely basis. Updates include information related to each project, obviating the need for team members to track down colleagues on the other side of the country at odd hours because a key document is missing.

Fuentek company policy requires that all work be submitted through the IPAMS. Resistance to the new system has been minimal, and not just because Schoppe signs the checks. The company's IPAMS is an essential tool for a virtual team to collaborate efficiently. Team members use the tool because they want to, not just because they have to. In this way, the New Small has an easier time collaborating, a subject discussed in much greater depth in Chapter 17.

Management Philosophy and Trust

Schoppe has heard the objections to a completely virtual workforce before: "You can't run a successful company that way." Although Fuentek has proven the naysayers wrong, not *every* company can exist without a formal office. "This isn't for everybody," Schoppe admits. "You have to take a look at the type of work you do, and most important, the type of employees you have."

The New Small understands the importance of these two factors. First, by employing very bright, responsible, and independent people who have high standards for themselves, Schoppe's management headaches aren't nearly as severe as skeptics might expect. "I never have to babysit my staff," she notes. Second, some kinds of work can be performed virtually—not all can. Even collaborative technologies have their limits. As we see in the case of RedSeven (Chapter 14), a physical presence is sometimes required.

In Fuentek's case, most of the work is project-oriented and of an hourly nature. These conditions also support the use of contractors, something covered later in this chapter.

Schoppe doesn't understand—nor do I—why companies hire employees and don't trust them to work at home. "Then why do you trust them to work for you at all?" Schoppe notes. It's a fair question, and I still haven't heard a good answer to this.[3] On a larger scale, this underscores a fundamental tenet of the New Small: a high degree of employee trust. To be sure, the emerging technologies described in this book can be used for productive purposes—as well as for nonproductive ones. Fuentek minimizes potential technology abuse by employees through emphasizing accountability. The company hires only employees and contractors who demand accountability of themselves and each other. Those who refuse to be accountable just don't last very long.

Compare this to large organizations, many of which ban social networking sites or filter certain websites. The implication is that employees will spend all day tweeting or mindlessly surfing the net. Such restrictive policies often stifle employee creativity and concurrently deprive companies of the benefits of social technologies. As for slackers, if blocked from certain sites, they'll find another way to waste time. In essence, the New Small just doesn't make this mistake. They don't punish the many because of the actions of a few. They find the few—and get rid of them.

Schoppe trusts her staff. That's not to say that this trust is unconditional, especially with newly hired employees or contractors. To this end, the Sophia system flags projects that require too many hours. In fact, the application precludes overbilling—either by accident or intentionally. Sophia alerts Fuentek that there is a problem. Schoppe is quick to note that such scenarios are not always—or even usually—the result of dishonesty. Often, the issue stems from either miscommunication or some type of misunderstanding. When required, she does not have difficult conversations at the end of a quarter or year; she immediately calls or e-mails the person to find out what happened. "I don't mind mistakes being made," Schoppe says. "I just don't want the same mistake made twice."

The previous content management system did not have this red flag functionality—not that Schoppe's constantly using it by any stretch. This is just another example of how the New Small intelligently uses the Five Enablers.

[3] Schoppe appeared as a guest on my podcast, *Technology Today*. She made this very point on my show. See *http://tinyurl.com/phil-laura-podcast*.

Technology, Choice, Culture, and Costs

Aside from the SaaS-based IPAMS, Fuentek employees use the following tools to work seamlessly across the country:

- E-mail
- Group scheduling
- Instant messaging (IM)
- Teleconferencing
- Intranet (company procedures and training materials)
- Forums
- Webinars and screen-sharing tools

"We're always looking for new tools and capabilities," Schoppe notes. Many of the company's technologies are piecemeal in nature (because most are free). Realizing that this may not be ideal, Fuentek plans to adopt a more enterprise-centric suite of collaborative tools, perhaps from companies such as Yammer, 37signals, or Google. The current collection of applications does not easily apply to multiparty chatting, something that certainly would benefit Fuentek staff. Noticeably absent from the preceding list of tools is videoconferencing, especially when compared to others in the New Small. Schoppe herself is not a fan of the medium but admits that she'll have to come around to it eventually.

Fuentek associates use their own computers, whether they are Macs or PCs. The company lets staff members decide how to do their work. The same applies for Internet service and cell phones; Fuentek doesn't provide them. Further, it does not mandate that staff members use specific applications, beyond Microsoft Office and Sophia for obvious reasons.[4] Associates can use whatever e-mail application, browser, or instant messaging (IM) app they want, as long they're secure and compatible with applications used by others. It's not lost on Schoppe that forcing people to use particular applications would increase ramp-up time and cost, especially for new hires. Getting the job done efficiently trumps doing it with a specific application. The results are more important than the means to achieve them.

As it does for many in the New Small, Fuentek's philosophy provides benefits in several ways:

- It reinforces a culture predicated on pragmatism.

---

[4] It does provide guidance around applications such as anti-virus software and how to integrate Fuentek e-mail with industry-leading client applications. Not requiring that associates use a contemporary product would expose the company—and its clients—to significant risk.

- It reduces IT costs and headaches.

- It shows a near-constant willingness to adapt.

- It increases employee engagement.

- Employees feel empowered because the company refuses to enforce strict standards on how to work—and with which tools.

The Symbiotic Relationship between Technology and Culture

Fuentek's use of—and philosophy regarding—different technologies suits the company. What's more, it promotes and reinforces the company's culture on a daily basis. The cultural alignment between many companies and their employees is sorely lacking in many organizations. I have seen too many times how an organization's systems and applications encourage one sort of behavior at the same time that managers pontificate about the need for everyone to act in a different manner. The New Small minimizes this disconnect.

The intelligent use of the Five Enablers provides Fuentek with several major advantages over companies that lack such a progressive culture. First, it sets the tone for the entire company. Creative ideas and suggestions from others are not immediately rejected because "that's not the way that we do things here." New staff members are required to add basic applications to their computers, but Fuentek is a two-way street. Employees often bring knowledge of other useful applications to the table, a topic about which Schoppe often asks. For example, a few years ago, Fuentek had difficulty scheduling conference calls with more than a few people. Like many companies, it relied on cumbersome e-mail threads. That all changed when a new hire recommended a couple of free scheduling tools to facilitate this task. (Fuentek uses Tungle[iv] because it supports multiple platforms and several time slot options in one meeting invitation.) Admittedly, this is a bit of a workaround and, as mentioned, Fuentek will soon adopt an enterprise suite of collaborative tools.

Second, extensively using emerging technologies minimizes the chance that the company as a whole becomes complacent. It can constantly push against its limitations and do things better, faster, and cheaper. Think about it: a company that decides to junk its useful and historic proprietary system isn't likely to resist something as easy to install and as beneficial as webcams.

FOSS and Changing Technology Needs

In addition to SaaS, Fuentek embraces free and open source software (FOSS), particularly with regard to communications. The New Small uses these tools, however, for only as long as they make sense, as evinced by the Fuentek scheduling tools. These companies are not afraid to blow something up when a superior alternative exists, especially when the tool is critical to its very being.

As Fuentek has grown, its technology requirements have changed. "We don't have the same needs with 40 people as we did with 3," Schoppe notes. Focusing merely on the number of employees is myopic, however. Any company that adds so many new employees (as a percentage, if not an absolute number) works with different *types* of people. Forget about cloning; small businesses add different types of people at different points in their history, and their tools need to reflect this. For example, let's say that a small business is mostly composed of hard-core techies, relying on very tech-savvy applications to do even the most basic of things. At 50 employees, it begins to hire marketing and HR/administrative personnel. Is it realistic to expect these new hires to use complicated tools far beyond their skill sets? The New Small recognizes that not everyone is a computer wizard.

Social Technologies: Blogging and Tweeting with a Purpose

Many companies misunderstand the power of emerging technologies. Perhaps no greater example of that exists than with social technologies such as Twitter. "You don't tweet just to tweet," Schoppe says. Rather, Fuentek embraces the social technologies because they provide a way for Fuentek's staff and customers to share company news or ideas related to a salient issue. She adds, "I'm sure nobody cares that I'm running to the store."

Schoppe is a proponent of tweeting and blogging at conferences. While at the 2010 CEO Forum in Raleigh, she and coworker Jack Spain sent a series of tweets about the conference's central message on a triple bottom line (social, environmental, and financial). However, she resisted the temptation to announce that Ben and Jerry (the keynote speakers) had brought ice cream samples. "You have to be careful about what you're putting out there," Schoppe says, advocating the reasonable and professional use of social media—at least on company time.

For someone who's admittedly not a social media expert, Schoppe knows more than many self-anointed ones. Many organizations make the mistake of blogging for the sake of blogging, lacking genuine or interesting content. Some blogs are thinly veiled marketing attempts and typically fail to gain traction, reinforcing the belief that social technologies are a waste of time. Others hit the wall after a few months and "go zombie," unable to keep the momentum going. Schoppe is well aware of these mistakes and takes steps to ensure that they don't happen at Fuentek. Every Monday, the company posts about topics such as best practices in technology transfer or running a virtual business. On Thursdays, readers expect a post about a specific client's technology or project. Schoppe also understands that "Google likes blogging" and the SEO[5] benefits of the medium.

Bench Strength and a Flexible Workforce

That Fuentek treats its staff maturely and with respect is a function of a number of factors. Schoppe argues that it's just a better way to run a business. Part and parcel to her largely hands-off management style is the type of consultants and contractors hired by the company. Many Fuentek consultants have MBAs, PhDs, or other terminal degrees in their fields. Moreover, the company shies away from hiring new graduates or pure academics, preferring those with significant and relevant work experience.

Like many in the New Small, Schoppe realizes that she may be able to save a few dollars per hour by using more junior professionals. However, the company never falls for the temptation, and truth be told, the temptation is really not all that compelling. At the New Small, hiring the best resources is typically worth the premium.

Jack Spain joined the company in late 2005, and like Schoppe, had a traditional background working in large companies and managing technology personnel. Schoppe realized that managing five employees was fundamentally different from managing multiples of that. She sought Spain's help to share the responsibility of hiring and managing Fuentek associates.

Although subcontractors add flexibility and reduce fixed costs (relative to hiring W-2 employees), they also introduce additional risk. Good people may be easier to find in a downward economy, but never mistake easier for easy. Spain readily admits that there are inherent risks involved with not being able to offer full-time employment to highly specialized folks. It is expensive to hire and train people. What's more, if you can't engage them on a full-time basis, they may seek other opportunities that offer greater stability. Fuentek is structured to provide hours needed only for the jobs on hand, and this often fluctuates throughout the year. This is not a comfortable situation for everyone, another reason that Fuentek seeks experienced consultants who can weather the ebb and flow of billable hours. In addition

---

[5] Search engine optimization (SEO) is the process of improving the visibility of a website or a web page in search engines in a natural, unpaid manner. This is in direct contrast to paying for placement on the right-hand side of Google results, for example.

to being completely virtual, this part-time structure sets Fuentek apart from most other businesses. You might think this arrangement is a recipe for transient staff, but Fuentek has found it to be quite the opposite. It is able to attract smart people looking for a better work-life balance than they can find in other employment arrangements. The New Small is sometimes reluctant to hire people on a W-2 basis; using contractors allows these small businesses to try before buying.

Happy Clients Mean Happy Employees

From Schoppe's perspective, Fuentek has two main clients:

- Those who they provide services for (and who cut the checks to them)
- Those who do the work and represent Fuentek (they get a check from Fuentek)

Schoppe believes that her associates are happy if they are well suited for their jobs. This requires achieving the right balance between being in one's comfort zone and being challenged. Associates need to feel that their work is recognized and appreciated. A healthy dose of respect doesn't hurt either. Schoppe has seen firsthand how happy employees are more productive and loyal than those who merely punch a clock each day. Employee satisfaction ultimately translates into better service and products for her clients—who are more likely to be happy as well.

Of course, Fuentek isn't utopia. Schoppe gets quickly and directly involved when core values are violated. This has led to firing employees as well as clients.[6] The New Small knows that the customer is *not* always right, or at least not always the right fit for the company. These companies are not afraid of saying no to clients and employees who represent more trouble than they are worth.

Future, Results, and Challenges

Fuentek continues to look for new technologies as they become available and evolve. The right tools maximize company efficiency and effectiveness. Fuentek will continue to use its staff flexibly to match its clients' needs. For example, if Fuentek signs up more aerospace clients, it will look for additional mechanical and aerospace engineers with industry experience.

---

[6] I'm a big advocate of businesses firing high-maintenance clients. See http://tinyurl.com/phil-fire-clients.

In 2001, Fuentek was a three-person company with annual revenues of several hundred thousand dollars. Fast forward to today: Fuentek is a 40-person team comprised of a web of employees, contractors, and partners. The company's annual revenues now exceed $2.5M. Remarkably, its already stable client base actually *increased* during the recession.

Schoppe continues to speak at conferences, sharing best practices and improving Fuentek's recognition and reputation. She is also writing a how-to book with a focus on technology transfer. The company has won many awards, including 2008 Triangle Business Journal Women in Business Award, Business Leader Entrepreneur of the Year, and the 2009 Chamber of Commerce Pinnacle Award for Small Business.

SUMMARY

This chapter has shown how one company has overcome traditional telecommuting obstacles. Fuentek proves that a dispersed workforce is not an inherent or unsolvable problem. Trust, accountability, and technology all play key roles. Careful management of people and technology means that being a virtual company is not any type of limitation. On a different level, Fuentek demonstrates the necessity of retiring outdated technologies, no matter how much a key person is emotionally tied to a specific tool.

Endnotes

i   http://www.fuentek.com/
ii http://www.npr.org/templates/story/story.php?storyId=123406526
iii http://www.wellspringworldwide.com/index.php
iv http://www.tungle.me/Home

Chapter 14

THE COMPUTER BUDDY

Efficiency is intelligent laziness.

—David Dunham

Most people aren't like Michael Cady, and he is well aware of this. The self-described *hyper-geek* has always enjoyed fiddling with computers and different technologies. He even admits to winning a science fair for programming in BASIC[1] when he was 12.

One thing led to another, and years later Cady found himself working as a process engineer in a factory in Arizona. Although it wasn't the world's worst job and provided adequate pay and benefits, Cady's heart wasn't entirely in it. "I realized that I was miserable," Cady admits.

His passion had always been in technology, and after about 10 years of working for "the man," he decided to return to his true calling. In 1997, during his spare time, he started building computers for his friends. It wasn't long before he was sucked back in to the world he knew as a kid.

Cady never lost his touch with computers, and eventually, his friends just wanted too much of his time. "I figured that maybe this could be more than a hobby," Cady says. He opened a little office in 1999 near Arizona State University (ASU) in Tempe, AZ. At first, the office was open only part-time.

---

[1] *BASIC* stands for Beginner's All-purpose Symbolic Instruction Code. It is a family of high-level programming languages. People in my general age range grew up programming in it on Commodore 64s.

Cady saw customers by appointment only. He still had his full-time job and wasn't entirely convinced that he could make a living by fixing computers.

Cady was faced with a dilemma not uncommon to many of the New Small or, more broadly, those contemplating career changes. Should he be unhappy in his current job or starve himself for a few years? Could he make a go of it as his own boss? For better or worse, Cady decided to take the plunge. "I left a fairly lucrative career and started from scratch."

One of his friends, Nick Coons, had started his own technology company reselling Internet service. Cady and Coons started talking and realized that they both shared a vision and passion for delivering friendly computer service. The two felt that many support specialists at the time belittled end users, making them feel stupid for even asking questions. Against that backdrop, RedSeven was formed.

Finding the Right Path

It took a while for the company to gain traction. "Early on, we made the same mistake that many small businesses make," Cady says. "We tried to be everything to everybody. We tried to sell computers and parts, set up websites, and configure networks. Offering a full array of products and services ultimately just muddied our brand." Although the company had grown to 18 employees at that point, something just wasn't clicking—and its founders knew it.

By 2005, Cady and Coons came to a realization: their company really wasn't as specialized as they had initially envisioned. The two felt that their shop was becoming what they despised—a big company that does many things, none of them particularly well. RedSeven subsequently narrowed its offerings, focusing on providing quality components and service. This is a key point: while relatively rare, New Small companies are willing to make difficult strategic decisions, even when buoyed by some level of success.

Enter phase two of RedSeven. The company started building its own computers with high-end motherboards, RAM,[2] and power units. RedSeven computers cost more than mass-produced equivalents from Dell and HP, although RedSeven provided a lifetime warranty. Unfortunately, most potential customers focused on the price tag, not the quality of the components inside the computer. What's more, consumers recognized big brands; they couldn't say the same about RedSeven. As a result, sales were relatively sparse. "Customers didn't want to hear that there weren't any Dell parts in a Dell computer," Cady observes. "It was a tough thing to explain to people in a short period of time."

---

[2] Short for *random access memory*.

Phase Three: Getting It Right

Cady and Coons realized once again that RedSeven needed to change direction. In early 2006, the company did just that. Cady and Coons kept asking its customers one simple question: what can we do to make RedSeven better for you? It turned out that hardware, parts, and speed meant very little to their customers. The two kept hearing words like *service*, *help*, and *support*.

When it sold one of its premium computers, RedSeven would configure the new machine for its clients. Not surprisingly, customers loved both the individualized attention and not having to deal with new machines' typical installation and configuration headaches. RedSeven realized the benefits of moving to a service-oriented model. The company could forsake traditional software and hardware sales and, at least in theory, expand indefinitely.

The Right Business Model

In early 2009, RedSeven launched its new service plan. The company would handle all of its clients' computing needs. "The computer is my responsibility, not the customer's," Cady says. "Think about it. You don't blame yourself when your cable television or cell phone doesn't work. You call those companies, and they are responsible for fixing the problem." RedSeven adopted the same model for computers.

The company discovered that its clients were willing to pay anywhere from $35 to $75 per month for a computer with an unlimited warranty and professional support. Cady likens the relationship to paying for a maid. Particularly with professionals, the price of the cleaning supplies, equipment, and someone's time exceed paying a service to do the same.[3] Ironically, most people would prefer to clean a toilet than try to remove a virus. Judging by the company's growth, RedSeven is on to something.

Clients and Services

Most RedSeven clients are small and home-based businesses (SOHOs). These people and companies require occasional technical support. They do not have large IT staffs supporting them, nor can they afford to hire a part-time IT professional. Common clients include:

- Real estate agents
- Insurance agents
- Outside sales professionals

---

[3] Economists refer to the latter as *opportunity cost*. In English, this equates to what else you could do with your time.

- Lawyers
- Doctors
- Dentists
- Chiropractors
- Photographers

Although not technologically inept, these people are certainly not experts at configuring computers, setting up networks, removing viruses and malware, and so on. They are more than happy to let RedSeven handle their technology needs at a reasonable monthly cost, especially if they can write off the expense. RedSeven leases computers to its clients, handling all computer-related problems. This is analogous to leasing a car. (Interestingly, much like many car dealerships, RedSeven gives its clients free loaner computers if it can't fix problems the same day that the computer arrives. This allows its clients to remain productive.) Customers enjoy peace of mind because they know an expert will solve their computer problems.

The car leasing analogy isn't *completely* apropos, however. At RedSeven, computers returned are not charged extra if they exceed the equivalent of car mileage limits. RedSeven does not put restrictions on how many hours someone can use a computer, nor are clients charged if they return computers with scratches. In fact, at the end of the two-and-a-half year lease period, clients can actually keep their computers—at no charge—and simply walk away, although few of them do. Instead, most turn in their computers for brand-new models with new warranties and extended support agreements. And much the same way that angry customers tell the world, happy customers do the same. In the case of RedSeven, its customers avidly proselytize the company. As a result, it spends virtually nothing on traditional marketing and advertising. Like many New Small companies, Red-Seven relies almost exclusively on word of mouth, the cheapest and most effective way to grow a company.

Effectively Matching Clients, Products, and Services

At its core, RedSeven is all about convenience and choice. With regard to the former, the company offers free walk-in estimates and makes frequent trips to its customers' homes and offices. Employees start by understanding their clients' businesses, what they are trying to achieve, and any preferences or restrictions. For example, although free and open source software (FOSS) may be a good fit for some clients, it's not for everyone. Some insurance agencies, technically independent, are in fact affiliated with much larger outfits, such as State Farm. Each agent needs to use very "standard" software such as Microsoft Windows and Office. For a standalone graphic designer, however, the same restrictions do not apply.

After that initial consultation, RedSeven recommends to its clients a general computing model, as well as specific software applications. Some customers have relatively simple computing needs, such as bookkeeping, web browsing, social networking, e-mail, and other basic applications. Others have much more complex requirements and need more sophisticated and proprietary applications.

RedSeven then moves its clients' old data (photos, music, contacts, files, individual records, and so on) from the old computer or server to the new one. RedSeven employees set up wireless networking, anti-virus software, and remote access tools if needed. "It's a very personal experience," Cady explains. "Some people just want us to do everything with no questions asked; others are very interested in the process and want to participate."

New Small companies often personalize their services, enabling a better customer experience. Of course, this is only possible when employees demonstrate a high degree of flexibility. At RedSeven, for example, employees don't say "that's not my job," although they may attempt to talk clients out of poorly conceived decisions. This increases the overall degree of trust among New Small companies, employees, and its clients. "Sometimes we have to overcome some pretty ingrained preconceptions with new clients," Cady says.

Providing Choices

RedSeven constantly identifies opportunities to save money for all of its clients, especially the budget-conscious ones. The company typically recommends many FOSS applications. "Proprietary software can account for more than 50 percent of PC ownership costs if people use the traditional tools," says Cady. "This doesn't have to be the case."

A few examples are instructive here. First, many companies require remote access for their employees—that is, the ability for people to use their computers when not in the office. Cady advises clients that they need not purchase GoToMyPC.[i] Instead, they can use VNC,[ii] a popular FOSS alternative. Second, for larger clients, Cady suggests monitoring software designed to prevent employees from accessing certain sites at work. (Use your imagination here.) Of course, any business can subscribe to services such as WebSense.[iii] Cady recommends FOSS reporting tools that allow employees the freedom to go where they want. At the same time, though, they allow managers to see whether employees are spending, say, 15 percent of their time on eBay. Cady knows that savings from FOSS applications and services add up, especially for small and home-based businesses.

Knowing the Limits of Free

In a word, RedSeven often *educates* its clients without being pushy. Although the company alerts its customers to largely unknown FOSS alternatives, RedSeven doesn't force its clients to use particular applications, services, or technologies. Cady and Coons firmly believe that both proprietary and FOSS software drive each other; they are often complements, not substitutes. For many specific business needs, such as running a dental practice, there are viable FOSS alternatives to proprietary applications. We saw this in Chapter 6 with HPD, a company that saved a great deal of money by using OpenDental. Had Drs. Lewis and Zima purchased proprietary dental software, they would have unnecessarily spent tens of thousands of dollars. But RedSeven recognizes that FOSS is *not* always the right way for a business to go.[4]

Using Technology to Minimize Internal Costs

Like many New Small companies, RedSeven itself makes extensive internal use of the Five Enablers. For example, it uses Ubuntu Linux throughout the company,[5] an open source operating system that obviates the need for Microsoft Windows. RedSeven also built its own CRM system with FOSS tools and deployed it in the cloud. The application allows employees to enter sales, customer status, and lead information from anywhere, including via a web-enabled phone. Although the Five Enablers may not yet allow people to do everything everywhere, New Small companies are working toward that goal. These companies want emerging technologies to make their employees as productive as possible.

RedSeven uses FOSS applications and tools instead of paid alternatives, including these:

- The LAMP stack[6] for basic database and web infrastructure
- Audacity[iv] for editing audio tracks
- OpenOffice for productivity
- AVG[v] or Avast[vi] for virus protection
- Gmail for e-mail
- Picasa[vii] for photo storing and editing (now owned by Google)

---

4 We will see this in the next chapter. Chaotic Moon Studios consciously decided to spend thousands of dollars on Adobe Creative Suite 5 (ACS5) because it is the *de facto* standard for creating exciting, graphic-rich content.
5 According to its site (http://www.ubuntu.com), Ubuntu is a secure, intuitive operating system that powers desktops, servers, netbooks, and laptops. Ubuntu is, and always will be, absolutely free.
6 In his book *Open Source Web Development with LAMP: Using Linux, Apache, MySQL, Perl, and PHP*, James Lee defines LAMP as "an acronym for a solution stack of free, open source software, originally coined from the first letters of Linux (operating system), Apache HTTP Server, MySQL (database software), and PHP, principal components to build a viable general purpose web server."

- HomeBank[viii] for accounting

Using these programs allows the company to pass additional savings along to its customers—and keep internal expenses down.

Happy Clients and Employees

RedSeven is a fun place to work, and Cady can't see ever going back to his job as a process engineer. The company hires personable and talented local college students, paying them above-market wages. Cady targets those studying to be network engineers or programmers. The same holds true for recent graduates. These people are ideal: many twentysomethings grew up with computers and today are extremely proficient with them.

RedSeven customers often become fiercely loyal to individual employees, in many cases not wanting to talk to Cady himself when he answers the phone! Cady understands that his clients develop deep personal relationships with specific employees. They mean no offense in refusing his requests to help. In fact, this loyalty is a testament to RedSeven. The company turns the stereotype of aloof and indifferent IT support folks on its head. Personable and patient RedSeven employees enjoy the one-on-one interaction with customers, solving problems and demystifying confusing issues. The company helps its clients navigate the perplexing sea of choices out there vis-à-vis technology in a friendly manner.

A Cool Culture

The culture at RedSeven is extremely laid back and intentionally "uncorporate." Cady's not joking when he says, "When customers visit, they usually think they've entered a bar or a nightclub." Employees typically walk around in sneakers and Beatles T-shirts. Posters adorn the walls. This informality no doubt contributes to the company's low turnover rate. Rather than the typical shop with gray cubicles and folding tables, RedSeven's showrooms have a very chic and modern feel to them. "We're *not* a typical computer repair shop," Cady says with pride.

Future, Results, and Challenges

RedSeven has not gone unnoticed; it has received its fair share of publicity over the last few years. "The IT world profits from your misfortune. In our system, the opposite is true. We want people to know it's our problem, not theirs," Cady said when interviewed recently by *The Arizona Business Gazette*.[ix]

After several changes in direction, RedSeven has found its niche and turned the corner. The company has grown to three locations in the Phoenix area and now offers mobile support. Revenue-per-employee has increased more than 100 percent in the last two years. Looking into his crystal ball, Cady is intent on expanding RedSeven. The company is working on building a more repeatable model via cloud computing.

SUMMARY

Many companies struggle trying to understand their client bases and, for various reasons, are simply out of touch with their customers. As this chapter has shown, this is not a problem with RedSeven. New Small companies try to develop intimate relationships with their customers. Through a combination of personalized service, enthusiastic employees, and the Five Enablers, RedSeven is able to cater equally well to the most tech-challenged people and the most tech-savvy ones—and everyone in between. Cady understands that not everyone is like him: energized and challenged by technology. As we have seen throughout this book, some people just want to run their law firms and dental practices without their computers crashing. People like these are RedSeven's bread and butter clients. By handling frustrating situations, the company meets its clients' needs, making owning a computer as simple as leasing a car.

Endnotes

i   https://www.gotomypc.com
ii   http://www.realvnc.com/vnc/index.html
iii   http://www.websense.com/content/products.aspx
iv   http://audacity.sourceforge.net
v   http://free.avg.com/us-en/homepage
vi   http://www.avast.com/index
vii   http://picasa.google.com
viii   http://homebank.free.fr
ix   http://www.azcentral.com/business/abg/articles/2010/08/12/20100812abg-small-biz0812.html

Chapter **15**

THE VIRTUOUS CYCLE

Don't ever take a fence down until you know why it was put up.

—Robert Frost

William Hurley grew up around computers. He fondly remembers that his fifth-grade computer science teacher told his parents during a routine conference that he wouldn't be able to get a job at McDonald's when he was older. The reason: according to his teachers' predictions, computers would soon run everything—even the cash registers. Rather than let a technology-oriented future intimidate him, he found the idea strangely appealing.

Growing up, Hurley played bass guitar in a funk band. Upon graduating from high school, he gave no thought to attending college. He had aspirations of making it big in the music industry. Unfortunately, his dream ended ominously on Friday, April 13, 1991. Hurley was involved in a serious car accident, an event that he calls "a life-changing experience." Although his playing days came to an end, his love of music and computers did not. They were about to coalesce.

He bought a digital recording studio and began scoring digital music for video games and CD-ROMs. Back then, proper, professionally produced CDs cost a great deal of money to make, a far cry from today. His skills and passion for technology fed each other, and he began to make a name for himself. In 1994, Hurley joined Apple Computer as a telephone support representative for the company's high-end users, such as movie studios. Back then, Apple used to deliver its software training courses via CD. Hurley quickly figured out a way do it over the nascent Internet by using a single

FTP[1] server. Customers could download courses and updates immediately. They would no longer have to wait for a physical CD to arrive in the mail. And it saved Apple hundreds of thousands of dollars in the process. Not surprisingly, it wasn't long before Hurley was promoted. He took on a number of increasingly senior roles in his three years with the company.

With his drive, knowledge, and results-oriented approach, Hurley quickly climbed the corporate ladder. He landed senior management-level jobs at tech stalwarts IBM (where he was named a Master Inventor[2]) and BMC Software. At the latter, he eventually held the title of Chief Architect, Open Source Strategy. Not bad for a self-taught ex-musician without a college degree.

Despite working in traditional corporate environments, the affable Hurley never relinquished his entrepreneurial drive. After a series of startups, he founded Chaotic Moon Studios[i] with longtime friends Mike Erwin and Ben Lamm in January of 2010.

A Diverse Portfolio of Products and Services

Chaotic Moon Studios is a particularly interesting case study. Its business model casts a wider net than those of the other companies profiled in this book. At a high level, it's a software development outfit that helps companies with their mobile needs. Its widely diverse clients hire the company to take its apps[3] from concept to reality. Based in Austin, TX, the company offers four types of *complementary* mobile-oriented services:

- Custom development
- Content publishing
- App resurrection
- Mobile strategy

Custom Development

The popularity of Apple's iPhone (as well as other mobile devices) has resulted in a deluge of custom apps for all sorts of purposes. For consumers, Apple, and developers, this has been a boon. However, many organizations have struggled with mobility. They might have ideas for interesting mobile

---

[1] File Transfer Protocol (FTP) is a standard network protocol used to copy a file from one host to another over a TCP/IP-based network, such as the Internet.

[2] An IBM Master Inventor is an individual selected through a rigorous process by IBM. The qualification and appointment to Master Inventor is governed by the value to IBM of an inventor's contribution to the patent portfolio, and through defensive publication (http://www.ibm.com).

[3] App is shorthand for mobile application.

apps but lack the skills and resources to develop them. Enter Chaotic Moon Studios. The company creates a range of products:

- Casual games
- Business-oriented utility apps
- Enterprise class apps for infrastructure management
- High-end augmented reality[4] gaming titles

Many organizations are struggling with the whole concept of mobility. Mobility can confuse or frustrate those who believe in its power, yet are unsure about how to harness it. To use Hurley's words, the company's mobile strategy is "wide and deep." Let's delve into this a bit more.

Content Publishing

Chaotic Moon works with its clients to manage everything from mobile brand strategy to ongoing maintenance and all parts in between. This work can be broken down into four areas. First, the company handles original and existing intellectual property (IP) from third parties. Second, it ports IP from other publishers. For example, the company takes video games written for one console (say, the Microsoft Xbox) and makes them available on another, such as the Wii. Chaotic Moon works with developers who create apps for the iPhone and want to make them available on Windows Phone 7 or the Android.

Third, and perhaps most creatively, the company assists individuals and other small businesses in distributing their content to the world. For instance, let's say that I wanted to create an application to go along with this book you're reading, and that Chaotic Moon believed that such an app had a viable market. I could engage the company to create the app, and we'd share the revenue.[5] But Chaotic Moon doesn't stop there. It markets the app and attempts to license it to other companies. Fourth, the company enables the streaming of television content on mobile devices.

Perler Beads

The *Los Angeles Times* recently profiled the company in an article entitled "Companies Help Non-Techies Create Killer Apps for iPhones."[ii] Chaotic Moon created an app for an individual who produced printable beading patterns. Richard Goodman, a product marketing manager in Austin, had

---

4 *Augmented reality* is a term for a live direct or indirect view of a physical real-world environment whose elements are augmented by virtual computer-generated imagery.

5 I would have to use a company like Chaotic Moon because I have absolutely no idea about how to create a mobile app. I would have to read a book like *Tapworthy* by Josh Clark.

an idea for an application to create Perler Beads.[iii] Unfortunately, he had no time, money, or skill developing apps. Enter Chaotic Moon.

The company worked with Goodman to create and launch the app *beadit!* The total time from concept to reality: an astonishing two weeks. You can find it now in Apple's App Store.[iv] The app allows users to easily create their own custom patterns for wildly popular Perler projects. They can design their own patterns by simply choosing an existing photo or taking a new photo using their cameras.

App Resurrection

Perhaps most intriguing, the company breathes new life into existing but underperforming or moribund mobile apps via its Application Resurrection program. This work typically involves adding to an existing app new code, better art, an improved user experience, more robust features, or a better marketing plan. Chaotic Moon buys promising intellectual property (IP) that has the potential for greater growth.

Hurley describes this service as "secret ninja coding." Chaotic Moon works behind the scenes on apps that are poorly conceived or designed, and as a result, poorly reviewed. As discussed in Part I of the book, today customers are increasingly social. App stores allow—and even encourage—product reviews. An app facelift can have a dramatic impact, as the company has shown with FlightAware, a flight tracking application for mobile devices. The first iteration of FlightAware did not do well, in large part because its interface was clunky. It was clearly not meeting the needs of its customers.

Enter Chaotic Moon. Hurley and company rewrote the app, dramatically improving it in the process. Chaotic Moon possessed the technologies and expertise to overhaul the application—and the results have been astounding. Thanks to Chaotic Moon, the product now contains geolocation functionality and provides a greatly improved user experience. Users can easily see which planes are flying above them in real time via Google Maps.[v]

These improvements have not gone unnoticed. FlightAware's user base is much happier with the new version of the app. One-star reviews have largely disappeared with its latest release, replaced by positive ones. As of this writing, nearly all of the 7,000 online reviews gave the app five stars (out of five). FlightAware is now "the world leader in flight tracking with over two million monthly users offer[ing] the only free flight tracking application for the Apple iPhone and iPod Touch."[vi]

As a case study, Chaotic Moon is instructive on a number of levels. On one hand, it shows how the New Small recognizes the limitations of existing applications and technologies—both for internal use and for its clients. Although anyone can complain, the New Small actually does something about these issues. These companies quickly and efficiently put ideas into action, often with the help of the Five Enablers. To expedite development efforts, the New Small takes full advantage of existing resources, refusing to reinvent the wheel. In this case, Chaotic Moon used—among other things—the Google Maps application programming interface[vii] (API) to integrate FlightAware with real-time geolocation information.

There is no better case study in this book than Chaotic Moon's use of the Five Enablers as it relates to FlightAware. The company used FOSS, mobility, and social technologies in concert to turn a nascent and flawed mobile app into a vastly more powerful and popular one. In turn, this success bred additional business and word of mouth for the company.

Careful Client Selection

Of course, Chaotic Moon could not have successfully overhauled FlightAware had its client not let it. This illustrates another common characteristic of New Small companies: they are often pickier—if not just plain picky—about their clients, especially after some initial success. "From day one, we all had the basic start-up mentality," Hurley notes. "We would take whatever clients we could get." That ephemeral train of thought has given way to greater selectivity. Hurley is experienced enough to know that there is such a thing as bad business, something that many organizations of all sizes just don't understand. With more work than the company can handle and a desire to expand, Chaotic Moon only takes on clients with the greatest upside and the fewest internal obstacles. Hurley goes on to say, "We've reached the point where we're not afraid to tell prospective clients, 'We're just not the right company for you.'" This long-term focus is very common among New Small companies.

Learning from Other Companies

Without question, Chaotic Moon employees are smart and talented individuals. However, they realize that there are other people and companies out there doing creative, innovative, and neat things with emerging technologies. Why not learn from them?

Hurley tells a story of a small video game company (SVGC), also based in Austin, that has had a large impact on Chaotic Moon and its founders.[6] Back in 1998, SVGC looked at other companies that had created successful video games for the PC and offered to port these to the Mac, for example. At that point, there was a dearth of games for Apple computers. SVGC made a

---

[6] Although I am calling it *SVGC* here, that is not the actual name of the company. Hurley requested that I use a pseudonym for the real company's name.

killing by taking a game built for one platform and making it available on another. Hurley thought that the idea made sense, so he implemented it years later.

As Chaotic Moon shows, the New Small is not afraid to employ a copycat strategy when it makes sense. Contrast this with companies—both large and small—that stigmatize products, tools, and ideas not invented internally.

Funding and People Philosophy

Like most New Small companies, including PeerPort (Chapter 9), Chaotic Moon is self-funded. "We really don't believe in venture capitalists," Hurley says. "Because of our growth, we've had offers from VCs." Although he wouldn't rule out such a move in the future (with an accurate valuation), Hurley and his founders are content calling the shots without outsider influence or interference, at least for now.

Chaotic Moon hires only the best people, choosing to pay them extremely well. Hurley has "been there and done that" with previous start-ups and knows the trap into which many fall: they become obsessed with the number of employees. Chaotic Moon knows better. The company would rather have 20 top-tier employees than a mixture of 40 with varying levels of skill. Hurley notes the difference between *being* a management team at a start-up and *doing* what start-ups do. This philosophy isn't for everyone, as many old-school managers are comfortable only being full-time managers. At Chaotic Moon, managers need to get their hands dirty on projects as situations warrant; you won't find people who operate only at 30,000 feet.

The company leaves a writer or storyboard artist position open for months, rather than filling it just for the sake of doing so. In a fast-paced company such as Chaotic Moon, no one has time to babysit people who lack the requisite skills, attitude, or knowledge. Although there's a great deal of collaboration on different projects, employees need to be able to contribute good work right away. Perhaps most important, employees have to have the passion of the founders. Chaotic Moon enhances existing apps and creates new ones for its clients. This type of work obviously involves a great degree of creativity. In other words, theirs are not typical IT maintenance jobs, such as help desk support or network engineering. To create killer apps, one needs to have passion, creativity, and a vision.

Using Emerging Technologies to Minimize Internal Costs

Like some of the other companies profiled in this book, Chaotic Moon takes advantage of FOSS and SaaS-based software. Although these may not be the most widely approved tools of their type, they are good enough and allow the company to minimize internal costs:

- HighRise[viii] for CRM
- Basecamp[ix] for project management and collaboration
- Google Apps (free edition)
- Drupal for its website and content management system
- Initially, FreshBooks for invoicing clients, although the company has since moved to an open source alternative
- PayPal for receiving payments
- ADP for payroll

Minimizing the costs of the applications and services it uses gives Chaotic Moon tremendous flexibility. What's more, those savings allow the company to spend money on proprietary software for which there are no legitimate FOSS equivalents. Adobe Creative Suite 5[x] (ACS5) certainly comes to mind because it includes PhotoShop, Acrobat Pro, and other industry-standard applications. These tools are absolutely vital for creative types. Although these aren't inexpensive, Chaotic Moon received a number of free licenses by virtue of participating in the Adobe's Influencer program (since discontinued). New Small companies often use FOSS but simultaneously aren't afraid to pay for proprietary software, especially when necessary. ACS5 enables Chaotic Moon's employees to create exciting and dynamic content and apps. Using less powerful applications to save a few thousand dollars just doesn't make sense. The New Small understands that free software has its limits; the key is striking the right balance between FOSS and proprietary applications.

Future, Results, and Challenges

Many old-school organizations pour a great deal of money into sales, marketing, and business development efforts, much of which is tied up in employee salaries and campaigns of questionable success. Chaotic Moon has been so successful that it has been able to forgo these traditional expenditures. Although not bragging, Hurley goes on to say that "Companies just call us and talk to one of the founders."

Without question, Chaotic Moon's recent press from different articles has helped it generate a decent amount of buzz, something expanded by the company's liberal use of social media. It is active on the major social media sites—that is, on Facebook, Twitter, LinkedIn, and the like. Moreover, word of mouth about the company should intensify because of the following:

- A filmmaker is in the process of shooting a documentary about the company.
- Consumers who buy applications developed or enhanced by Chaotic Moon stumble upon the company.
- Other developers are likely to want to work with them, especially after they hear about the success of projects like FlightAware.
- The company just released an app that uses augmented reality to help color-blind people use the iPhone to identify different colors. This is just plain cool and socially impactful.

For these reasons, the future is bright for Chaotic Moon. The company will be a featured player for three new platforms coming out in the next year, including many tablet computing devices and new mobile operating systems. For example, when the new version of Windows Mobile is launched, Chaotic Moon will sell about 25 apps from its online store from the day the new version is available. This first-mover advantage can be huge.

Hurley recognizes the need to remain as lean as possible. He has no crystal ball, and although things at Chaotic Moon are humming along nicely, the last thing that it needs is a bloated staff or excessive fixed costs, particularly in the way of employee salaries.

Of course, success breeds imitation. Many other companies have already jumped on the mobile bandwagon. Fortunately, mobile apps are an enormous market. Juniper Research estimates that it may reach $25B USD by 2014.[xi] None of this worries Hurley, though. Although hardly complacent, he's justifiably confident that his company will continue to do great work—and be a great place to work.

SUMMARY

It shouldn't be terribly surprising that companies rooted in emerging technologies use them so pervasively. To be sure, not all of the New Small live and breathe technology. Although companies such as Hanover Pediatric, Chef Tony's, and Skjold-Barthel extensively use the Five Enablers, they aren't in the technology business. Dentists, chefs, and attorneys are rarely successful when they try to act as hard-core programmers and developers—just as the opposite is certainly true.

This same cannot be said about Chaotic Moon. Hurley and his employees embrace the Five Enablers. Ultimately, this mindset increases the strength of his company. Immersing themselves in all things technology benefits the company, its employees, and its clients—the very definition of a virtuous cycle.

Endnotes

i   http://www.chaoticmoon.com
ii http://www.latimes.com/business/la-fi-app-goldrush-20100624,0,7112327.story
iii http://www.eksuccessbrands.com/perlerbeads
iv http://itunes.apple.com/us/app/beadit/id357412484?mt=8
v   http://maps.google.com
vi http://flightaware.com/iphone
vii http://code.google.com/apis/maps/index.html
viii http://www. http://highrisehq.com
ix http://www.basecamphq.com
x   http://tryit.adobe.com/us/cs5/designpremium/promo1.html?sdid=IBERA
xi http://www.atelier-us.com/e-business-and-it/article/juniper-mobile-application-market-worth-25b-in-2014

Chapter 16

THE CHIEF SEAFOOD OFFICER

There is no sincerer love than the love of food.

—George Bernard Shaw

Tony Marciante isn't your typical chef or restaurateur. He's tinkered with computers all of his life, not that he's a programmer by trade. A 23-year veteran of the industry, since 2007 he has owned and run Chef Tony's,[i] a seafood restaurant located in Bethesda, MD.

Marciante is a self-described "geek" and, in particular, a long-time Applephile. He's had an iPhone since the product's first incarnation, has bought multiple Macs, and plans to buy an iPad. He constantly looks to merge the two sides of his brain: food and technology.

Marciante is an industrious and engaging guy. He uses his restaurant to also build his personal brand. Along those lines, he maintains a separate website[ii] devoted to his other endeavors, including speaking and consulting to the restaurant industry. In this chapter, you see how a restaurant employing eight full-time employees has a reach far beyond that of many of its larger competitors.

Exceptional Use of Social Technologies

Because of the explosion of popular and powerful social technologies, our world is considerably more connected and social than even five years ago. In his book *Six Pixels of Separation*, Mitch Joel writes:

We no longer live in a world where there are Six Degrees of Separation (where any one person is connected to anybody else through fewer than six degrees of separation). We are all intrinsically connected through technology, the Internet, and our mobile devices. These digital channels break down the notion of "it's who you know," because we all now live in a world where we can know anyone—and everyone can know us. And we're not connected by degrees anymore; we're simply connected.

As a group, the New Small understands that harnessing the social web can yield enormous benefits. Although most of these companies use these social technologies to some extent,[1] Marciante is at its vanguard, perhaps in a class by himself. "If I'm not in the kitchen or running my place, I'm in front of my computer updating my websites, working on social media campaigns, or just keeping in touch with people," Marciante says. "It's not about making direct sales as much as it is being a part of conversations." To him, that overriding goal supersedes important but potentially misleading statistics such as website hits, returning visitors, and converted clicks.

Constantly fiddling with his websites, Marciante makes extensive use of social technologies. Although the mediums vary, he consistently provides meaningful content to his followers, listeners, and readers. At a high level, he uses social technologies to

- Connect with his customers
- Arguably more important, to allow his customers to connect with him
- Enable his customers and employees to connect with each other

Marciante avoids the cardinal mistakes made by most companies using social technologies (discussed in Chapter 3). For example, he doesn't use them for overt marketing. Nor does he hire a self-anointed expert who has no clue about his company's culture and customers.

Marciante is what Malcolm Gladwell calls a connector in *The Tipping Point*. The gregarious chef often links customers who might be able to help one another. For example, a woman recently laid off had her farewell lunch at Chef Tony's. Marciante asked her about her future plans. She mentioned her intent to start a new crocheting business. The woman wasn't terribly familiar with website design. Marciante gave her some tips and then

---

[1] In fact, I only found out about Marciante in August of 2010 through—you guessed it—social media. I posted an update on Facebook to the effect of "Looking for tech-savvy restaurateurs." Within an hour, I had spoken with Chef Tony himself. The rest, as they say, is history.

introduced her to a photographer friend of his starting a studio and looking for subjects. Marciante figured that the two of them might benefit from an introduction. They did—and both now love Marciante for his gentle meddling. Because he promotes goodwill and karma, they in turn reciprocate down the road.

Examples like this manifest a few important things about the New Small. First, these companies get the word out in innovative ways—not in pushy ones. Theirs are the antithesis of forceful and obnoxious sales techniques. Marciante understands the fine line between raising awareness and overdoing it. Sites such as FriendFeed[iii] and Facebook allow him to keep tabs on his friends and customers—and vice versa. Second, particularly on slow days, the New Small doesn't just wait around for things to happen; they *make* things happen, typically through the use of social technologies. Marciante is always creating videos, thinking of new ideas, and writing blog posts. Such zealousness rubs off on employees who appreciate the way that he builds his business.

At a high level, the New Small uses social technologies to start conversations, not to shove unwanted information at their customers. "Social media is about representing yourself in your community," Marciante plainly states. "It's about being available." Of course, being available and producing quality content—both of which Marciante does exceptionally well—take a great deal of time. What's more, the results are not likely to be immediate. Just because a company starts a blog or opens a Twitter account does not mean that its sales will double overnight.

Blogging

Although he started blogging before he really knew what he was doing, Marciante was a quick study. Today, he runs several WordPress blogs in which he disperses knowledge about what he does.[iv] Recent topics have included:

- Thoughts on seafood and a gulf update
- Soft shell crabs coming into season
- A yummy caramel sauce recipe

In January, Marciante posted his year in review, including this passage:

> I want to reach out to you, and ask…What other types of subjects/questions/show topics would interest you? Please e-mail me any thoughts,[2] and we can incorporate them into our show! I plan also to interview other industry players and introduce my listeners to other great local restaurants, because for me,

---

[2] This included a link to his e-mail address.

no one is competition, we're all just players in the restaurant game with different flavors. I understand and embrace that peoples' tastes may change from night to night, and I certainly realize that we all have some great foods, just depends what you want![v]

Marciante asked how he can better meet the needs of his customers. This gesture is characteristic of the New Small; these companies do not arrogantly believe that they have all of the answers. A know-it-all mentality is the first step in losing touch with its customer base.

The Generalized Tornado

Although the topics Marciante covers vary, they generally fall into two categories: instructional and personal. His instructional videos involve anything from how to look for and buy the best tuna at a fish market to how to properly sear scallops in a pan. Personal videos allow him to put a human touch on his sites. He strives to be both informative and personable, and judging from the popularity of his site, he knows what he's doing.

Regardless of the type of video or podcast he's creating, Marciante's style is informal. He doesn't mind if a video is a little raw; in fact, he'd prefer that to being too polished or staged. His customers appreciate the natural element of his content; he provides an authentic behind-the-scenes look at his business online and in the physical world. Chef Tony's sports an open kitchen in which customers are allowed to see what's going on and even talk to Marciante while he's preparing meals. Although that might not appeal to everyone (certainly not restaurant traditionalists), Marciante believes that his perspective resonates with more customers than not. "They like being involved in the process," Marciante says. "They don't feel like there's a barrier."

Marciante broadcasts videos via sites such as these:

- Viddler[vi] is especially useful because users can easily embed a company logo in a video, increasing brand awareness.

- TubeMogul[vii] allows for easy distribution of a video to multiple networks, which obviates the need to separately post to different sites.

- Other video-related sites, including: Break.com, Mevio.com, Veoh.com, Metacafe.com, and Vimeo.com.

Rest assured: making videos for social media is hardly Marciante's exclusive daily focus. He constantly searches for ways to multitask and make efficient use of his time via emerging technologies.[3] He often records a podcast while he's simultaneously cutting fish or making fresh mozzarella in his kitchen. Sometimes he asks an employee to record a quick video of him in action and upload it for the entire world to see. His videos often quickly spread among customers, family, and friends. A series of informal videos shot by a new employee garnered over 3,000 hits on YouTube within six months.

And Marciante has seen the benefits of his social media investment pay off. "I've had people walk in the door and feel comfortable with me immediately," he says. "They'll say, 'Hey Tony. What's up?' before we've ever met." Marciante builds bonds with many of his customers even *before* they enter his establishment. The New Small knows that this social media can produce such results, *but only if it is done well*. Marciante astutely calls social media both a "generalized tornado" and a "virtual salesperson always working for free."

As for pictures, Marciante is a fan of Jing,[viii] a simple screen capture and posting service. Jing is particularly helpful in quickly sending pictures of new menus to the web, allowing customers to see what's currently available. Marciante posts these screen captures on Twitter and Facebook. This is one of the creative ways in which the New Small uses technology to unobtrusively get the word out.

On the microblogging front, Chef Tony has nearly 5,000 fans on Twitter[ix] as of this writing. He uses Twitter to promote Free Martini Fridays. He holds tweetups[4] on a regular basis, with attendees numbering 30 to 50. These are events in which people who tweet meet in person for the first time.

In sum, Marciante uses all of the different social media channels and networks to tell a story about a guy very passionate about food—something to which his customers can relate. That passion comes through in the form of videos, podcasts, blog posts, tweets, and—arguably most important— in person when customers step through his doors. In this sense, Marciante takes his cues from social media expert, best-selling author, and speaker Gary Vaynerchuk—aka "The Wine Guy."[x]

Understanding the Limitations of Social Technologies

"Social media isn't the be-all and end-all," Marciante says. "You have to get out from behind the counter and computer and let people put a face to a name." Marciante knows full well that social technologies complement personal relationships. That is, they are not replacements.

---

[3] I am reminded here of the quote from Henry David Thoreau: "It is not enough to be busy. So are the ants. The question is: what are we busy about?"

[4] These are meet-ups on Twitter.

Mobility

Marciante doesn't just know on an abstract level that mobility is huge; he sees it every day in his restaurant. His customers are constantly using their phones to text, take pictures, send e-mails, and post updates to social networking sites. He is currently working on a mobile website and iPhone app customized for his restaurant. Marciante uses services and sites to reach mobile customers—and keep them in his restaurant after they arrive. These include

> ▦ Opt-in text-based advertising service Fanminder[xi] to reach local customers, particularly for those Free Martini Fridays. Customers merely show up with a text from Tony to collect a free drink.[5]

> ▦ Überpopular mobile sites like Foursquare[xii] and Gowalla[xiii] allow for real-time connections with local customers.

> ▦ The OpenTable[xiv] seating system to facilitate online reservations, although he notes that the one-way nature of reviews on that site needs to change.

> ▦ After a recent upgrade to Comcast Business Class,[xv] the restaurant now offers its customers free Wi-Fi access.[xvi]

Using services such as these is typical New Small: rather than build something from scratch at considerable effort and cost, these companies use existing and effective sites, platforms, and tools.

Customer Rescue

Marciante realizes the power of the social customer, especially in this day and age. Although he can't make each and every one of his patrons happy, he can certainly try to understand the source of customer dissatisfaction—as the following story illustrates. In 2009, a customer had an unsatisfactory experience at his restaurant and left upset. That customer would soon let the world—or at least his readers—know about it on his blog.[xvii]

Marciante's Google Alerts[xviii] picked up that customer's post soon after it was published. Marciante reached out, and, within an hour, the two were talking. Marciante apologized to the customer and asked what he could do to remedy the situation. A few weeks later, the customer returned to the restaurant, enjoyed his meal, and amended his initial blog post. Examples such as these prove two things. First, technology allows interested companies

---

5   Of course, most stay for more than that. The Chef makes a killer martini.

to track the social customer. Second, as I know from personal experience,[6] customer rescue works. You can turn detractors into advocates.

Marciante's anecdote serves as an important lesson: each angry or dissatisfied customer represents an opportunity for a business to turn a negative experience into a positive one. Companies like Chef Tony's and DODOcase have successfully used social technologies to redress less-than-ideal situations. Although there are no guarantees, merely reaching out to a disgruntled customer often helps. More often than not, it can diffuse a potentially volatile situation.

To the extent possible, Marciante focuses on what his customers are saying *everywhere*, with particular emphasis on popular social review sites such as Yelp.[xix] Too often, companies ignore the word on the street, either intentionally or because they are unaware that they can actually monitor customer sentiment and comments. New Small companies don't make this mistake.

Other Technologies

To run his business in the most cost-effective manner, Marciante uses tools commonly found at the New Small, including these:

- Google Docs
- Skype
- WordPress
- TweetDeck[xx] for managing Twitter
- Hardware such as the iPhone, Flipcam, Mac, and Snowball Mic[xxi] for podcasting

Future, Results, and Challenges

Marciante is interested in introducing iPad-type devices at his restaurant. These would enable instant communication between waiters and kitchen staff. If his business continues to grow, he'll be able to hire additional people. In turn, this will allow him to focus on social media and more creative endeavors. Again, this type of mentality is prevalent in the New

---

[6] To make a long story short, I contacted someone who gave a one-star review to *Why New Systems Fail* (my first book) on Amazon.com. His sole reason: "Not available for the iPad." Since I have no control over what my publisher and the folks at Amazon.com do, I contacted the guy, explained this to him, and sent him an autographed copy of the book at my cost. In turn, he blogged and tweeted positively about the experience. It isn't that hard to turn a detractor into an advocate.

Small. Rather than being comfortable with the way things are and feeling like they've done enough, New Small owners understand that there's essentially unlimited opportunity out there.

Marciante is working on a membership site as well as a book to teach others in small business how to harness the power of social media. He knows that the restaurant business isn't easy. Although the failure rate for individual restaurants may be grossly overstated,[xxii] success is anything but easy in any economy—much less in the Great Recession. Many people have scaled back the frequency with which they dine out. As a result, competition among restaurants has intensified beyond anything seen for quite some time.

Marciante does not attempt to *prove* the effectiveness of social media. He knows that it's working for at least two reasons. First, the mere fact that his restaurant is still open in the midst of a crippling recession is a testament to his stick-to-itiveness. Many of his competitors have not been as lucky or resilient. Second, he has noticed an increase in check averages, a common barometer in the restaurant business.

The company's effective use of social technologies has paid dividends beyond reaching new customers. He admittedly spends less than $5,000 USD each year on traditional marketing efforts. Although employee turnover in the restaurant industry is notoriously high for many reasons (including the age of the workforce), Marciante describes his attrition as "below average" and says that his employees "like to show off that they work at a cool place."

Despite these challenges, guest counts at Chef Tony's have risen, as patrons drop in to both socialize and enjoy a meal. Marciante sees this as a direct result of starting conversations early through social media, leading to real-world conversations at the bar or in the restaurant.

SUMMARY

Marciante understands that everyone is potentially connected and not merely through traditional mechanisms. He welcomes customer and employee feedback through multiple channels. He invites people into his world, sharing pictures of his kitchen and allowing others to take them with their mobile devices. This allows him to grow his social network while on the job.

Chef Tony's stands in stark contrast to how many short-sighted organizations mistakenly use social technologies. For example, many believe that a simple Facebook page is sufficient for communicating with—and engaging—customers. It's not. New Small companies understand that social technologies represent unique opportunities to interact with customers in very meaningful ways. Companies like these cast a wide net of communications and engagement— but it doesn't stop there. Customers extend that net, virally engaging others in ways that traditional marketing campaigns typically cannot. Rich relationships develop organically.

Endnotes

i   http://ChefTonysBethesda.com
ii http://whatdoestonydo.com
iii http://www.friendfeed.com
iv http://blog.visionsbethesda.com
v   http://blog.visionsbethesda.com/2010/01/11/hows-your-year-in-review-heres-ours
vi http://www.viddler.com
vii http://www.tubemogul.com
viii http://www.techsmith.com/jing
ix http://twitter.com/cheftony
x   http://garyvaynerchuk.com
xi http://www.fanminder.com
xii http://www.foursquare.com
xiii http://www.gowalla.com
xiv http://www.opentable.com
xv http://business.comcast.com
xvi http://blog.visionsbethesda.com/2010/04/20/wireless-is-always-free-at-visions
xvii http://theupstatelife.blogspot.com/2008_02_01_theupstatelife_archive.html
xviii http://www.google.com/alerts

xix http://www.yelp.com
xx   http://www.tweetdeck.com
xxi http://www.bluemic.com/snowball
xxii http://www.businessweek.com/smallbiz/content/apr2007/sb20070416_296932.
     htm

Part III

BECOMING ONE OF THE NEW SMALL

No company can guarantee the successful adoption of new technologies—even those in the New Small. There's just no silver bullet. A point from before bears repeating: *Relative to large organizations, New Small companies have an easier time deploying the Five Enablers. But easier doesn't mean easy.*

This part of the book takes a step back. It covers the ways in which New Small companies overcome challenges and obstacles when deploying emerging technologies. It asks and answers the question, how can these companies collaborate so well? The management and technology lessons from Part II are examined and generalized. We see how New Small companies carefully and intelligently select the tools, people, and partners that make sense—and quickly get away from those that no longer fit the bill. They don't immediately and unilaterally embrace every technology that comes along. What's more, they balance immediate short-term needs with long-term prospects for growth. New Small companies know that although the Five Enablers are powerful, they are no panacea. Just like everything else, they have to be viewed through the right lens. It is just plain foolish to ignore their costs, risks, and contexts.

Chapters

Chapter 17

TRUE COLLABORATION

*A lie can get halfway around the world before
the truth can even get its boots on.*

—Mark Twain

A long with *Web 2.0* and *social media*, perhaps no other business term is as prevalent and overused today as *collaboration*. As they do with many buzzwords, many people throw around the term without a clear understanding of what it actually means in the workplace. This chapter discusses:

- The definition of collaboration

- Collaborative work environments and types of software

- How New Small companies successfully collaborate

- Why large organizations struggle embracing true collaboration

The New Small doesn't just embrace the notion of collaboration. For them, survival *depends* on it. By contrast and as a general rule, large organizations are still struggling with collaboration on two levels:

- Adopting specific tools

- Arguably more important, adopting the mindset necessary to foster successful collaboration

We have seen how technology has exploded faster than most enterprises can effectively handle. Perhaps nowhere is the distinction between New Small and old-guard companies more pronounced than in the successful adoption and use of collaborative technologies. In the big corporate world, collaboration is slowly catching on, although not to the same extent everywhere. It varies by company, industry, and department. Many big companies are stuck in their ways; some departments and people simply ignore collaborative tools. Old habits die hard.

New Small companies understand that deploying a new technology designed to promote collaboration does not guarantee results. Anyone can buy a tool, deploy it, and politely request that people use it under certain circumstances. That is, deploying new tools for the sake of doing so serves no purpose. To justify the time, money, and effort involved in creating and adopting collaborative tools, organizations of all sizes need to effectively use them. By virtue of their size, small businesses are simply in a better place than their corporate counterparts.

Let's explore why.

Collaboration 101

The term *collaboration* began to permeate popular business culture at the end of 2006, thanks in large part to the extremely successful book *Wikinomics: How Mass Collaboration Changes Everything*, by Don Tapscott and Anthony D. Williams. Today, there are two major types of collaboration:

- **General**—A cooperative arrangement in which two or more parties (which may or may not have any previous relationship) work jointly toward a common goal.

- **Knowledge management (KM)**—An effective method of transferring know-how among individuals, which is critical to creating and sustaining a competitive advantage. Collaboration is a key tenet of KM.[i]

It's no coincidence that business folks didn't hear a great deal about collaboration until relatively recently. Let's say that *Wikinomics* was never written. I'd argue that we would still be hearing a great deal about collaboration today for the following reasons:

- Recent trends in the economy and technology
- The explosion of the social web and broadband
- The direction of software development over the last five years

Look at it another way. As of 2000, most websites were unidirectional glorified brochures. Sure, eBay, Amazon.com, and other online stores allowed for e-commerce, but the majority of sites and software didn't promote real-time interaction and collaboration. In other words, going back a few years, how exactly were people supposed to collaborate? In the 1990s, the concept of a *wiki* as we know it now simply didn't exist. Many corporations experimented with intranets and knowledge bases only to find that the majority of key documents still resided on employee hard drives. Employees typically shared documents largely through the cumbersome process of sending e-mail attachments back and forth (typically with a new version number after it), a process hampered by dial-up speeds and strict corporate limits on the sizes of e-mail boxes.

In hindsight, Collaboration 1.0 wasn't terribly collaborative at all. To effectively work on a document or project, most of the time people needed to be in close physical proximity to each other. The technology didn't allow for anything better. That has changed. Unfortunately, for many companies, the overreliance upon e-mail has not.

Collaborative Work Environments (CWEs)

Today, the days of intranets, shared drives, and dial-up connections seem quaint. Emerging technologies have ushered in a new wave of collaboration, especially at New Small companies. They are becoming collaborative work environments, equipped with the following technologies:

- E-mail—the web's first killer app
- Task and workflow management tools, such as Google Wave[ii]
- Instant messaging (IM)
- Screen and application sharing
- Videoconferencing
- Collaborative workspaces such as DropBox[iii] and Google Docs
- Document management
- Really simple syndication (RSS) feeds
- Group- and community-based wikis
- Mutliuser blogs, such as those from WordPress 3.0[iv]
- Microblogging sites such as Twitter and their business equivalents (Yammer[v] and Noodle from Vialect[vi])
- Other tools evolving as I write

In short, no longer does technology prevent us from collaborating with our colleagues and partners. If anything, there just might be too many options for effective collaboration these days. Of course, to embrace the future, one has to let go of the past, something with which many organizations continue to struggle.

Embracing Alternatives and the Limitations of Old Standbys

With regard to collaboration, perhaps the biggest advantage for the New Small is its collective willingness to let go of old standbys:

- The E-mail Is Collaboration mindset
- Bulky and dated e-mail programs
- Microsoft Office programs never really meant for collaboration

The E-Mail Is Collaboration Mindset

E-mail is a powerful and useful medium in a digital age, and only a fool would advocate its elimination. However, too many people rely on it too much and to do too many things for which it isn't terribly well suited. So, let me dispel a myth: *e-mail is not collaborative.*

On his well-read blog, ZDNet Editor in Chief Larry Dignan acknowledges that many people continue to benefit from e-mail—almost too much. Dignan writes that e-mail is "inefficient, unruly, cumbersome, and in serious need of a complete overhaul. And that's just from the user's perspective. On the IT side of things, e-mail is also a malware magnet, a drain on resources, and a governance headache."[vii]

E-mail will probably never die altogether because, to be honest, what's the alternative? To claim that it is collaborative in nature, however, is bunk. Yet many businesses of all sizes continue to misuse e-mail; they fail to adopt tools specifically designed to enable people to work together more effectively. Thankfully, New Small companies do not have this problem. You're not likely to find 40 e-mail chains at these companies.

Truly collaborative tools (read: not e-mail) hold enormous promise. Wikis[1] and comparable tools contain amazing features designed to:

- Facilitate document sharing and updating
- Improve intrateam communication
- Rid the organization of its dependency on e-mail

Collectively, these collaborative tools can greatly improve project management and product development. Although this sounds good in theory,

---

[1] *Wikis* are websites that allow non-technical folks to easily add new content and edit existing content. Perhaps the biggest wiki is Wikipedia.

unfortunately and all too frequently, the promise of these tools is far greater than their actual benefits.

But why is this the case? Collaborative tools are only as good as the people who use them. Lamentably, usage is inconsistent at best throughout many organizations. Old habits (read: e-mail) die hard. E-mail may be the Internet's first killer app because work-related messages convey important information about tasks, events, and projects. From a collaboration standpoint, however, e-mail is hardly ideal for several reasons:

- E-mails are often deleted or lost. They do not update wikis or websites.

- E-mails tend to be more difficult to find and search than content posted on wikis.

- People constantly forget to copy others on e-mails.

- Most e-mails are downloaded to individual PCs, making them suboptimal for future reference.

To be certain, wikis will never obviate the need for e-mail. What's more, not every piece of information on a project should be posted on a wiki. E-mails should constantly reference collaborative sites to reinforce the notion that the wiki governs the project, not 100 separate e-mails.

The New Small ensures the optimal use of collaborative tools by doing the following:

- Starting at the top

- Holding team members accountable for updates on wikis

- Cross-referencing wikis in e-mails

Starting at the Top

The head of the company sets the tone for everyone; New Small founders understand the importance of leading by example. This type of leader also encourages those who rely on e-mail to use better collaboration tools and update their documents properly.

Holding Team Members Accountable for Updates on Wikis

New Small companies understand that buying Microsoft SharePoint or rolling out wikis does not guarantee their effective use. People must use collaborative tools in a consistent and timely fashion in order for these applications to live up to their hype. Employees cannot occasionally—and belatedly—update their own availability and progress on a particular task or project. Rather, collaborative tools need to be at the epicenter of all internal communications. They need to immediately include all project plans, status updates, test scripts, design requirements, training materials, and so on. Obvious exceptions include confidential or politically sensitive material.

Cross-Referencing Wikis in E-Mails

Today, many people now routinely read e-mail via a BlackBerry, iPhone, or other mobile device. This isn't changing anytime soon. To that extent, it's simply foolish to expect people to completely abandon e-mail. However, e-mails should contain URLs referencing relevant content on wikis. Doing so will help minimize conflicting or missing information.

The Evolution of E-Mail Programs

Although e-mail existed in the 1970s,[viii] most people received their first electronic message in the 1990s. At least in the corporate world, those were the halcyon days for industrial-size e-mail applications, such as IBM's Lotus Notes and Microsoft's Outlook.[2] Those two programs were prevalent for one simple reason: there just weren't too many alternatives for corporate e-mail.

Think about it. As e-mail became essential in the mid-1990s, where were large, conservative organizations going to go? IBM and Microsoft had two of the strongest brands back then, and both represented safe choices for securely transmitting electronic communication. Even today, Outlook and Lotus Notes accomplish their primary objectives: to send and receive e-mail.

Of course, technology never stands still. In this case, what we want from e-mail applications now is much different from 15 years ago. Many end users now demand additional features from their e-mail programs. Microsoft and IBM both responded with the introduction of web-based e-mail, allowing people to access their messages from a web browser—often only if connected via a virtual private network (VPN). However, each e-mail application was a poor choice for many companies, especially the New Small. For several reasons, New Small companies tend not to use Outlook, and none use Lotus Notes.[3] First, web-native applications are very simple to deploy. Second, Zoho and Gmail typically cost far less than traditional alternatives. Open source alternative Zimbra[ix] is free. Third, new e-mail tools keep improving at a rapid rate.[x] Consider Google's recent announcement to allow

---

[2] Of course, as Ed Brill (head of Lotus Notes at IBM) consistently points out on his site (http://www.edbrill.com), the product is much more than a mere e-mail application. Many organizations use Domino Designer to create blogs, wikis, RSS aggregators, CRM, and Help Desk systems. Also, to be fair, Outlook can do more than handle e-mail. It provides calendar, contact, and task management.

[3] I have not used Lotus Notes in over eight years but talk quite a bit with people who do. Most people still do not consider it a user-friendly application. It completely deserves its reputation as a clunker. In all of my travels, I have never met a true Notes fan. Google "Lotus Notes sucks," and you'll see that I'm not alone in this viewpoint.

Gmail users to make calls directly in the application.[xi] New Small companies simply love one-stop shopping and constantly improving products. Fourth, the needs of many end users grew beyond merely exchanging e-mails. New programs often contain additional functionality enabling enhanced collaboration and communication.

Finally, although they are still stable and reliable, older e-mail applications just haven't kept up with recent technological advances. IBM and Microsoft built Lotus Notes and Microsoft Outlook, respectively, well before social networks, instant messaging, and collaboration became popular. With varying degrees of success, each company has enhanced its programs to include important new functionality. In fact, in July of 2010, Microsoft announced the introduction of a connector between Outlook and profile information in Facebook. As Irwin Lazar, vice president for communications research at Nemertes Research, writes on the Enterprise 2.0 blog:

> The service works by matching a user's e-mail address to their Facebook profile. So if one of your contacts in Outlook is on Facebook, you will see whatever information is publicly available from their profile within Outlook (or whatever information you can access if you are "friends"). Microsoft previously announced a similar integration between Outlook at LinkedIn.[xii]

Kudos to Microsoft for recognizing the importance of social networking. However, advances like these do not change the fact that Outlook and Lotus Notes do not integrate emerging technologies to the same extent as Gmail, Zoho, and their ilk. Today, many IT managers or CIOs at large companies privately admit to the shortcomings of mature e-mail programs. My hunch is that relatively few would select either for their enterprises today if given the choice. Of course, large organizations cannot easily migrate from one e-mail application to another. For better or worse, many are stuck with antiquated e-mail programs that employees are required to use. The tools are typically ill-suited for real collaboration.

To address this widening gap, large software vendors are working with smaller companies that specialize in add-on functionality. Eric Lai writes in *ComputerWorld* about companies that see opportunity in the state of traditional e-mail programs. In January of 2010, FewClix[xiii] introduced a plug-in for the much-maligned Lotus Notes to improve the following features:

- **Archiving**—Although Notes lets users archive batches of e-mail by date, FewClix offers archiving by any combination of factors, such as recipient + before date + attachment. The beta requires users to search archives separately from the main inbox, but that condition will be changed by the general release, CEO Madan Kumar says.

- **Folders and Groups**—Rather than forcing users to set rules that route e-mails into various folders, FewClix allows users to keep their e-mails in the inbox but reduce clutter by creating different *Groups*.

- **Performance**—A slick demo Mr. Kumar showed involved a Notes database with 12,000 e-mails. He said FewClix's in-memory index enables "very good" performance for mailboxes as large as 200,000 e-mails.[xiv]

Note that there is a similar plug-in for Outlook from Xobni.[xv]

The Problem with Plug-Ins

I am a huge fan of plug-ins, especially for my Firefox browser and my own website. But plug-ins have their limitations, especially for large organizations that use big e-mail applications. First, remember that Outlook and Lotus Notes are very prevalent *corporate* e-mail applications—although many people use Outlook for personal e-mail. Most IT departments in large organizations do not sanction employees' downloading third-party plug-ins to use in this manner. Plug-ins can cause IT departments major security and connectivity problems.

Second, what does it say about an essential application (such as e-mail) when plug-ins have to address *basic* features, such as archiving, search, and performance? We're not talking about a cool new theme or the ability to add fish swimming in the background. This is core functionality.

Advantage: The New Small

New Small companies don't force their employees to use clunky applications to perform essential tasks, especially when much more user-friendly alternatives are readily available. Of course, none of this is rocket science. These companies know that e-mail remains critical, although they have made great strides with collaborative tools. Although plug-ins can extend the capabilities of e-mail applications, those applications should not be so limited that they require third-party plug-ins to provide basic functionality.

Microsoft Office Programs

The 1990s represented the acme of Microsoft's hegemony. With a lock on operating systems (Windows) and office productivity applications (Office), it's no coincidence that the company consistently made billions of dollars every year. At one point in 1999, Bill Gates was worth more than $100B USD, a simply astonishing number.

Take a look at Microsoft's stock price over the last few years. Yes, the company loses significant amounts of money via software piracy, something that it now fights with professional investigators and even a piracy hotline.[xvi] But there's another reason that the Redmond giant has been struggling as of late: the cash cow that is Office no longer is the only game in town.

Only in 2010 did Microsoft create a web-based version of Office. By then, many small businesses had already tried and successfully adopted similar products from OpenOffice, Zoho, Google, and other software. That is, many companies tried different applications (often via a freemium model) and found others that worked for them.[4] They didn't wait for Microsoft to catch up and provide now-essential functionality to facilitate collaboration.

The willingness of many New Small companies to go beyond Office represents a key window into their collective mindset. If a software application doesn't meet their needs, they will find one that does. The New Small will not be beholden to deficient or overly expensive software with a recognized brand. Nor will these companies wait indefinitely. They will try, buy, or build another one until they find one that can meet their business needs. This type of independence and decisive action is commonplace at the New Small.

Requirements for Effective Collaboration

Now, anyone can throw out facile bromides such as, "Collaboration is important" and "We need to do a better job at collaborating." This is analogous to consultants saying, "It's all about execution." Lines like these are rightly mocked. But how does a company of any size ensure that its employees, partners, vendors, and suppliers actually collaborate? Moreover, relative to large corporations, why are New Small companies better at collaborating?

The New Small understands that effective collaboration is a function of three things:

- Vision and belief
- Tools
- Culture and accountability

Let's explore each.

Vision and Belief

New Small companies recognize the benefits of collaboration, and as we have seen, practice what they preach. This starts with the common vision of the founders and the employees.

---

4 Of course, some stayed on Office.

Tools

Vision and belief are all fine and dandy. Before I swing, I can believe that I'm going to hit a golf ball long and straight, but that alone doesn't guarantee that it will happen. It helps if I own decent clubs, practice, remain calm during my swing, and keep my head down as I strike the ball.

The same applies to collaboration. Throughout this book, we have seen that New Small companies make the requisite investments in technology to allow employees, partners, contractors, and suppliers to work and communicate effectively. The New Small gives people the tools required to do their thing.

Culture and Accountability

As discussed earlier in this book, the New Small has an inherent advantage over big companies. Smaller company size makes it easier to get everyone on the same page—and keep them there. Contrast this with the different tribes of big companies. They are typically unable to agree on what to do, much less how to do it. New Small companies can move nimbly precisely because they lack big-company impediments. They make important decisions quickly, and should those decisions not turn out as expected, swiftly change direction.

New Small companies hold people accountable when they don't collaborate and fail to meet the requirements of their jobs. Whereas many big companies move dead weight into less visible roles, no such roles exist in New Small companies. This isn't to say that these companies' cultures are highly stressful or cut-throat. On the contrary, they are typically anywhere from pleasant to outright fun, as Michael Cady of RedSeven showed us in Chapter 14. Everyone recognizes, however, that all employees play important roles in the success of their companies. The New Small does not have a perfect batting average vis-à-vis hiring employees and using contractors. It becomes quickly evident which people don't quite fit, and when they don't, the parties go their separate ways.

The Limits of Collaboration

At the same time, however, the New Small understands that collaboration has its limits. As we have seen with many small businesses profiled in Part II of the book, sometimes decisive action is needed to seize an opportunity. Many windows rapidly close, and these companies understand the benefits of first mover advantage. For example, the founders of DODOcase knew that the launch of the iPad created a unique opportunity to create a product and grab market share. Although Buckley and Dalton agreed on business strategy and many specifics, they did not force themselves to agree on every detail. There's still something to be said for intelligent division of labor. The New Small can effectively make these types of judgments.

SUMMARY

This chapter looked at how and why the New Small collaborates so much better than larger organizations. For one, there are often no such things as formal departments or organizational charts. Beyond that, however, employees who fail to embrace essential tools aren't able to hide to the same extent that they can in a large, potentially bloated organization. It becomes readily apparent who is and is not using tools to facilitate collaboration and communication.

Endnotes

i   http://www.businessdictionary.com/definition/collaboration.html

ii   https://wave.google.com/wave/?pli=1

iii http://dropbox.com

iv http://mu.wordpress.org

v   https://www.yammer.com

vi http://www.vialect.com

vii http://www.zdnet.com/blog/btl/forrester-email-may-be-here-to-stay-but-it-definitely-needs-an-overhaul/35114?tag=readInner;readability-content

viii http://tools.ietf.org/html/rfc561

ix http://www.zimbra.com

x   http://www.sfgate.com

xi http://www.nytimes.com/2010/08/26/technology/internet/26google.html?_r=1

xii http://enterprise2blog.com/2010/07/the-social-wall-springs-a-leak/

xiii http://www.fewclix.com/

xiv http://www.computerworld.com/s/article/9144818/FewClix_e_mail_plug_in_may_help_you_love_Lotus_Notes_again_

xv http://www.xobni.com/

xvi http://www.microsoft.com/piracy/reporting/default.aspx

Chapter 18

FINDING THE RIGHT PEOPLE AND PARTNERS

Adventure is just bad planning.

—Roald Amundsen

More than ever, today no company is an island. The labor market, economic forces, and technology trends discussed in Chapter 3 make isolation virtually impossible—and certainly undesirable. Because of these factors, many if not most businesses today deal with each of the following groups:

- Employees
- Consultants
- Partners
- Contractors
- Vendors[1]

As we have seen, New Small companies are no exception to this rule. They maintain close relationships with these different players. But, in comparison to larger companies, the nature of these relationships at the New Small is somehow different. These relationships are more important,

---

[1] I collectively refer to employees, consultants, partners, contractors, and vendors in this chapter as *players*.

sensitive, and—should that relationship sour—potentially destructive. Remember that, at their core, these are small businesses. It's no exaggeration to say that one failed venture, ill-advised partnership, or bad hire could mean the death of the company.

New Small companies are not like the massive organizations that can afford—*and even expect*—a decent percentage of their relationships to disappoint. Although big companies also suffer from these letdowns, their size means that they are, generally speaking, better positioned to withstand them. Fuentek's Laura Schoppe echoes this sentiment:

> At large companies, one bad hire may go unnoticed for quite a while and, depending on the circumstances, may not do a great deal of damage in the whole scheme of things. At small companies like ours, however, the same bad hire can have a devastating impact. Short-term costs such as the salary of the unproductive employee can be significant, but the long-term ramifications can be ruinous. These potentially include lost business opportunities, a negative impact on team dynamics, or a permanently damaged reputation with a major client.

Despite the inherent risks, New Small companies march onward, leaning heavily on various players in a wide variety of capacities. But how do they find the right players with which to do business? As we have seen throughout Part II, this is often easier said than done. Many would-be employees or contractors are simply not cut out to work with these progressive small businesses. Although it can be difficult, New Small companies have no choice: they simply must find experts capable of handling often complicated and nebulous tasks and ongoing responsibilities.

Let's see how they do it.

Employees

Many books have been written about attracting, retaining, and motivating the right people. Finding the right folks is much more art than science. There's no secret sauce. Irrespective of company size, sometimes the most promising new hires just don't work out. Here, the New Small is just like every other company. Whether publicly or privately held, big or small, in one industry or another, sometimes companies just plain get it wrong. Consider Hanover Pediatric, for example. You saw in Chapter 7 how several times the company has had to part ways with people who, just a few months before, seemed to be perfect fits.

Six Key Traits

Those drawn to—and most successful working with and for—the New Small tend to exhibit the following characteristics:

- Low maintenance
- Willingness to help others
- Ability to wear multiple hats
- Comfort with ambiguity
- Multiple skills
- Willingness to learn

Let's look at each in more detail.

Low Maintenance

I'm hardly the first to observe that managing low-maintenance folks is fundamentally easier than managing their high-maintenance counterparts. Nowhere is this truer than at the New Small, whose owners and employees tend to have plenty of real work to do. As Holly Lewis and Drew Zima from Hanover Pediatric know all too well (Chapter 6), the New Small is no place for employees who require constant handholding, especially for mundane tasks. Employees who constantly bring their personal issues to work are also poor fits. This is not to say that the New Small is comprised of heartless owners who don't care about their employees' problems. On the contrary, these small environments allow people to get to know one another very well, perhaps better than at large companies. At the same time, though, independent folks who leave their personal baggage at home do much better.

Willingness to Help Others

As discussed in Chapter 17, real collaboration is absolutely essential at the New Small. Effectively working with others is a *sine qua non*. Employees don't help each other out because they have to; they do it because they want to. You're not likely to find folks unwilling to show colleagues how something works or solve a problem. On the contrary, they actually enjoy what they're doing; they're not threatened by sharing knowledge. This is a refreshing change for those used to working in highly guarded workplaces in which people keep their cards close to their vests out of fear, insecurity, or some other personal reason.

Ability to Wear Multiple Hats

Perhaps the biggest distinction between New Small employees and their counterparts in large companies is in the definition of roles. Big companies tend to have many departments, each of which is comprised of people with different responsibilities, experiences, skills, and interests. What's more, they often have different goals. Rare is the large company in which everyone is on the same page about what needs to be done, much less how to do it.

As a general rule, New Small employees just don't look at the world in this way. There are fewer—if any—formal departments, and it's not uncommon for things to suddenly change, forcing people to take on different responsibilities. You're not likely to hear the words, "That's not my job" at any of these companies. In fact, employees actually enjoy doing different things. They like being lynchpins.

Comfort with Ambiguity

Part of wearing multiple hats is a fundamental comfort with ambiguity. This is not to say that every day is an adventure. Although business varies from day to day and week to week, Chef Tony knows when to expect the dinner crowd. To some extent, William Hurley of Chaotic Moon can manage his company's workload by agreeing to take on a limited number of mobile development projects. Regardless, these are very dynamic work environments. Things happen. You won't find detailed job descriptions or formal schedules; these are the antitheses of strict union shop workplaces.

Multiple Skills

As we saw in Chapter 13, Laura Schoppe intentionally hires people who can do more than one thing. After all, it's hard to wear multiple hats if you know how to put only one on. This is not to say that New Small employees do everything on every day. These are not completely anarchic environments in which anything goes. However, employees often need to pinch hit because of business needs, personal circumstances, or some other type of crisis. Employees who can muddle their way through something until the incumbent returns—without causing irreparable harm—provide enormous value to New Small companies.

Willingness to Learn

Finally and perhaps most important, New Small employees need to enjoy learning on the job. Why do these companies place a primal importance on nearly constant learning? In part, the answer stems from the fact that the New Small is not a complacent lot. We saw many times in Part II how readily these companies move in a different direction, abandoning one application, platform, or system because another comes along that's better suited to their needs than the status quo. Companies like this cannot afford to be held back by stubborn or change-resistant folks. Legitimate objections and concerns are one thing; outright refusal is quite another.

On occasion, learning takes the form of classroom instruction, as we saw in Chapter 8, with Voices.com sending its employees—at considerable cost—to Toronto for a week of Salesforce.com training. More often, however, this knowledge transfer takes place on the job—or after hours. Employees roll up their sleeves and figure something out.

It's folly to think that *all* employees want to learn. Some people simply want to check in each day; not everyone is looking for a challenge at work. For those who embrace opportunities to improve their skill sets, the New Small offers another critical element: *employees who go out on a limb are not crucified for making mistakes.* These companies understand that not all projects and endeavors proceed in a linear fashion. Employees who attempt to build a better mousetrap might stumble, even though their minds and hearts are in the right place. In other words, when they work in encouraging and risk-tolerant environments, employees need not worry about catastrophic results for making mistakes. In the long run, they'll figure things out, benefitting themselves and their companies in the process.

The Bottom Line

A certain type of personality flourishes at New Small companies: one that embraces risk, uncertainty, opportunities to learn, and chances to wear multiple hats. Those who prefer to do the same thing every day don't do well in these dynamic, often unpredictable environments. New Small companies know that it's best to hire slow and fire fast.

Consultants

Many small business owners view consultants as necessary evils. After more than 10 years in the field, I have been called worse. Much worse. Many owners and founders of the New Small have worked with consultants before, especially if they came from large corporations before going out on their own. What's more, many companies are somewhat justifiably reluctant to employ consultants. I'll be the first to admit that, as a group, we have a less-than-stellar reputation—and it's not hard to understand why. Consider stories like this.

In June of 2010, Marin County in California filed suit against consulting firm Deloitte and Touche (D&T) for $30M USD over a botched SAP[2] implementation. According to an article from *ComputerWorld*:

> The 38-page complaint alleges that Deloitte was lying when the company promised to assemble a team of its "best resources" for the project and when it claimed to have "deep SAP and public sector knowledge" when marketing itself to the county.

---

[2] SAP makes very large and powerful Enterprise Resource Planning (ERP) software used by some of the biggest organizations in the world.

Deloitte's misrepresentation of facts resulted in a defectively designed and deficiently implemented project that resulted in the county having to pay millions of dollars to remedy, the lawsuit alleged.

Meanwhile, Deloitte is claiming that it fulfilled all of its obligations under the contract. The company filed an administrative claim last week with the Marin County Board of Supervisors seeking more than $444,000 in unpaid dues, and an additional $111,000 in late charges.[i]

Ouch. Unfortunately, things like this happen, despite what many software salespeople and slick consultants would like potential clients to believe.

A Few Notes

I want to make a few things very clear here. First of all, not all consultants and firms are created equal. As mentioned in Chapter 1, small businesses are very unlikely to use *large* consulting firms, and D&T is one of the largest in the world. The Five Enablers are specifically built for easy deployment and adoption, even for small businesses. In many cases, as shown in Part II, these technologies have obviated the need for 1990s-style consulting engagements that take years to complete. Second, the Marin project was simply enormous, as evinced by its budget. Big projects often result in big failures. Third, I can tell you from personal experience that rarely is the big bad consulting firm solely at fault when lawsuits are filed. There's typically a great deal of blame to go around—such as for poor communication of requirements, and so on. Fourth, I cited the Marin-D&T example only because it occurred recently. D&T is hardly the only large consulting firm to face legal action, nor is it proof that these firms (much less D&T in particular) are inherently incompetent or greedy.

The preceding example illustrates one critical point: although not perfect, New Small companies have much better batting averages in adopting the Five Enablers compared to large organizations. Blame aside for a moment, most small businesses—and certainly New Small companies—*can't* let a project get out of hand nearly to the extent that Marin County did.

Case in point: an employee recognition and rewards company by the name of O.C. Tanner, profiled in the book *Small Giants*—originally mentioned in Chapter 5. Bo Burlingham tells the story of how O.C. Tanner struggled to implement an enterprise resource planning (ERP) system:

Like most companies that put in ERP systems, O.C. Tanner initially relied on consultants to do the installation. "At one point, we have eighty-five consultants from Arthur Andersen working on it," Murdock[3] said. "But the consultants had it wrong. They said it was a project with a beginning and an end. It was more than a project. It was a huge transition. They miscalculated the time line. They didn't understand our business or its complexities. Finally, we fired all the consultants and did it ourselves."

O.C. Tanner saw things spiraling out of control and took decisive action. Of course, this doesn't prove that consultants aren't necessary across the board. In fact, I have never encountered an organization that has successfully implemented a major enterprise system entirely on its own. The key point here is that well-run small companies do not let massive IT projects continue to run behind schedule and over budget.

Does the New Small Need Traditional Consultants?

Today, most companies are lean by necessity. Many can't afford to hire the people with which to successfully lead organizational change and the adoption of new technologies. Consultants primarily exist to get a specific job done when the organization lacks the internal expertise to do so. Because of trends discussed in Chapter 2, the need for companies of all sizes to hire consultants for particular jobs and projects is not going away anytime soon.

As for the ideal dynamic today, the Five Enablers differ from their predecessors. On technology projects in the 1990s, for example, large organizations typically defined hundreds of requirements and went through protracted RFP processes in search of the best software and system integrator. Long and expensive consulting engagements often miss their marks. This was essentially the subject of my first book, *Why New Systems Fail*.

The New Small understands that the ideal environment for using consultants involves collaboration, transparency, and the alignment of high-level objectives. For example, garnering a better understanding of customer retention might be the goal of a project, not checking off pages and pages of detailed requirements from the old system and ignoring powerful new features of the new one.

Consultants in an Age of Google

The New Small strikes a balance between doing things on their own and realizing that it's much easier—and typically less expensive—to outsource a job or use consultants for the same purpose.

Now, some of you may be thinking, "I'm pretty net-savvy. I can Google any of the technologies or vendors in this book and figure things out on

---

[3] Kent Murdock, the third CEO of O.C Tanner, a company that specializes in employee recognition awards and programs.

my own. I don't need high-priced consultants telling me what I already know." And to be honest, maybe you're right. Based on your background, you might know more about emerging technologies—and how to deploy them—than I do.

As we have seen, the New Small is extremely capable and independent. At the same time, though, it is pragmatic. Its owners know that they cannot completely *and independently* change their companies' technology backbone without significant risk and incident. The New Small knows that the successful adoption of a powerful new technology hinges on using people who know what they're doing—and have done it before. These companies may not need to hire a formal consultant. Perhaps a friend can lend a hand, as we saw with Marisa Smith of The Whole Brain Group helping Megan Torrance of Torrance Learning. Maybe a family member can assist, as Holly Lewis's husband Ben did at Hanover Pediatric. In any event, the New Small does not slam the door on using consultants.

The Bottom Line

The New Small understands that consultants are just like any other people, including employees and temps. Some are better, more honest, more affordable, and more willing to share than others. The New Small does not let a bad experience with a consultant color its view of the group—and the important roles that they often play transforming businesses.

Think of it this way: would you vow never to see a doctor again because your physician was a bit rude to you? I sure hope that you don't skip the dentist's office because you were once kept waiting for an hour.

Vendors

As we saw in the case of Fuentek and Voices.com, sometimes New Small companies need to replace systems, applications, or technologies that have reached the ends of the useful lives. Even in niche spaces, there are often many proven alternatives. What's more, with the Five Enablers, development of a new alternative is not necessarily difficult and horribly expensive, as PeerPoint discovered in Chapter 9. This begs the question: how does the New Small select the right vendor?

Although there's no one right answer, the New Small considers several factors when selecting vendors to address its technology needs. At a minimum, the New Small avoids onerous contracts. David Ciccarelli of Voices.com signed a one-year deal with NetSuite; he surely would not have signed a longer one with an unproved application, no matter how promising. In fact, some SaaS vendors and technology service vendors now offer 30-day contracts, allowing unhappy clients to freely walk away from arrangements. The New Small avoids long-term deals and expensive licensing agreements, especially during first-time negotiations.

Savings can come from areas as prosaic as phone service, as Alan Berkson, head of the Intelligist Group[ii] points out:

> These days, small businesses can get services with more features, at lower cost, and without making long-term commitments. For example, a decade ago, phone systems cost about $10K to $15K just to install. Telco vendors insisted upon multiyear from their clients. Fast forward to today. Now small businesses can get up and running with sophisticated phone systems for as little as $20 per month per phone line running through an existing high-speed [Internet] connection.

The New Small looks for savings wherever and whenever it can, especially when initially selecting vendors. Although the savings can be dramatic, perhaps the greatest benefit to these companies is maximum flexibility if business needs change. These companies are not beholden to long-term contracts that no longer meet their needs.

Partners

As discussed throughout this book, New Small companies have a strong need for partners, perhaps because of their size. However, the wrong choice of partners could have devastating consequences. As a result, the New Small chooses carefully among the many opportunities for strategic relationships, making sure that all parties are in accord. These companies don't skimp on due diligence. For example, Chaotic Moon entered into a mutually beneficial—and ultimately very successful—partnership with FlightAware to improve the first version of its mobile app. The relationship between The Whole Brain Group and Torrance Learning has continued to be fruitful because it meets both companies' objectives. Marisa Smith, head of The Whole Brain Group, describes partnerships as follows:

> The mentality at The Whole Brain Group can best be described as "it takes a village." We expect this with our employees, contractors, and partners. We prefer to excel at a few things and work with partners who excel in complementary areas. We find that this makes everyone more capable of succeeding. Our favorite partners send us referrals for projects and potential employees. They share best practices and identify opportunities for collaboration for one simple reason: they aren't just thinking of themselves all the time. And we do the same for them.[iii]

What's more, the New Small isn't afraid to pull the plug on unsuccessful partnerships. The founders would rather do without a particular service than continue to work with companies that don't embody their beliefs and advance their causes. Harmony is especially important in long-term partnerships.

Contractors

For a variety of legal reasons, companies of any size incur less risk by using contractors instead of employees. U.S. labor laws cover a wide variety of areas, including medical leave, discrimination, whistle blowing, and disability. By and large, these laws do not apply to contractors. Although employees have more rights relative to contractors, the latter are hardly unprotected targets of verbal or physical abuse, discrimination, and the like. Companies can rid themselves of contractors much more easily—and with far fewer potential consequences—than employees.

But not all contractors are created equal, as we learned in Chapter 12 with Torrance Learning. Some can talk a good game, charging above-market rates for a set of skills that they may not ultimately possess. Even in a tough economy, the best contractors often have their pick of opportunities.

Five Key Traits

The New Small finds contractors who exhibit the following characteristics:

- Openly communicate their availability
- Make themselves expendable
- Provide frequent updates
- Know when to punt
- Honestly estimate and report hours worked

Let's look at each in more detail.

Openly Communicate Their Availability

Contractors often enjoy the flexibility of being able to take assignments that meet their personal, professional, geographic, and financial needs. Whereas employees have to show up at work every day, many contractors have their fingers in multiple pies. On a personal level, I take consulting assignments but sometimes decline them when I'm in the middle of a major project—like the book you are reading.

To be sure, contractors often possess very specific skill sets—not to mention solid reputations with the New Small. As such, they advise their potential clients well in advance that they're engaged on another assignment and won't be available. This allows the New Small to make alternative arrangements, eliminating the need to scramble when a business need arises. Although the contractor-client relationship is always tenuous, basic courtesy and the Golden Rule go a long way.

Make Themselves Expendable

The best contractors transfer knowledge to anyone and everyone. They don't hoard key pieces of information, processes, or tricks. This may seem counterintuitive to some. After all, by revealing some of their secrets, they are ostensibly risking their own future earnings. Although there's some merit to the argument for contractors keeping the tricks of their trade to themselves, the New Small will simply not continue using contractors who protect their secret sauce. Ultimately, the New Small has to answer questions about the nature of the work long after the contractor has moved on to different engagements. Constantly replying, "I don't know" to a client's queries puts the New Small in an untenable position.

Provide Frequent Updates

Nothing frustrates companies—and the New Small in particular—more than not knowing where things stand. Organizations bring in contractors to complete a specific and often time-sensitive task. Even an update of "still waiting on X" is preferable to saying nothing.

Also, because most of the New Small use collaborative tools, an over-reliance upon e-mail tends to confuse people more than convey timely updates. Most collaborative tools allow administrators to easily add new users, whether that user is an official employee or not.

Know When to Punt

The best contractors know their limitations and will burn bridges with the New Small if they falsely claim to be qualified for a job. There just aren't too many places to hide in the New Small, and shoddy work becomes apparent pretty quickly to everyone at the company. What's more, people talk. The contractor who misrepresents his skills runs the risk of alienating his current—and future—clients. The New Small has no problem cutting the cord with those who do not meet its needs; these companies respect those who honestly refuse work based on availability, other projects, and skills that are incompatible with the job.

Honestly Estimate and Report Hours Worked

Sometimes even ostensibly trustworthy contractors fudge numbers, something that Megan Torrance learned in Chapter 12. This is arguably easier—if still unethical—when that contractor is working remotely. These less-than-ethical contractors take advantage of the New Small's general aversion to micromanage.

Fudging can also apply to estimates of the hours required to complete a task. To be sure, it's damn near impossible to precisely predict in advance the number of hours required to write a report, develop or customize an application, or the like. The New Small understands this, because it often has to craft estimates. The best contractors provide a list of explicit assumptions and a range. Further, they would rather estimate high and come in low than vice versa.

The Bottom Line

The New Small knows that the best contractors don't act like hired guns. Rather, they go above and beyond the call of duty, broaching issues and having difficult conversations as needed. The best contractors don't look at a particular engagement as a one-time endeavor, burning bridges in the process; they approach the job as the start of a potentially prosperous long-term relationship with very progressive and innovative companies.

SUMMARY

This chapter has covered a great deal of ground, providing tips on finding the best employees, consultants, vendors, partners, and contractors. To be sure, the characteristics of these groups and individuals vary, as do the circumstances in which each is used. However, the New Small ethos rarely wavers. These companies expect value for their dollar and will quickly move in another direction if that isn't happening. They simply won't tolerate deficient performance, dishonest or onerous terms, or other conditions often accepted—at least to some extent—at larger organizations.

Endnotes

i   http://www.computerworld.com/s/article/9177655/Deloitte_hit_with_30M_lawsuit_over_ERP_project
ii   http://www.intelligistgroup.com/
iii Personal conversation, 8/19/2010

Chapter 19

NEW SMALL GENERAL MANAGEMENT PRINCIPLES

All progress occurs because people dare to be different.

—Harry Millner

Technology continues to change while the business imperative remains constant. We saw this in Chapter 1 with Kranzberg's Six Laws. Businesses continue to adopt different technologies at different times for different reasons based on different needs. This has always been the case. Indeed, the vast majority of my writing over the last two years has focused on one central question: how do companies effectively deploy and use technology?

Although many small businesses have dabbled with the Five Enablers, relatively few have embraced them nearly to the same extent as the New Small. I would put the laggards into three general categories.

First, there are those that are open to emerging technologies but lack the time, resources, budgets, or knowledge to adopt them. These might be precarious new businesses or precarious old businesses trying their best in a difficult economy.

Second, many small businesses are still swimming against the stream. They are actively opposed to different—and often better, more efficient, and less expensive—ways of doing things. This is not to say that resistance to new things is the exclusive domain of small businesses entrenched in their ways. I have encountered more than my fair share of companies of all sizes stuck in their ruts, in many cases victims of their own success. Returning to the Preface for a moment, remember my friend Tim and *The Innovator's Dilemma*.

Third, some small businesses are merely skimming the surface with the Five Enablers. For example, consider companies that have established accounts on different social media sites. Because they have set up a Facebook fan page and have registered with Twitter, these businesses claim that they are doing social media. Paradoxically, many of these same companies concurrently forbid their employees from using Facebook or Twitter on company time. They just don't understand that the use of social technologies is not a box for a list item that can be checked off and then ignored.

As discussed in Chapter 3, part of the resistance to the Five Enablers—and technology in general—stems from one simple fact: they force many folks to break out of their comfort zones. For now, consider two examples. First, cloud computing means that IT departments no longer control their data and applications. Second, social technologies allow employees to easily waste time.

New Small companies mitigate these risks, and it's time to look at how. This chapter covers the major management principles to which the New Small subscribes. We'll see that, by and large, these companies do the following considerably better than others:

- Manage up
- Accept failure and learn how to fail well
- Admit mistakes
- Remove problem employees
- Find a tolerable level of risk
- Avoid egolock
- Delegate
- Recognize the primary importance of people
- Act decisively but find acceptable compromises
- Minimize the Waterfall
- Start small and expand cautiously
- Keep it simple
- Keep customers and employees happy
- Use add-on tools
- Embrace change

- Employ hybrids
- Tread carefully with customizations
- Recognize the different focuses of consultants
- Understand the nuances of technology projects[1]

The New Small is not wedded to antiquated technologies and ways of doing things. In fact, as you can probably tell from having read about them, they embrace change and *enjoy* finding ways to do things better, even if that means retiring an application that has served the company well. The New Small doesn't stop there, though. Let's cover some of their general management practices.

Manage Up

Part II of the book showed us how New Small companies introduce new technologies in a manner very different from other types of companies—even many small ones. For one, they don't exclusively rely upon a top-down approach. At companies like Fuentek and Torrance Learning, new tools are often introduced organically, from the bottom up. Employees are encouraged to experiment with free and open source software (FOSS). If those experiments turn out to be successful, those tools become part of the fabric of the company.

This is not to say that the use of the Five Enablers at the New Small is *completely* user-driven—nor should it be. Imagine the chaos that would result if 10 employees used 10 different applications for accounting or CRM. However, for collaborative tools such as Yammer, trying before buying makes complete sense on many levels. Like many companies, Yammer operates on a freemium model, allowing for mass adoption of the tool within a company before formal contracts are signed and checks are cut.

Accept Failure and Learn How to Fail Well

Google is simply a fascinating company to watch for all sorts of reasons. This is especially true for the New Small. As we have seen, many New Small companies use Google applications and services to run their businesses. Forget its ubiquity; Google is actually a really big company with nearly 20,000 employees, and it makes billions of dollars.[i] Astonishingly, it often acts like a small business, and it does have something in common with the New Small: Google isn't afraid to fail.

---

[1] It's not lost on me that Chapter 19 contains 19 management principles. I'm not trying to be cute here. Pure serendipity, I promise.

In fact, Google fails at loads of projects. Consider a few biggies:

- Its social media website, Orkut, has failed to catch on in many countries, although there are some notable exceptions.[ii] To be sure, no one is mistaking it for Facebook.[iii]

- In August of 2010, Google announced the discontinuation of Google Wave as a standalone product.[iv] In a post on the company's official blog, Urs Hölzle, senior vice president, operations and Google fellow, noted that, "Wave has not seen the user adoption we would have liked."[v]

- Its public relations blunders are well documented, including its overreach on Google Maps (with facial recognition) and the initial incarnation of Gmail lacking a Delete button.

These examples prove that not everything Google touches turns to gold. By all accounts, the company has hundreds of projects in different stages of development at any given point. Some degree of failure is to be expected in creating something new, something great. Rare is the unalloyed success. Even the company's wildly popular and profitable search engine has been an evolution, as Ken Auletta writes in *Googled: The End of the World as We Know It*.

No company *likes* to fail, and New Small companies are certainly no exception to that rule. However, as Diane Von Furstenberg once said, "Life is a risk." That is, New Small companies realize that, to be successful, they must occasionally go out on a limb. The key is to take *intelligent* risks. The New Small understands this.

These companies also know the futility in trying to avoid failure altogether. That's pretty much impossible. More apropos are questions such as these:

- How can we minimize the chance of failure?

- If we do fail, then what can we learn from it to avoid the same mistakes next time?

- What are the pros and cons of taking on a project, client, or new technology?

- What represents an *acceptable* risk?

As we saw in Part II, the New Small doesn't shy away from risks. It carefully balances risks with rewards, knowing well before undertaking any major endeavor that its outcome is uncertain.

Admit Mistakes

The New Small readily admits when it makes mistakes and focuses on correcting them and ensuring that they don't happen again. Consider what happened to me on the penultimate day of a consulting engagement with a very large organization in early 2010. This would *never* happen at the New Small. The project manager (PM) literally dropped 10 custom report requests on my desk that I had requested several times over a three-month span. His timing couldn't have been worse; I was in the middle of another crisis at the time that involved employee paychecks. The PM offered a lame apology but quickly added that he knew that these reports were "*ad hoc, not enterprise reports.*"

The New Small doesn't play games like this or rely on semantics; they just call a spade a spade. Equivocating merely increases the amount of damage done to one's credibility and reputation.

Remove Problem Employees

The New Small differs from larger companies on another level as well: the former does not tolerate high-maintenance folks. Large corporations are often reluctant to cut the cord with a problematic employee, preferring instead to move him or her to a place in which the damage is minimized. There really are no such roles for the New Small; each employee and contractor has the ability to harm the company, so New Small companies avoid carrying dead weight. As Martin Traub-Werner, president of Raybec Communications, says:

> When a company has fewer than 20 employees, it is very visible when one isn't pulling 100 percent of his weight. The fewer the employees, the more visible—and painful—that situation can be. This underscores the importance of hiring for fit. It's critical for everyone to easily deal with ambiguity and, if necessary, quickly change directions. We've had some spectacular hires and some shaky ones. I've learned that the smaller you are, the more important it is to give employees a sense of purpose. If they lose that sense of purpose, or if you don't reiterate it on a regular basis, it's very hard to keep them pulling for you.

Find a Tolerable Level of Risk

I have worked with many types of organizations. As a general rule, I have found that they fall into three categories with respect to risk tolerance:

- Zero-risk organizations
- Oblivious organizations
- Acceptable-risk organizations

Let's examine each with respect to the New Small.

Zero-Risk Organizations

Several years ago, I worked on a project for an organization that would not do anything if there was even the smallest risk. To that end, it employed a full-time internal auditor to carefully monitor all IT projects. He reported his findings to the CIO.

So, you may ask. What's wrong with this?

In the abstract, nothing. But the process of deploying a new technology is never abstract. Actions have consequences. The project consistently suffered as the implementation team attempted to address his concerns, and he had a bunch. Sure, many of them were well founded, but an organization cannot concurrently assuage an auditor's concerns and make up time on a delayed project.

The New Small understands that introducing the Five Enablers to replace antiquated equivalents—or to add new functionality altogether—by definition introduces *some* level of risk. They realize that even doing nothing does not eliminate risk. The New Small is wise enough to know that risk cannot be eliminated; it can only be mitigated.

Oblivious Organizations

Now, consider the other end of the spectrum. This type of organization is perhaps best epitomized by one of my previous clients. The mentality could be described as: there is no such thing as risk. Period. The company routinely implemented new systems in this haphazard manner. According to lifers at the company, *every* system that the company implemented in the last 10 years was managed the same way. Senior management instructed them to proceed as if nothing is every wrong.

This was a shock to just about every consultant on the project. Good consultants have been trained to identify and *attempt* to minimize risks throughout projects. Sadly, the CIO did not want us "editorializing." Translation: keep your mouths shut. We don't like naysayers.

This is just bad management, plain and simple. The consultant or employee who broached a legitimate issue was silenced, and if he or she persisted, was removed. Paradoxically, those who kept their mouths shut had to answer questions such as, "Why didn't you tell us about this?" Organizations like these have a high employee rejection rate; it takes a certain personality type to accept the risk of lawsuits, audits, and generally appearing foolish as you expose yourself and others to excessive levels of risk.

Acceptable-Risk Organizations

The New Small falls comfortably into this category. These companies understand risk and possess more than a modicum of perspective. They take serious risks seriously. Further, key people understand the time-sensitive nature of many problems. They know that risk is always a function of information, time, and money.

Of course, no organization has unlimited information, time, and money. Trade-offs need to be made. Fortunately, most New Small companies fall into the category of acceptable-risk organizations. They understand the nature of risk and are likely to make the right calls—or at least the best calls possible given imperfect information. Things won't always go flawlessly, but these realists create contingency plans in the event that things break bad.[2]

Avoid Egolock

The New Small avoids egolock, defined by BuzzWhack as "a situation in which an executive makes a bad decision, refuses to admit it, and holds steadfast until the bitter end."[vi] Like most consultants, I have regularly encountered egolock, especially when I had to tell people that their company's current technologies may be inadequate. In 2005, I did some consulting for a fairly large telecommunications company that had outgrown its internal systems. I remember being nervous about a pending talk with a mid-level manager who had built many of those systems. Call him Steven. I had to tell Steven that those systems were probably not sufficient to support the company's long-term growth objectives. When I delivered the news, Steven surprisingly said something to the effect of, "I thought so. No worries."

I was floored. Although he had spent *years* developing these proprietary systems, he understood the limitations of his "babies" and opted to get on board with a more robust enterprise solution. I had grown so accustomed to egolock that I had come to expect it. My fears were misplaced.

Although egolock is common at many midsize and large organizations, it is exceedingly rare at New Small companies, if not nonexistent. These owners and founders do not stick to their guns when faced with evidence that something isn't working—and cannot easily be triaged. We saw this in Chapter 13, as Laura Schoppe of Fuentek retired a system that was

---

[2] *Breaking Bad* is the amazing show on AMC about a high school chemistry teacher who, after discovering that he has terminal cancer, begins to produce crystal meth.

admittedly dear to her heart. It was the right business move and, personal feelings aside, she knew that it simply had to be done.

Delegate

Many extremely bright, dedicated, and capable small business owners simply have a hard time delegating. Call it a God or Superman Complex,[3] but some people just don't know their own limitations—or even believe that they have any. For two reasons, it's somewhat understandable when successful folks have great difficulty ceding control. First, consider the fact that most small businesses fail, even during normal economic conditions. The U.S. Small Business Administration (SBA) estimates that more than 50 percent of small businesses fail within the first five years.[vii] One can only imagine those odds in a dismal economy. Despite unfavorable odds, many driven individuals persevere and build relatively successful companies from the ground up. Often, the owners of these businesses become accustomed to doing *everything* themselves. They just don't think to ask for help. Second, some have sought the assistance of others only to get burned by disappointing employees, bad consultants, or back-stabbing partners. The burnt hand teaches best, as they say.

It's always fun to speculate about people's motivations. Perhaps these anti-delegators feel invincible or have fundamental control and trust issues.[4] Some of them may justify this stubborn and unhealthy isolation in the name of cost savings. Maybe they believe that old adage "If you want something done right, you have to do it yourself." And, who knows? Maybe for some people, good help is really *that* difficult to find, at least in the short term. As a general rule, however, these are all just rationalizations. By insisting upon doing everything—up to and including less valuable work, anti-delegators typically inhibit the growth of their businesses.

Throughout this book, we have seen how the New Small successfully uses employees, consultants, partners, contractors, and vendors to play a wide variety of valuable roles. I will never criticize anyone for working hard, and by this point, it should be obvious that I have tremendous admiration for people who hang out their own shingles. It ain't easy out there. Still, something just doesn't make sense when overworked small business owners insist upon doing absolutely everything themselves—from their own accounting to trash disposal.

---

[3] It's simply impossible for me to use the term *God Complex* without mentioning Alec Baldwin's amazing scene in *Malice*. See http://www.youtube.com/watch?v=8g2dkDh4ov4.

[4] I should point out here that I would much rather work with people who want to do everything than with people who want to do nothing.

Everyone needs help, sometimes—even me. I consider myself a pretty capable guy and, over the past five years, have hired a book cover designer, several editors, a financial consultant, an accountant, a web designer, and many others to help me run my little company.

Let's return to 90s Sites for a moment, originally discussed in Chapter 5. If you look at the primitive websites of many businesses, I can pretty much guarantee you that they fall into one of the three following categories:

- They have been built by people too frugal or obstinate to hire proper web designers.

- The owners believe that their websites don't really matter. Put simply, these people are wrong. Although these companies "save" a few tax-deductible dollars,[5] they probably cost themselves 10 times that much in lost sales and referrals.

- The owners are simply unaware of the presence of powerful and user-friendly tools that enable easy website and content creation.

Brass tacks: Today, there's just no reason for any company to lack an effective web presence. In the words of Chris Nakea, head of Nakea[viii], a leading provider of robust, interconnected, easy-to-use online tools, "Websites are an integral part of the way we do business these days—and have been for quite some time. In the past, businesses used to spend thousands of dollars to build a website and a substantial amount of money on monthly maintenance. With today's new tools and services, even non-technical users have the ability to create rich, functional websites for just a few dollars per month."

Anti-delegators live by the same clocks as the rest of us. They can work only 24 hours per day. In addition to being really tired, they have less time to do their most important work: generate new sales, leads, and clients. New Small owners know which activities are most important and where they should spend their time. They recognize the opportunity cost associated with personally doing low-value activities and neglecting key tasks such as website design and content creation. Further, while occasionally pinch-hitting is necessary, they know two things:

- They cannot possibly do everything.

- Their businesses can flourish only through prioritization and using the considerable skills of other groups and people.

---

[5] Don't let anyone tell you that you need to spend thousands of dollars for a professional website.

Recognize the Primary Importance of People

As discussed throughout this book, we are living in an exciting time with regard to emerging technologies. Companies can build new tools or choose from a vast array of existing ones. The web is in full force, as the shackles of desktops, laptops, traditional networks, and client-server architecture are being removed. The New Small understands that we have entered a period in which just about anything is possible on a technology front.

Yes, the continued importance of people and intelligent decision making cannot be understated. Put another way, just because a company can deploy a technology doesn't mean that it should. The Five Enablers are *very* flexible and can be implemented in myriad ways—some far superior to others. Because of this, the role of intelligent business decisions regarding design, architecture, user interface (UI), and the like is *more* important than before, not less. The New Small gets it: people matter, big time.

Act Decisively but Find Acceptable Compromises

We have seen throughout the book how Fuentek, NSI Partners, and Voices.com took decisive action when their existing technologies no longer met their needs. Rather than hemming and hawing on the future direction of the company, each went in a specific direction—refusing to ceaselessly debate the pros and cons of every conceivable alternative. In each case, the costs of inaction exceeded the costs of action.

When undertaking any project, it's foolish to ignore very real problems and mindlessly plow ahead. (I have seen firsthand many large organizations make this fundamental mistake.) New Small companies understand that the best-laid plans often go awry. In many instances, projects can recoup valuable time if features and functionality are removed from the immediate plan and postponed until a later time. The New Small determines in advance which features are essential and which are merely desirable. If necessary, these companies drop the latter for the overall good of the project and the company.

Minimize the Waterfall

At a very high level, all technologies can be deployed in one of two ways:

- **Via a Waterfall or sequential methodology**—This involves gathering business and technical requirements, designing the system, testing it, and activating it all at once. Development and implementation progress in a linear fashion, culminating in a big bang. In theory, there should be no issues. In practice, this is never the case.

- **Via iterative or agile methods**—This involves multiple releases of the product or application. Each version provides new functionality and fixes to previously discovered issues. There may never be a "final" version of the product.

Although there are exceptions, we have seen that New Small companies strongly favor rolling out new tools and products via agile methods. Torrance Learning in Chapter 12 served as a particularly instructive example. Iterative development and deployment offer a number of advantages, perhaps the most significant of which is the ability to catch problems much sooner than via the Waterfall method.

Large organizations are typically reluctant to cut functionality from Waterfall-based projects for one simple reason: there's typically (and mistakenly) a now or never mentality. In other words, key stakeholders believe that if all functionality isn't present when the application goes live, they'll never see it.

This hazard may or may not be real. Delays, budget cuts, internal politics, and key employee turnover often mean that the best intentions regarding future rollouts are derailed. I'd argue, however, that continuing down a parlous path because you're afraid that internal obstacles will prevent you later on is a fundamental misstep.

New Small companies grasp the concept of phases. They are more likely to sacrifice "nice to have" functionality if it's likely to increase organizational risk. Project teams, developers, and senior management know that the next version of the software (or the next phase of the project) can easily incorporate enhancements. There's no burning-plank mentality here: there will be a next version, and it will come soon.

Start Small and Expand Cautiously

As corollary of *avoid the Waterfall*, the New Small is loath to *boil the ocean*. When deploying the Five Enablers, rarely does it make sense to try to do absolutely everything at once. It's better to have one little victory than a bunch of failures. The New Small ensures that the scope of a project makes sense from the beginning. Also, it extensively uses agile methods of software development and deployment.

Keep It Simple

Using the Five Enablers is not the same as flipping burgers.[6] However, it's important to keep in mind that, at least at a fundamental level, most of the Five Enablers have simple objectives, such as these:

- Improving employee communication and collaboration
- Reducing costs
- Improving the quality of information—and access to it

The New Small knows that it must remember the purpose of an emerging technology throughout a deployment. Remaining true to a mission is a good general rule of thumb. Superfluous complexity benefits no one. The New Small realizes that its business needs are probably not unique. All else being equal, these small businesses would rather make do with a generic software configuration than build an albatross that requires cumbersome and expensive maintenance and support.

Keep Customers and Employees Happy

The New Small doesn't skimp on things such as employee pay, staffing levels, or internal opportunities for advancement. These companies attempt to cultivate an egalitarian culture in the workplace. The New Small knows that there's something to be said for treating everyone with respect on a project, including external folks such as consultants. Although times may be tight, projects need to have sufficient resources. Consider this: it's hard to simultaneously flip burgers, watch the fries, and mop the floor. Imagine the difficulties with setting up and testing network security on a new application while concurrently doing your day job. Multitasking has its limits.

But keeping *everyone* happy just isn't feasible. In the words of 80s rocker Bryan Adams, "One man's nightmare is another man's dream."[7] As it applies to the Five Enablers and the delicate nature of change, I couldn't have said it better. As technology marches onward, improving the functionality of existing applications and introducing entirely new ways of doing things, not every end user is going to be happy. Within the same organization and across different ones, different people deal with change in very different ways.

New Small employees are not tied to legacy applications and outmoded processes. They are generally more open to technology changes than employees of large corporations. The latter are often wedded to a particular

---

[6] I should know. I did my nine months at McDonald's in Wyckoff, NJ, as a teenager.
[7] From his song "Heat of the Night."

way of doing things and resent having to learn something new. Many fight new technologies tooth and nail.

Such resistance doesn't fly at the New Small. As we saw repeatedly in Part II, the companies hire employees based upon both skills *and* attitude. Those employees who pose unnecessary risks don't last very long.

Use Add-On Tools

New Small companies often do not possess the resources—or the desire—to customize their applications in the traditional sense. At the same time, however, a software vendor's standard application may not meet some of its business needs. What to do? The New Small uses technology to create e-mail alerts, enable document sharing, and maximize overall collaboration. These complementary technologies improve productivity while currently minimizing complexity and the resultant strain on internal resources.

Embrace Change

Unlike many large organizations, New Small companies quickly recognize when they are not using technology in an optimal manner. What's more, they actually do something about it. Rather than take a "That's just the way we do things around here" approach, the New Small searches for and openly embraces new ways of doing things. This typically starts with the founder and cascades down to everyone else. New Small companies ask other consultants, new hires, partners, and even competitors questions, such as, "Have you seen other companies do this better?" and "How do other businesses resolve this issue?" These companies don't stop there, however. As we saw repeatedly in Part II, after assessing the problem and evaluating potential solutions, they quickly formulate plans and put them into action.

Employ Hybrids

Many companies suffer from what I call the *technical-functional disconnect*. In short, techies don't understand what business folks say or mean—and vice versa. These two groups of people typically think in vastly different terms and often use different words to communicate. A great deal is often lost in translation. Beyond fodder for *Dilbert* cartoons, this problem has derailed many technology initiatives in companies of all sizes.

New Small founders are extremely aware of this problem. To combat it, they employ people who can wear many hats and who can serve as interpreters between these two groups. In many cases, this is a techie with front-end application knowledge or the opposite: a functional end user who likes to get under the hood of applications and mess around with code.[8] We saw this with both Torrance Learning and Chaotic Moon. In essence, these folks are problem solvers. By using those with a more complete understanding of emerging technologies, New Small companies minimize the traditional technical-functional disconnect.

Tread Carefully with Customizations

Over my years as a technology consultant, I have seen many organizations mishandle the work of customizing their applications. On many a project, the functionality of a commercial, off-the-shelf (COTS) application[9] did not meet my clients' current business practices. Invariably, this would beg the thorny question, should we customize the system or change how we do things?

There's no one right answer to this question even for New Small companies. Depending on many factors, some businesses should customize their systems or applications and some should not. In either case, the New Small carefully considers the ramifications of going down that road sooner rather than later. When it's appropriate, they ensure that they have allocated the financial and human resources to effectively handle the customization.

New Small founders are certainly not above getting their hands dirty. In fact, they enjoy it. For example, consider Colin Hickey of PeerPort (profiled in Chapter 9). He is hardly a programmer by trade, but he's far from a neophyte around a keyboard. He does not want to have to rely upon external developers to make changes of basic or medium complexity. He knows enough to adopt a limited do-it-yourself (DIY) mentality. Note two fundamental differences between technologies today and those of 15 years ago:

- Getting under the hood to change some basic HTML or PHP code is very different from modifying COBOL.[10] The latter could very well cause unintended consequences in other parts of large enterprise systems.

- Depending on whether a company's apps exist in a single- or multi-tenant environment, *significant* customizations may or may not be possible. The same holds true for private or public clouds. The

---

[8] Of course, many New Small founders are hybrids themselves.
[9] *COTS* is a term defining a ready-made and available system for sale, lease, or license to anyone.
[10] COmmon Business-Oriented Language (COBOL) is a computer programming language first conceived in the 1960s.

New Small asks these kinds of questions *before* making key choices about platforms and vendors.

New Small companies typically forgo excessive and expensive customizations to their core technologies. *Staying vanilla*[11] lets them avoid the pitfalls faced by tweak-happy organizations. First, version upgrades and application patches do not break these customizations. Second, they need not rely upon that one individual who knows where the bodies were buried. This is just plain smart. We saw this in Chapter 8 with Voices.com using the widely deployed Force.com development platform to extend the native capabilities of Salesforce.com.

Recognize the Different Focuses of Consultants

Businesses often forget one fact when they engage consultants: clients and consultants often have unique and different focuses during business hours.

The Consultant

As a consultant, my focus at a client site is singular when I am engaged to implement a new system, write reports, teach a course, and so on. That is, I don't have a separate day job in the company that would divert my attention in the event of a problem with a client's current applications. Even if I did, many times I wouldn't know where to start. Issues such as these are often well beyond my scope or ability to handle:

- I don't know how to resolve an accounting issue in a client's legacy system because I have never worked with it before.
- I can't extract data from a client's application because the extraction tools are antiquated, I have no access, or I have no experience with them.

For the moment, let's assume that I do have the knowledge of a client's legacy systems and *can* pitch in. Assume further that the small business is comfortable with the "all hands on deck" approach. From an insurance and liability perspective, however, I may not be able to participate in the effort because the statement of work (SOW) typically does not cover my working on applications with which I am not familiar. Or perhaps, from a

---

[11] A term for using the generic version of an application or system, opting not to customize it in any way.

Sarbanes-Oxley[12] perspective, I may not legally be able to get involved. In other words, for the consultant, *willing* and *able* are often not the same.

The Client

Clients, on the other hand, are constantly balancing (or trying to balance) present and future priorities. The former almost always defeats the latter, typically causing project delays, cost overruns, critical oversights, and minimized knowledge transfer. This problem is particularly acute at understaffed organizations. Heaven forbid that one of the following scenarios occurs:

- An organization loses a key contributor unexpectedly.
- That end user's responsibilities are not (sufficiently) documented, much less understood.
- The organization is confronted with an emergency requiring the immediate and undivided attention of current end users.
- The project has a hard stop for budgetary and/or date reasons.

The result is that the organization is more susceptible to major problems, oversights, and project failures.

Understand the Nuances of Technology Projects

The New Small also understands the following technology management principles.

Ease of Deployment

Organizations often call me about their ostensibly easy technology projects. I often hear things such as, "We just want to upgrade our system" or "It's a simple set of report requests." Most of the time, the task or project is much easier said than done. IT projects that look or sound easy might conceal nuances that few of the projects' originators have considered until someone like me begins asking very specific questions. I then often hear things such as, "Oh yeah, we forgot about that."

Small Errors and Major Problems

Project estimates often consist of strategic wild-ass guesses (or SWAGs, in common parlance). If you're facing tight deadlines, an estimate of two weeks that winds up being even a few days more can be catastrophic. Why?

---

[12] Sarbanes-Oxley is a U.S. financial law passed in 2002 after a number of accounting scandals, such as Enron and Tyco. In a nutshell, it calls for greater financial transparency for publicly traded companies.

All future tasks and goals now have to be postponed. Unfortunately, many projects are tied to key dates, such as end of the quarter or the year. You might have no time to make required adjustments.

Risks and Rewards

At crucial points of projects, there's something to be said for taking a justifiable risk. For example, conducting limited system testing without all of the components often manifests key issues that otherwise would have remained dormant until later in the project. However, as the project's go-live date becomes closer, politics, budgets, or other factors often cloud the risk-reward calculus. I have seen many downright silly decisions made when the risks were much greater than the rewards.

Second Guessing

Projects that grossly exceed budgets and time lines (or are canceled altogether) are the golfing equivalent of a snowman.[13] In a project post-mortem, each person has the benefit of hindsight. Things unknown then are no longer unknown, and as a result, it's very easy to question poor project management decisions.

The Difficulty of Maintaining Consistency

Few technology projects are consistently in the zone. Ups and downs affect just about every endeavor, no matter how simple. I have never worked on a project of any duration that did not deliver some surprises.

SUMMARY

With respect to the Five Enablers, we are in the early innings of deployment. As more small businesses successfully use these technologies, more change will emerge. Change takes time. This chapter has covered the characteristics that separate the New Small from its peers.

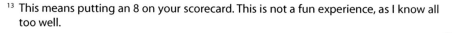

---

[13] This means putting an 8 on your scorecard. This is not a fun experience, as I know all too well.

Endnotes

i   http://investor.google.com/corporate/faq.html#employees

ii   http://www.orkut.co.in/MembersAll.aspx

iii   http://news.cnet.com/Googles-antisocial-downside/2100-1038_3-6093532.html

iv   http://www.infoworld.com/d/applications/google-drops-google-wave-908

v   http://googleblog.blogspot.com/2010/08/update-on-google-wave.html

vi   http://www.buzzwhack.com

vii   http://usgovinfo.about.com/od/smallbusiness/a/whybusfail.htm

viii   http://www.nakea.net

Part IV

THINKING
AHEAD

The final section of the book looks at the reasons that New Small companies succeed—and what might derail their success. It also provides conclusions, a summary, and a look toward the future.

Chapters

Chapter 20

PREDICTIONS AND CONCLUDING THOUGHTS

All know the way; few actually walk it.

—Bodhidharma

Well, we've reached the end of our journey. This book has covered a great deal of ground. We have discussed the Five Enablers, the New Small, and the many ways in which this new breed of small businesses is harnessing the power of emerging technologies. This concluding chapter covers

- The greatest risks facing the New Small
- Why the New Small is successful
- Final thoughts

The Greatest Risks Facing the New Small

As we have seen, the New Small is not a conceited bunch. Although these companies—and the very talented people who run them—don't have crystal balls, they attempt to proactively address issues. In fact, by virtue of their size and their heavy reliance upon the Five Enablers, they face challenges about which their larger brethren need not worry. These include:

- Key departures
- Creative destruction
- Staying current

Note that New Small companies face specific risks associated with each of the Five Enablers, as discussed in Chapter 3. Also, it should go without saying that all businesses face similar risks in a capitalist system. These are related to the economy, credit markets, cash flow, competition, the regulatory and political environments, and myriad other factors.

Key Departures

Although changes in technology have largely benefitted New Small companies, they still face inherent risks because of their size. These risks start with people. As a general rule, compared to larger organizations, small businesses have shorter benches. In the event of a key departure, there may be no logical backup. In *Talent on Demand: Managing Talent in an Age of Uncertainty,* Peter Cappelli writes:

> …there may very well be situations in which the chance that a particular executive will leave truly puts the organization at risk in an immediate way. This is especially likely in smaller organizations, where the performance of an individual can have a huge effect and where systems and procedures are not sufficient to offset many of the distinctive competencies of individuals.

Cappelli tells the story of a small London-based company concerned that its CFO might leave without an appropriate successor. That company retained a search firm to identify external candidates. Although not as good as having the backup in-house, such a strategy has become relatively common for small businesses and serves as a decent proxy.

Although it's unlikely that William Hurley would leave Chaotic Moon or Michael Cady would depart from RedSeven anytime soon, each plays such an important role at his company that his loss would not be easy for his companies to overcome.

Creative Destruction

Technology has always provided opportunities for people willing and able to embrace it—and it simultaneously creates anxiety for those with vested interests in maintaining the status quo. For example, consider Apple Computer. In the mid-1990s, it was an also-ran before digital music and the iPod made it one of the most valuable brands today. Now, thanks to the iPad, iPhone, and AppStore, the company is thriving. Or consider social technologies. They have allowed people to connect with others in ways simply unimaginable 20 years ago. The same forces that have allowed the New Small to flourish concurrently threaten their existence.

In the early twentieth century, an obscure German sociologist named Werner Sombart wrote about *creative destruction*. In a nutshell, it means that technology creates jobs while destroying others; technology giveth and technology taketh away. In the years since, the term has had remarkable staying power. Consider some of the massive changes caused by technology in just the last 15 years:

- ATMs have eliminated countless bank teller jobs.

- Sites like Travelocity[i] have had a similar effect on travel agents.

- Thanks to the Internet, the futures of traditional print publishing and paid journalism aren't exactly promising. Typewriters are more likely to be found in museums than in offices. Products such as CDs are on the brink of obsolescence, while others face uncertain futures.

- People are increasingly forgoing landlines for cell phones.[ii]

The New Small is not immune to the risks and dangers associated with rapidly changing technologies. But these companies tend to have a better handle on rapid change than their counterparts. Nevertheless, continued success is hardly guaranteed.

Staying Current

New Small companies have successfully adopted emerging technologies faster than their competitors—and with fewer problems. However, today more than ever, advantages are fleeting in all areas of business—absent a monopoly or some form of patent protection. Any company can make cool iPad cases and try to take market share from DODOcase. Skjold-Barthel is hardly the only law firm with a cost advantage stemming from its use of cloud computing. New Small companies must continue to balance growing their businesses with staying on top of an incredibly dynamic area: business technology. New Small founders and employees have to keep questions like these in mind:

- What would cause them to go from technology leaders to laggards?

- How can they prevent becoming victims of their own success?

- Can they get burned by being *too* far ahead of other companies?

- Will the advantages of working for small companies wane in importance?

- What would cause the leaders of these companies to leave?
- Can their mistakes allow their competition to overtake them?[1]

Why the New Small Is Successful

This book tells the stories of 11 dynamic companies. Although New Small companies share many similar traits, they are by no means identical. They differ on many levels, including the specific technologies the companies deploy and how they are deployed. For example, one company (NSI Partners) chose to purchase and fully adopt Microsoft's suite of online tools. Other companies continue to meet their needs by using a variety of tools from different vendors.

The bottom line is that there's no one "right" set of technologies; each company uses the tools appropriate for its individual business. Something else is equally clear: there's no technology-based formula for success. Adding one part cloud computing to two parts social technologies does not translate into success. Too many factors are at play. By the same token, as a group, the New Small follows the general management principles outlined in Chapter 19.

Moreover, it's completely farcical to claim these companies so successful for any one reason—and that reason certainly is not technology. Plenty of promising small companies with good products, state-of-the-art applications, talented employees, and solid foundations struggle for all sorts of reasons, including these:

- An inability to retain key employees
- Poor customer service
- Insufficient cash flow
- Bad senior management
- Changing market conditions
- Bad luck

So now it's time to ask, "Beyond the intelligent use of emerging technologies, why are New Small companies so successful?" To this query, I offer seven relatively brief answers:

- Visionary leaders
- Flow and hyper-focus
- Lack of the principal-agent problem

[1] I am reminded here of how Japan overtook the U.S. after World War II with respect to infrastructure.

- A willingness to go above and beyond
- An openness to change
- Alignment of people, culture, and technology
- The inherent advantage of being small

Visionary Leaders

It should be obvious by now that New Small companies would not exist without the drive, vision, and leadership skills of the people in charge. The remarkable individuals in this book have created something out of nothing. They foster workplace cultures imbued with creativity, innovation, flexibility, and many other elusive qualities to which many companies aspire. It's simply hard to imagine the New Small without these people.

Flow and Hyper-Focus

During my conversations with New Small owners and founders, many common themes emerged. Perhaps most striking was the *flow* they felt while working on particularly important projects. I can think of no better example than David Ciccarelli of Voices.com launching his company's mobile website over a single weekend—*without any related experience*. It is not uncommon for New Small owners and employees to become hyper-focused, so locked in on a particular task that they don't rest until it has been completed.

Let's just say that I can relate. Permit me a personal story. In 2007, I was working on a project in upstate New York involving a system upgrade for a regional hospital system. The team had manifested a problem with the new application that was vexing me. It was around lunchtime, and two very nice women (Carol and Debbie) wanted to grab a bite with me. We sat at the table and got to know each other a bit better. But I just couldn't concentrate on eating my meal. I knew that our system problem had to have a logical solution, and I was determined to figure it out, turkey sandwich be damned. I just couldn't make small talk while this problem remained unsolved.[2]

After about five minutes of not eating, Carol looked at me, smiled, and said, "You're thinking about that problem, aren't you?" I just smiled back and said, "Guilty." I could tell that they weren't offended; they knew that my singular focus comes from a good place. That's just how I'm wired, I suppose. Lest I leave you hanging, I solved the problem within the hour, and from my perspective, all was right with the world.

---

[2] Perhaps this is some form of OCD, but I have never been officially diagnosed.

It turns out that plenty of people are wired this way. In his book *Flow: The Psychology of Optimal Experience*, Mihaly Csikszentmihalyi writes:

> In the course of my studies I tried to understand as exactly as possible how people felt when they most enjoyed themselves, and why. My first studies involved a hundred "experts"—artists, athletes, musicians, chess masters, and surgeons—in other words, people who seemed to spend their time in precisely those activities they preferred. From their accounts of what it felt like to do what they were doing, I developed a theory of optimal experience based on the concept of *flow*—the state in which people are so involved in an activity that nothing else seems to matter; the experience itself is so enjoyable that people will do it even at great cost, for the sheer sake of doing it.

New Small founders and owners exhibit an infectious enthusiasm and seem to actively seek these optimal experiences. This begs the question, why? Although it's probably impossible to generalize, and I'm no psychiatrist or psychologist, I do have a few theories. First, perhaps it is because these people immediately see the fruits of their labor. They don't have to wait until their next annual review and hope for recognition via a minor bonus or raise. Second, maybe they are just acutely aware of the obvious: if they don't do something, it just won't get done. There is no backup. Third, remember Csikszentmihalyi's observation that they are actually enjoying themselves despite—or perhaps because of—these challenges.

I doubt that there's one unifying answer to this question of why, and ultimately, it doesn't matter. In fact, flow might be the effect—not the cause—of something else. The bottom line is that, when confronted with a problem, they become bulldogs.[3] They are stubborn and determined to accomplish their tasks, refusing to let anyone or anything get in their way.

Lack of the Principal-Agent Problem

For many reasons, the small businesses profiled in this book—and many others that were not—are extremely successful. Perhaps most important, they have tremendous leaders. These businesses are owned and run by very smart, pragmatic, and driven folks. They take care of their clients because they know that, if they don't, someone else will. They deliver

---

[3] Without question, English bulldogs are the sweetest, most adorable animals on the planet. I smile every time that I see one. In Manhattan a few years ago, I saw a small woman of no more than 100 pounds trying to walk her bulldog (Billy) across the street. Billy wasn't having any of it; he liked where he was, thank you. I laughed as the woman gave up trying to move him after about two minutes. For those who don't know, fully grown English bulldogs are very strong and compact; they can easily weigh 55 pounds.

high-quality products and services and stand behind them. They look for ways to innovate and cut costs. They make intelligent choices and pull the plug on a technology that doesn't seem to be working—or is not working as well as it should. They benefit from dedicated and creative workforces happy to contribute to companies that largely reflect their own values. But there's more going on here.

In the process of writing this book, I noticed other commonalities of the New Small. Regardless of size, industry, and product or service provided, these companies are successful because just about everyone is on the same page. There's a singularity of mission and purpose lacking at other companies. That is, the New Small doesn't suffer from the principal-agency problem, defined as

> …conflict arising when people (the agents) entrusted to look after the interests of others (the principals) use the authority or power (given to them, directly or indirectly, by the principals) for their own benefit instead. It is a pervasive problem and exists in practically every organization whether a business, church, club, or government. Organizations try to solve it by instituting measures such as tough screening processes, incentives for good behavior and punishments for bad behavior, watchdog bodies, and so on but no organization can remedy it 100 percent because the costs of doing so sooner or later outweigh the worth of the results. [This is] also called [the] principal-agent problem or principal-agency problem.[iii]

Perhaps avoiding the principal-agent problem is the single greatest advantage for the New Small and the biggest reason for its collective success. Remember that these companies are privately held. Contrast this with publicly held organizations that often suffer from deep conflict among the following parties:

- Shareholders
- Banks and other financial institutions
- Senior management
- Rank-and-file employees
- Unions—at least in some organizations
- Customers
- Different departments and divisions[4]

---

[4] I am surprised to this day how much departments at large organizations with normatively similar goals bicker about how to achieve them. For example, when I used to

- Regulatory agencies
- Other parties, such as consulting firms, software vendors, suppliers, and strategic partners

With so many groups and different self-interests at these companies, it often shocks me that anything ever gets done at all. Many large companies almost breed a certain level of dysfunction and poor decision making. For example, up until fairly recently, Dell Computer acted as if customer service was an annoying expense to be minimized. Only after being lambasted in many customer satisfaction surveys did the company reaffirm its commitment to those who purchased its products.[iv] Dell's reputation and bottom line took substantial hits because the company forgot about the importance of the people who buy their products.

Let's not excoriate Dell here. Problems like these are quite common at large companies. They are typically compounded by things like internal politics, poor or misused technology, cultural issues, and the inherent tension between short-term profits and long-term strategy. Against this often contentious backdrop, it doesn't take long for a previously successful company (such as Dell) to show signs of fissure. Big companies often stumble as they try to be everything to everybody. Interests begin to diverge, gaps become chasms, and key employees leave. Books such as *Billion-Dollar Lessons: What You Can Learn from the Most Inexcusable Business Failures of the Last 25 Years*[5] and *How the Mighty Fall: And Why Some Companies Never Give In*[6] address these topics in great depth. Long story short: it becomes increasingly difficult for companies to remain successful as they continue to grow.

A Willingness to Go Above and Beyond

New Small companies actually value their employees and work with them to solve problems—even when they're not legally required to do so. In other words, by virtue of being small, New Small companies face far fewer government regulations. They are not subject to much U.S. labor legislation. Many laws contain specific small businesses exemptions, such as the Family Medical Leave Act (FMLA). It applies to all public agencies, all public and private elementary and secondary schools, and companies with 50 or more employees. New Small companies tend to fall well below this threshold. Legally speaking, these companies are not compelled to grant family leave to their employees.

---

work in the pharmaceutical industry, people in the sales and marketing departments would come nearly to blows about the best way to increase sales.

5 By Paul B. Carrol and Chunka Mui.
6 By Jim Collins.

But they do it anyway for a few simple reasons. First, it's the right thing to do. Second, these companies care a great deal about their employees, as we saw repeatedly in Part II of this book. These family-friendly companies have forged solid relationships with their employees. *Why wouldn't they develop flexible arrangements with new mothers and fathers?* The question of whether these companies are obligated to adhere to FMLA is irrelevant. What's more, by going above and beyond they need not concern themselves with administrative headaches, such as related paperwork and reporting.

An Openness to Change

Many businesses cling to older methods and technologies out of routine, fear of the unknown, and so on. This resistance to change is endemic to companies with long-time employees in key positions relatively insulated from the outside world. Many old-guard companies continue to struggle because they don't know that there are better and more efficient ways of doing something. Others have fought attempts by external parties, such as consultants and newly hired employees, to introduce change.

Transformative technologies don't leave business processes unaltered. Anyone taking on new technology will have to change processes as well. The New Small knows that, despite changes, challenges, and occasional disruptions, the Five Enablers make things better. In fact, that's one of the major points of using emerging technologies: they represent means to different ends—not ends in and of themselves. The organization that doesn't regularly try to improve things contributes to its ultimate demise.

Alignment of People, Culture, and Technology

In a way, New Small companies are the same as every other. All businesses are ultimately run by people. Technology is certainly important, but individuals—not computers—make business decisions regarding these matters:

- Which technologies to deploy—and not deploy
- When to deploy them
- How to deploy them
- Who will deploy them

The New Small is successful not only because of the absence of conflict (see previous section). However, it's facile to claim that any company does well simply because people and departments don't fight with each other. The New Small succeeds because its technologies, cultures, and people are all tightly aligned. Although not perfect, their size allows these companies to deal with minor—and even major—issues quickly.

The Inherent Advantage of Being Small

Because New Small companies are privately held, they avoid financial reporting and shareholder hurdles faced by publicly traded organizations. Owners are not under pressure to cook their books, attempting to make their businesses appear to be more profitable than they are.[7] This sense of fairness and honesty is in keeping with treating employees and customers well. In turn, this reinforces a culture conducive to sustained growth, fulfilling work, and other positive attributes beyond the reach of most corporations. In short, in the New Small, interests among various parties are closely aligned.

Don't mistake *closely* with *perfectly*. These companies do not operate in a perpetual state of harmony, and the owners of the New Small don't make that claim. However, a small company size means that issues can be solved quickly. For example, it's just easier for employees to approach their bosses with problems. At the New Small, there's often no formal complaint process handled by the HR department because there's typically no HR department.

Final Thoughts

Technology continues to fascinate me, especially from a historical perspective. In a general way, nothing has really changed in the last few centuries. Technology has always presented different issues, challenges, and opportunities. The need to communicate and share information is just as important now as it was in 400 BC. Of course, Plato didn't tweet. At the same time, however, our daily proximity to technology couldn't be more different from earlier times. Both the pace of technological change and the array of choices are unlike anything that I have ever seen. Amidst today's incredibly dynamic environment, there is at least one constant: Some people and organizations have always resisted change and new technologies.

Not the New Small. These companies do not succeed because they are magically able to avoid all problems. Nor can they predict the future. Rather, they *embrace* change and new technologies. They anticipate. They quickly and effectively deal with issues. They overcome challenges and seize opportunities.

Let's return to Voices.com, profiled in Chapter 8. The company experienced a number of major problems after implementing NetSuite, a new internal customer relationship management (CRM) application. Employees and accountants struggled with the new system; they could not easily enter and obtain basic information. These problems threatened the company's

---

[7] This is certainly not to imply that all or even most publicly traded companies do this.

current operations and future growth, and if they were left unaddressed, perhaps its existence altogether.

Now, think about the typical company. What if it had the same problem—the introduction of a major technology adversely affecting the business? This scenario happens all the time. When an application does not work as advertised, it is extremely unlikely that the average company would even consider replacing it—and even then, not for at least several years. Politically, financially, logistically, and sometimes even legally,[8] change just isn't feasible in many companies, especially large ones. These companies just bite the bullet and suffer the consequences of another IT project gone amok.

Accepting an untenable status quo isn't an option at New Small companies. Voices.com rapidly went in another direction in *a matter of weeks*. That it made the change so quickly and successfully stemmed from three main things:

- Its size enabled rapid change.
- Moving to Salesforce.com was the right business decision.
- The company's founders realized that the costs of inaction exceeded the costs of action.

Today, Voices.com is much better off for moving to a new CRM system—Salesforce.com. This story underscores the underlying theme of this book: ultimately, the emerging technologies discussed in this book are merely reflections of the remarkable and dynamic people behind them.

Thermostats, Not Thermometers

In his autobiography *Open*, tennis legend and my personal doppelgänger Andre Agassi[9] tells an amazing story. Agassi was nervous about asking out Steffi Graf and went to his friend J.P. for a pep talk. J.P. obliged, saying to Agassi, "…some people are thermometers, some are thermostats. You're a thermostat. You don't register the temperature in the room, you change it." To make a long story short, the encouragement worked. That was all that Agassi needed. He is now married to Graf, and they have two kids.

I can't describe the New Small, its founders, and its employees any better than that: they are thermostats, not thermometers. They create more than they maintain. They inspire themselves—and others. They react and anticipate. They move and build. They facilitate and enable. But, most

---

[8] Such as when lawyers are involved in contract disputes with system integrators and software vendors.

[9] As a big tennis fan, I had to include at least one related reference before ending the book. And yes, I've been told more than a few times that I look like the man. I only wish that my backhand was half as good as Agassi's.

important, they change and adapt. In other words, they're just like the technologies themselves.

And they're not stopping anytime soon.

Endnotes

i   http://www.travelocity.com
ii   http://www.technewsdaily.com/americans-give-up-landlines-for-cell-phones-0569
iii http://www.businessdictionary.com/definition/agency-problem.html
iv   http://news.cnet.com/2100-1042-5162141.html

A HUMBLE REQUEST
FROM THE AUTHOR

Thank you for buying *The New Small*. I truly hope that you enjoyed the book and learned a great deal while reading it. Beyond enjoyment, I also hope that it helps you in some way.

And perhaps you are willing to help me. I am a self-employed author, writer, speaker, and consultant. My professional livelihood depends in large part upon my reputation, coupled with referrals and recommendations from people like you. Collectively, these allow me to make a living.[1]

You can help me by doing one or more of the following:

- Write a review on amazon.com, bn.com, goodreads.com, or other related sites. The more honest, the better.

- Mention this book on your blog, Facebook, Digg, Twitter, LinkedIn, and other websites that you frequent.

- Recommend the book to family members, colleagues, your boss, friends, small business owners, and budding entrepreneurs.

- Give it as a gift.

- If you know people who still work in newspapers, magazines, television, or industry groups related to the content and message of this book, tell them about it. Although social media is incredibly important, traditional media still matters.

You might think that doing these things won't have any impact. I respectfully disagree. As the book you have just read has shown, individuals and small businesses are doing some amazing things as we speak. What's

---

[1] My friend, fellow author, and Carnegie Mellon alumnus Scott Berkun added a similar section to the second edition of his excellent book, *The Myths of Innovation*. It's a smart move by a really smart guy.

more, today we live in a very social world. You never know what will spark people's interest.

I write books for four main reasons:

- Although Kindles, Nooks, and iPads are probably the future of books, I really enjoy holding a physical copy of one of my books in my hands. The sense of accomplishment justifies the long hours and sleepless nights.

- I have something meaningful to say—at least, I hope.

- I enjoy the process of creating something from scratch. I like writing, editing, crafting a cover, and everything else that goes into writing books. To paraphrase from the Geddy Lee album, it's *my favorite headache.*

- I believe that my books will make other good things happen for me.

At the same time, though, producing a quality text takes an enormous amount of time and effort. Every additional copy sold helps—and makes more books possible.

Thanks again.

—Phil

BIBLIOGRAPHY

Agassi, Andre. *Open: An Autobiography*. New York: Alfred A. Knopf, 2010.

Anderson, Chris. *Free: The Future of a Radical Price*. New York: Hyperion, 2009.

Anderson, Chris. *The Long Tail: Why the Future of Business Is Selling Less of More*. New York: Hyperion, 2008.

Auletta, Ken. *Googled: The End of the World As We Know It*. New York: Penguin, 2010.

Baron, Dennis. *A Better Pencil: Readers, Writers, and the Digital Revolution*. New York: Oxford University Press, Inc., 2009.

Bruch, Heike and Menge, Jochen, "The Acceleration Trap," *Harvard Business Review*. 2010.

Burlingham, Bo. *Small Giants: Companies That Choose to Be Great Instead of Big*. New York: Portfolio, 2007.

Cappelli, Peter. *Talent on Demand: Managing Talent in an Age of Uncertainty*. Boston: *Harvard Business School Press,* 2008.

Carnegie, Dale. *How to Win Friends and Influence People*. New York: Simon & Schuster, 2009.

Carr, Nicholas. *The Big Switch: Rewiring the World, from Edison to Google*. New York: W. W. Norton & Company, 2009.

Carr, Nicholas. *The Shallows: What the Internet Is Doing to Our Brains*. New York: W. W. Norton & Company, 2010.

Carrol, Paul B. and Mui, Chunka. *Billion-Dollar Lessons: What You Can Learn from the Most Inexcusable Business Failures of the Last 25 Years*. New York: Portfolio Hardcover, 2008.

Christensen, Clayton M. *The Innovator's Dilemma: The Revolutionary Book that Will Change the Way You Do Business.* New York: Harper Paperbacks, 2003.

Collins, Jim. *How the Mighty Fall: And Why Some Companies Never Give In.* New York: Jim Collins, 2009.

Covey, Stephen. *The 7 Habits of Highly Effective People.* New York: Simon & Schuster Adult Publishing Group, 2004.

Csikszentmihalyi, Mihaly. *Flow: The Psychology of Optimal Experience.* New York: Harper Perennial Modern Classics, 2008.

Dubner, Stephen and Levitt, Steven. *Freakonomics: A Rogue Economist Explores the Hidden Side of Everything.* New York: Harper Perennial, 2009.

Edwards, Paul. "Running a Business on a Social Networking Platform: A Small Business Case Study," IDC, 2009.

Ferriss, Tim. *The 4-Hour Workweek: Escape 9-5, Live Anywhere, and Join the New Rich.* New York. Crown Archetype, 2009.

Florida, Richard. *The Rise of the Creative Class: And How It's Transforming Work, Leisure, Community, & Everyday Life.* New York: Basic Books, 2004.

Friedman, Thomas L. *The World Is Flat: A Brief History of the Twenty-First Century.* New York, Picador, 2007.

Gladwell, Malcolm. *Blink: The Power of Thinking Without Thinking.* New York: Back Bay Books, 2007.

Gladwell, Malcolm. *Outliers: The Story of Success.* New York: Little, Brown and Company, 2008.

Gladwell, Malcolm. *The Tipping Point: How Little Things Can Make a Big Difference.* Back Bay Books, 2002.

Godin, Seth. *Linchpin: Are You Indispensable?* New York: Portfolio Hardcover, 2010.

Greenberg, Paul. *CRM at the Speed of Light, Fourth Edition: Social CRM Strategies, Tools, and Techniques for Engaging Your Customers.* New York: McGraw-Hill, 2009.

Gross, Neal C. "The Diffusion of a Culture Trait in Two Iowa Townships." M.S. thesis, Iowa State College, 1942.

Jackson, Maggie and McKibbien, Bill. *Distracted: The Erosion of Attention and the Coming Dark Age.* New York: Prometheus Books, 2009.

Joel, Mitch. *Six Pixels of Separation: Everyone Is Connected. Connect to Your Business to Everyone.* New York: Business Plus, 2009.

The New Small

Keen, Andrew. *The Cult of the Amateur: How Blogs, MySpace, YouTube, and the Rest of Today's User-Generated Media Are Destroying Our Economy, Our Culture, and Our Values.* New York: Doubleday, 2007.

Lee, James. *Open Source Web Development with LAMP: Using Linux, Apache, MySQL, Perl, and PHP.* Reading, Massachusetts. Addison-Wesley Professional, 2002.

Maslow, A.H. "Theory of Human Motivation," *Psychological Review* 50, no. 4 (1943): 370–96.

Michaels, Ed, Handfield-Jones, Helen and Axelrod, Beth. *The War for Talent.* Boston: Harvard Business School Press, 2001.

Mirchandani, Vinnie. *The New Polymath: Profiles in Compound-Technology Innovations.* Hoboken, New Jersey: John Wiley & Sons, 2010.

Parkhill, Douglas. *The Challenge of the Computer Utility.* Reading, Massachusetts: Addison-Wesley, 1966.

Perlman, Stacy. *In-N-Out Burger: A Behind-the-Counter Look at the Fast-Food Chain That Breaks All the Rules.* New York: Harper Paperbacks, 2010.

Pink, Daniel H. *Free Agent Nation: The Future of Working for Yourself.* New York: Warner Books, 2002.

Schor, Juliet B. *The Overworked American: The Unexpected Decline of Leisure.* New York: Basic Books, 1993.

Shirky, Clay. *Here Comes Everybody: The Power of Organizing Without Organizations.* New York: Penguin Group, 2009.

Simon, Phil. *The Next Wave of Technologies: Opportunities in Chaos.* Hoboken, New Jersey: John Wiley & Sons, 2010.

Simon, Phil. *Why New Systems Fail: An Insider's Guide to Successful IT Projects.* Boston: Course Technology PTR, 2010.

Spiegelman, Paul. *Why Is Everyone Smiling? The Secret Behind Passion, Productivity, and Profit.* Dallas: Brown Books Publishing Group, 2007.

Strauss, Randall. *Planet Google: One Company's Audacious Plan to Organize Everything We Know.* New York: Free Press, 2009.

Tapscott, Don and Williams, Anthony D. *Wikinomics: How Mass Collaboration Changes Everything.* New York: Penguin Group, 2010.

Unhelkar, Bhuvan. *Mobile Enterprise Transition and Management.* Boca Raton: Auerbach Publications, 2009.

Weinberger, David. *Everything Is Miscellaneous: The Power of the New Digital Disorder.* New York: Holt Paperbacks, 2007.

INDEX

The New Small

Via>Grapevine 148
Vialect 201
Viddler 190
videoconferencing 112, 119, 162
videos 21, 78, 107, 140, 189, 190, 191
Vimeo 190
Virginia Commonwealth University 89
viruses 42, 46, 172
Voices.com xx, 98, 99, 100, 101, 102, 103, 104, 105, 106, 107, 108, 109, 110, 141, 150, 214, 218, 232, 237, 247, 252, 253
VoIP 87, 118
Von Furstenberg, Diane 226
VPN 36, 204

W

W-2s 25, 165
Wade, Lisa 56
Wall Street 24, 73
Wall Street (movie) 48
Walmart 5
Wang, Ray xviii, 26
war for talent xxvi, 13, 18, 30
Waterfall method of software development. *Also see* Agile method of software development. 153, 224, 232, 233
Web 2.0 9, 47, 199
web browser xiii, 204
Weber Street Marketing Association 133
Weil, Ken 20
Wellspring Worldwide 159
WhatARacquet 10
Whole Brain Group, The 75, 151, 152, 218, 219
Wii 179
wikis 201, 203, 204
Wilde, Oscar 81
Williams, Evan 139
willingness to learn 79

Wilson, Fred 18
Wohl, Amy 81
word of mouth 18, 74, 95, 139, 140, 172, 181, 183
WordPerfect 3
WordPress 21, 42, 77, 189, 193, 201
workflow 22, 131, 159, 201
work-life imbalance 13
workplace policies 28
World War II 246
WYSIWYG 3

X

Xbox 179
Xobni 206
X-rays 91, 92

Y

Yahoo 118
Yammer 162, 201, 225
Yelp 23, 24, 193
YouSendIt 150
YouTube 140, 191

Z

Zima, Drew 89, 90, 92, 93, 95, 174, 213
Zimbra 204
Zoho 7, 127, 204, 205, 207

OTHER BOOKS
BY PHIL SIMON

Providing you with a better understanding of the latest technologies, including cloud computing, software as a service, service-oriented architecture (SOA), open source, mobile computing, social networking, and business intelligence, *The Next Wave of Technologies: Opportunities in Chaos* helps you know which questions to ask when considering if a specific technology is right for your organization. (John Wiley & Sons, 2010)

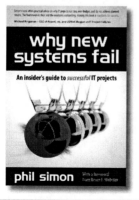

Organizations often lack the necessary framework to minimize the chance of system failure before, during, and after beginning IT projects. *Why New Systems Fail: An Insider's Guide to Successful IT Projects* provides such a framework, with specific tools, tips, and insights from the perspective of a seasoned, independent consultant with more than a decade of related experience. (Course Technology PTR, 2010)